Messy Ethics in Human Rights Work

Messy Ethics
in Human Rights Work

Edited by
SHAYNA PLAUT, NEIL BILOTTA,
LARA ROSENOFF GAUVIN, CHRISTINA CLARK-KAZAK,
and MARITZA FELICES-LUNA

UBCPress · Vancouver · Toronto

32 31 30 29 28 27 26 25 24 23 5 4 3 2 1

Printed in Canada on FSC-certified ancient-forest-free paper (100% post-consumer recycled) that is processed chlorine- and acid-free.

Library and Archives Canada Cataloguing in Publication

Title: Messy ethics in human rights work / edited by Shayna Plaut, Neil Bilotta, Lara Rosenoff Gauvin, Christina Clark-Kazak, and Maritza Felices-Luna.

Names: Plaut, Shayna, editor. | Bilotta, Neil, editor. | Rosenoff Gauvin, Lara, editor. | Clark-Kazak, Christina R., editor. | Felices-Luna, Maritza, editor.

Description: Includes bibliographical references and index.

Identifiers: Canadiana (print) 20230205887 | Canadiana (ebook) 20230205933 | ISBN 9780774868518 (softcover) | ISBN 9780774868532 (EPUB) | ISBN 9780774868525 (PDF)

Subjects: LCSH: Human rights – Moral and ethical aspects. | LCSH: Human rights workers – Professional ethics.

Classification: LCC JC571 .M47 2023 | DDC 323—dc23

Canada Council for the Arts Conseil des arts du Canada

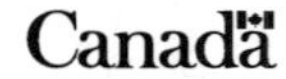

UBC Press gratefully acknowledges the financial support for our publishing program of the Government of Canada, the Canada Council for the Arts, and the British Columbia Arts Council.

This book has been published with the help of a grant from the Canadian Federation for the Humanities and Social Sciences, through the Awards to Scholarly Publications Program, using funds provided by the Social Sciences and Humanities Research Council of Canada.

Printed and bound in Canada
Set in Zurich Condensed, Sero, and Minion by Artegraphica Design Co. Ltd.
Copy editor: Robyn So
Proofreader: Helen Godolphin
Cover designer: David Drummond

UBC Press
The University of British Columbia
2029 West Mall
Vancouver, BC V6T 1Z2
www.ubcpress.ca

Contents

Acknowledgments

Ongoing conversations are at the heart of this book. We are grateful for the many people who engaged in these – at times difficult, but always generative – conversations. Dina Taha was part of the original discussions that led to this volume. Her personal and professional journey took her elsewhere, but we gratefully acknowledge her ideas and energy that remain at the core of our collective work.

The contributors took care and the time to thoughtfully share their experiences, challenges, and dilemmas. In an era of self-promotion and perfect social media personas, it takes courage, humility, and honesty to reflect on our mistakes, doubts, and work-in-progress as human beings working in human rights. This book would not have been possible without each author's commitment to reflexivity and relational ethics.

There were those who wanted to contribute but found that their lives during this time took them in other directions, with other priorities. They, too, were a part of these ongoing conversations and demonstrate the difficult practicalities with, and privilege of, prioritizing writing.

Randy Schmidt at UBC Press championed this book from the original proposal stage. He was willing to take on a non-traditional volume at an established, reputable Canadian academic press and shared our commitment to open access. The editorial board offered their support and suggestions that strengthened the book. The production team has invested their talents in translating our ideas into reality.

Two anonymous reviewers embraced our unorthodox approach and provided thoughtful, insightful comments that helped us grow as writers and as people committed to ethics. We are grateful for the time they took to read and comment on the manuscript, especially in the midst of a global pandemic.

Funding from the University of Ottawa's Faculty of Social Sciences and from the Social Sciences and Humanities Research Council enabled the production of this book as an open access title.

Danielle Gardiner Milln formatted the text and provided editorial assistance. Anahita Kazak troubleshot early Google docs issues, saving us hours of frustration.

This book was written during the COVID-19 pandemic and during births, deaths, and illnesses. As we worked from home, our families and loved ones inevitably shared space in our heads and hearts with this book. Like our professional work, our personal relationships involve ongoing conversations. We are grateful to those who care for us in our imperfect attempts at grappling with ethics in these daily relationships, both at home and at work.

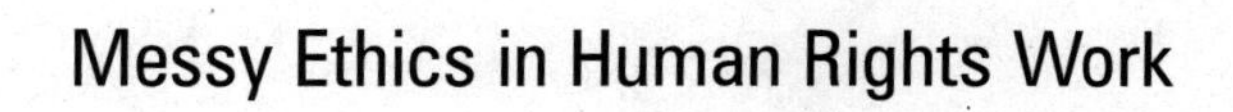

Messy Ethics in Human Rights Work

Introduction, or a Pitch for You to Read This Book

Maritza Felices-Luna

HOW WE GOT HERE

This book is part of an ongoing journey embarked upon by Shayna, Neil, Lara, Christina, and myself. Although some of us knew each other and were even close friends, we came together as a group in 2017, when Christina reached out to us with the idea of organizing a panel for the 2018 Canadian Association for Refugee and Forced Migration Studies conference. It quickly became apparent that we were (and continue to be) an odd bunch with multiple previous and current professional lives: a journalist-activist turned scholar constantly reflecting on, challenging, and engaging in human rights work through a multiplicity of venues; a social worker–practitioner turned scholar committed to decolonizing research in the field and providing a social justice–based training for future workers; an artist-activist turned scholar engaging in and facilitating knowledge production on post-conflict relations through meaningful long-term ethical relationships in the field; an ex-government worker turned scholar dedicated to transforming policies and practices on migration and development informed by ethics; and a migrant from Peru who became a criminology scholar in Canada without any previous professional life to speak of but with plenty to say about anything and everything given half a chance. Although the idea was to organize one panel, we had so many ideas and wanted to do so many different things that we ended up organizing three. Dina Taha was a valued contributor to those panels, but unfortunately her other considerable and meaningful commitments precluded her from joining us in our ensuing adventures. We sincerely hope to have the opportunity to work with her again sometime in the near future.

The success of the panels proved to us that we work well together and that there is much more that we want to accomplish collectively. Since that initial conference in 2018, we have organized other panels in other conferences[1] and have been building a strong synergy based on mutual respect and a commitment to working together ethically (and not just working on ethics). Aside from working together, we have been bonding: we have borne and raised children, buried loved ones, moved, and struggled through a pandemic. Most importantly, we learn from each other while striving to be kind to one another and to give back in our respective communities. We also have fun, lots of fun.

This book has been made possible not only by the bond we have developed between the five of us but also, above all, by the bonds with the many people who have crossed our individual and collective paths throughout our lives with whom we share an interest in ethics and human rights work. Those countless others have been incredibly generous in sharing with us their thoughts, experiences, and emotions whether in formal or informal settings; in public or private situations; over a conference table, a water cooler, or a beer; in tears, laughter, or serious thought. As a way to honour their selflessness and recognize their impact on our personal and professional ethical growth, we want this book to be an opportunity to pay it forward and to share our own ethical dilemmas and our processing of them in a transparent and, most importantly, accessible way. Accessibility for us means more than avoiding overly specialized jargon; it means committing to make the book an open access publication so that it can be of service to everyone and anyone interested in these issues. We take the opportunity, therefore, to thank the University of Ottawa and UBC Press for making it possible.

WHAT MAKES THIS BOOK DIFFERENT FROM OTHER ACADEMIC PUBLICATIONS?

A quick survey of the academic literature on ethics shows that there are millions of publications produced by a myriad of disciplines, in a multiplicity of languages, and from a variety of locations. Risking reductionism, I could say that this incredibly vast literature focuses on three distinct issues: the description and categorization of different ways of conceptualizing ethics; the identification and hierarchization of ethical principles; and the applied ethics or translation of principles in ethical codes or guidelines, including a discussion on the dos and don'ts to ensure ethical behaviour in a variety of contexts.

Although tedious, it is relevant to take a couple of minutes to provide you with a quick overview of some key elements discussed in the literature that somehow underlie many of the discussions within the book. This is not about providing readers with a thorough presentation of the academic literature on ethics (it would be impossible and would go against the grain of what we are doing in this book). It is simply about offering exploratory tools that might be helpful in navigating some of the issues we raise.

Across the book, we find five different types of ethics coming together or clashing against each other. *Deontological ethics* believe that action, in and of itself, can be determined to be right or wrong, good or bad, and, therefore, what is important is to establish codes of conduct or rules and to ensure that those rules are respected at all times, under any and all circumstances (Mattison 2000). *Consequentialist ethics* or teleological ethics, on the contrary, focus on the potential consequences of specific actions, so that an action is deemed ethical provided the consequences of said action are deemed positive or good; it is about the end result, not the means through which it is achieved (Chakrabarti and Chatterjea 2020). *Care ethics* are a form of intersubjective relationality experienced emotionally and affectively in a way that heightens responsibility between the self and other and necessitates considering context and history as well as place and location (Morgan 2020; Noddings 1984). *Relational ethics* value mutual respect, dignity, and connectedness as the basis for action (Baarts 2009) and require researchers to acknowledge our interpersonal bonds to others and, therefore, to take responsibility for our actions and their consequences (Ellis 2007). Although relational ethics and care ethics are closely related and sometimes used interchangeably, they are not the same thing (Caine, Chung, Steeves, and Clandinin 2020). Finally, *virtue ethics* are more interested in developing ethical individuals by instilling certain character traits and ideals rather than by determining correct ethical actions (Meara, Schmidt, and Day 1996). Virtue ethics seek to develop habits and behaviours in order to achieve moral and political good for everyone and, in doing so, acknowledge the intrinsic connection between the individual and the collective (Garlinton and Collins 2021). This is a continuous process requiring ongoing reflexivity and responsiveness (Dzidic and Bishop 2017).

The second focus of the academic literature is on determining what *should be* considered the essential or key ethical principles guiding our actions. Some of the most commonly referenced ethical principles are autonomy/self-determination, beneficence, non-maleficence, dignity, and distributive justice. Let me present succinctly what lies at the core of each one of these principles. Autonomy or self-determination refers to the right of someone to act according to their own wishes or beliefs and have others act in a way that enables, instead of hinders, their exercise of that right (Meara, Schmidt, and Day 1996). It not only requires having sufficient information to be in a position to make the right decision for oneself but also having the support to be able to carry out that decision (Juhila et al. 2021). Beneficence is based on the idea that our actions should seek to produce good for others and their communities or to enhance their welfare (Ellsberg and Heise 2002). Non-maleficence, or doing no harm, is the idea of not harming (physically, emotionally, psychologically, economically, legally, or through socially detrimental consequences) someone or a community through our actions or inactions (Goode 2001; Haggerty 2004). Dignity is about recognizing the intrinsic worth of every human being. It requires ensuring that our actions and interactions promote and value human life and that we treat people as ends in themselves and not as means to an end (Ross 2005). Finally, distributive justice is about non-discriminatory practices (Mackenzie, McDowell, and Pittaway 2007) and the equitable distribution of risk and benefits among those engaging in a particular activity (Ellsberg and Heise 2002).

There are a large number of scholars who criticize the above-mentioned principles because they are assumed to be universal and permanent, but also because the way they are conceptualized entails classist, sexist, racist, ableist assumptions of humanity (Baker 2022). As a result, scholars have been advocating for a reconfiguration of these principles, the development of new principles, or an acknowledgment of the value of other existing ethical principles. In this regard, Indigenous scholars have been bringing to the fore respect, relationships, reciprocity, relevance, responsibility, and representation as ethical principles that transcend the aforementioned criticisms by being grounded in the relationships we have with those around us instead of being justified through the presumed existence of a natural law (Brayboy et al. 2012; Grant et al. 2022; Kirkness and Barnhardt 1991; Parent 2011; Shotton 2018). As you read the book, you will encounter some of these and other principles being applied, discussed, or challenged by the contributors.

The third and final focus of academic literature is on how to act ethically. Aside from the book edited by Sashi Motilal (2010), which discusses the battle between human rights and human obligations as generating moral dilemmas from a theoretical perspective, most of the academic literature focuses on the (un)ethical logic of specific practices or the advantages/

disadvantages of specific courses of action, or it seeks to provide readers with tools to find their way out of ethical dilemmas. For instance, Ron Iphofen (2011) provides readers with a series of checklists to help them plan for and deal with any ethical dilemmas faced while conducting research, whereas Johan Bouwer (2019) presents a series of decision-making models available to those engaging in business when facing an ethical dilemma. Finally, Lisa Ehrich and her colleagues (2011) draw on four scenarios typically encountered by teachers in order to suggest a decision-making model that might help them work through any dilemma they might encounter.

Aside from those publications providing guidelines, models, or checklists, other academic publications focus instead on the ways incorporating certain perspectives or developing certain traits can help us make better decisions when confronted with ethical dilemmas. For instance, Samer Abdelnour and Mai Abu Moghli (2021) offer up a list of questions for researchers working in violent contexts to help develop political reflexivity as a means of engaging in ethical research, whereas Naomi Meara, Lyle Schmidt, and Jeanne Day (1996) suggest that experts would benefit from incorporating virtue ethics in their personal lives as well as in their professional practice. Marian Mattison (2000) also identifies the difficulty in implementing the social worker's professional codes of conduct and suggests a reflexive approach to ethical decision making that draws on past decisions and their personal value patterns.

While academic literature on applied ethics acknowledges the tensions and challenges of evaluating and deciding on the best ethical practice, the intent is to find the answer or to come as close as possible to establishing ethical practices (Bauman 1993). This is done sometimes by drawing on personal experiences or ethical dilemmas that people encounter during the course of daily life or engaging in a particular activity. For instance, in Daniel Bell and Jean Marc Coicod's (2006) book, contributors discussed specific ethical challenges encountered by international non-governmental organizations' human rights workers and evaluated their ways of dealing with those challenges. Heidi Armbruster and Anna Laerke's edited volume (2010) is specifically focused on researchers in various positionalities and relationships to the research "subjects," reflecting on their politically engaged field work. Our book fits within this literature of looking at ethics in action or ethical practice. However, instead of using personal experience on which to ground, justify, or base a series of checklists of dos and don'ts, our book seeks to contribute to the ethical thinking of those engaging in human rights work by generating questions, not by providing answers.

While ample scholarship explores ethics and human rights (Indaimo 2015; Monteiro 2014), minimal literature contemplates these complex social constructs in personal and deeply reflexive arenas. An example of this latter literature is the article by Peta Dzidic and Brian Bishop (2017), where they share their discomfort at being told by members of non-Indigenous institutions and communities to engage with an Indigenous community when they considered it to be unnecessary given the scope of their research. Dzidic and Bishop discuss in-depth the process through which they decided that the ethical thing was to *not* do what non-Indigenous institutions expected them to do as a way to be genuinely respectful of the local Indigenous community. Aside from articles such as this, we have only come across *Navigating Field Work in the Social Sciences: Stories of Danger, Risk and Reward,* edited by Phillip Wadds and his colleagues (2020), which looks at difficult situations encountered by researchers doing fieldwork in risky situations. Although they do not formulate those difficult situations as purely ethical dilemmas in human rights work, they could easily be read as such. Our book is similar to this marginal literature in that we all use personal stories to describe difficult situations and the way we processed them without attempting to come up with standardized solutions. Just as in the examples above, we are interested in providing the reader with material to explore their own thoughts and practices instead of prescribing the best course of action in a given situation.

Despite being insightful and thoroughly comprehensive, the scholarly literature on ethics tends to have as a target audience a specific discipline or a particular form of engaging in ethics. It is common to find works that examine how the ethics of foreign policy (Bulley 2009), public health (Holland 2009), Christianity (Witte and Alexander 2010), or morality (Hopgood 2006) inform human rights work from a unilateral lens. It is difficult to find discussions that transcend disciplines and speak at the same time to researchers, activists, scholars, students, practitioners, policymakers, and artists. This book attempts to fill this gap not only by bridging across disciplines but also, most importantly, by expanding the discussion beyond academia.

BEYOND ACADEMIA: HOLDING SPACE FOR CONVERSATIONS BETWEEN COMMUNITIES OF KNOWLEDGE

Academia is one of many places where knowledge is created, shaped, and shared and, as such, is a space of possibilities. However, it is also an intrinsically problematic and potentially harmful space. As scholars, we see the value of academic discussions on ethics. However, we are very aware that they are insufficient because academic processes exclude knowledges produced through means that traditional academe fails to acknowledge as legitimate. Consequently, important knowledges are systematically silenced or ignored by academia and within academia. Moreover, it has been well established that academia and the scientific knowledge it produces have been and continue to be interwoven with practices of exploitation, oppression, colonization, and epistemicide as well as the appropriation and commodification of a multiplicity of knowledges (de Sousa Santos 2016; Grosfoguel 2007; Mignolo 2001; Ndlovu-Gatsheni 2021; Smith 2012; Tamale 2020).

We, the editors of this book, believe that academia is a space that must be transformed, and this book is part of our continuous efforts and commitment to do so. As a way to challenge conventional academic practices, we chose to publish through an academic press a book that is *not* written solely by scholars for scholars. This book values and recognizes different means and sites of knowledge production; it seeks to create space for a variety of voices, experiences, and reflections that tend to be disregarded by academia; it supports and promotes different means and styles of communication; it supposes that knowledge is produced collectively through collaboration and exchange and not individually, as is usually asserted. This book is, therefore, a means to build bridges between different knowledge-producing communities and between different manners of engaging in human rights work. It intends to reach out to anyone and everyone somehow engaging in or interested in human rights work.

Human rights work takes place everywhere, everyday, and in every way. Artists, activists, journalists, policy-makers, practitioners, researchers, and volunteers unremittingly work with and for others to realize, protect, and advance the dignity, life chances, and quality of life of those who are oppressed, exploited, vulnerable, and thrust into marginalized positions. Engaging in such work confronts us on a daily basis with a series of irresolvable ethical dilemmas, in other words, moments in which we are at a loss about how to act as multiple moral values or duties converge and presuppose that we proceed in opposing or contradictory ways (Bouwer 2019). Through the publication of this book, we seek to generate much-needed opportunities for important conversations regarding the uncertainty of ethics when engaging in human rights work.

Professional, institutional, or even organic codes of conduct provide us with some dos and don'ts as a way to prevent, avoid, or resolve ethical dilemmas. These prescriptive tools often attempt to deter ethical dilemmas *prior* to carrying out the work. Although at times useful, such codified attempts at ethics often miss the point: ethical dilemmas emerge *in the doing* of the work. Human rights work often entails complex relationships of social, political, and economic power and responsibility that one can only experience and live through while actually *doing* the work. Due to the limitations and drawbacks of such codes (Matusek and O'Dougherty Wright 2010; Tapper and Millett 2014), it is important that as those engaged in human rights work, we continue to extend our ethical gaze and reflect on the ethical ramifications of our actions and inactions toward those we know, those we do not know, and those whom we do not know about regardless of the spatial, temporal, and relational distance that might separate us. Precisely because by engaging in human rights work we are particularly susceptible to thinking that "good intentions" necessarily bring about "good" processes, relations, practices, and results (Hopgood 2006), being ethically reflexive becomes the main antidote to the harms that can arise from our moral righteousness.

We conceived the book as a conversation starter to get us to think individually and collectively about how we are constantly confronted with ethical dilemmas in our work. Sometimes we are aware of them; we recognize them as such at the time. Other times we only became aware of them afterward, in hindsight. Either way, when living the situation or when acting in a particular moment, we are constantly (re)evaluating the situation and drawing on different emotions, values, principles, ideas, and imaginaries to decide how to act or to think about how we could do better, be better next time. This book seeks to lay bare some of those processes. Our ambition, then, is that anyone associated with this book (whether as editors, contributors, or readers) critically engage with its content, share with others their own ethical dilemmas, and commit to accompanying members of their own communities who are working through the complexities and irresolvability of their own ethical dilemmas.

We share a deep-seated conviction that the experiential is not anecdotal chatter; it is knowledge in a different form. If this knowledge is exposed and shared in the written form, we may have the possibility of imagining and nourishing a radically responsive and non-prescriptive ethos of engagement for human rights work in the twenty-first century. With such purpose in mind, we invited our contributors to think of a specific situation in which they were ethically stuck between the proverbial rock and hard place. We asked them to describe or share that specific situation with us, walk us through how they handled it. We wanted them to also reflect on the criteria they used to evaluate the situation and determine the options available to them, who they talked to about it (or not), where they sought guidance from (or not), and how they feel about the process now.

In this book, we candidly share ethical dilemmas we encountered that we did not know how to resolve, felt unprepared to face, and currently still feel unsure about a way forward. The chapters are about not knowing how to act ethically and not even knowing what acting ethically meant in that specific situation – showcasing not our successes but, rather, our failures or, at least, situations we are still uncomfortable with, still dealing with, still figuring out. The book seeks to make us all feel uncomfortable in our certainties and ethical righteousness and to provide us with food for thought. While some contributors share the lessons learned or what they would do differently next time, others provide ideas, strategies, tools, and principles to guide us through an ethical dilemma, to help us in our overall practices, and to minimize the harms we can cause in certain situations.

This book is not geared toward proposing templates for action or decision-making models for resolving ethical dilemmas, because it does not seek to be the end, the resolution, but, rather, the beginning. By sharing our stories, we want you to agree or disagree with us, and we want you to think about how you would have handled that specific situation. What would have been the ethical dilemma for you? What criteria would you have used to evaluate the situation and find a way to act ethically? Which values, principles, or ideas would you have drawn from? We want you to think about whether or not you would have identified or recognized a situation as an ethical dilemma. We encourage you to reflect on the problems/issues you see and how we handled them; we want you to problematize how we are talking about it, how we are thinking about it, how we are sharing it with you in this book; we invite you to seek out our oversights and attempt to become aware of yours. We want the book to be a source of personal reflection as well as of collective discussion. We would love for you to go out and tell people, "Hey, I read about this situation – what is your take on it? How would you have handled it?" In sum, we hope that many conversations will arise from this book.

YES, WE ARE NOT AS DIVERSE AS WE ENVISIONED AND WE MUST FIND A WAY TO DO BETTER

We intended this book to be a space of convergence where multiple voices could be heard: we reached out to artists, activists, journalists, practitioners, researchers, and volunteers from different countries, genders, races, class, (dis)abilities, immigration status. Despite having a positive response to the idea of the book, many declined the invitation or accepted but had to withdraw at some point during the process. As editors, we cannot but wonder to what extent individual realities played in making it (im)possible for some to contribute a chapter to this book, such as those who engage in paid versus unpaid human rights work and those whose professional settings count writing a book chapter as work and those who by being asked to contribute a chapter are being asked to (once again) engage in unpaid labour. Consider also those who are secure in their residency status and those who can be expelled from the country or see their citizenship revoked. Think about those who are used to being listened to and those who struggle to be heard, as well as those who navigate social life shielded by privilege and those whose lives are characterized by daily struggles. And there are those for whom English is an unproblematic means of communication and those for whom learning to communicate in English is the only way to have their thoughts and experiences taken into account; In other instances, specific events transformed the sociopolitical context, and contributors felt the need to step back and decide that *not* contributing a chapter was the ethical thing to do. This made us realize the importance of reflecting on the conditions that make it ethical to speak or not on a topic at a particular time as well as on the criteria we can draw from to determine the most appropriate venue for speaking.

We sincerely thank everyone who considered contributing to the book and who were able to submit a chapter. We want to particularly acknowledge those for whom writing the chapter and sharing their experiences, thoughts, and emotions put their livelihoods at risk and exacerbated struggles they face on a daily basis. The emotional toll and added stress that sharing publicly and in written form represents for potential contributors is an ethical issue we (editors, contributors, and readers) must contend with if we want to create space and opportunities for everyone engaging in human rights work to be able to actively participate in the conversation. We believe it is our collective duty to think about how we can support those who want to take part in these conversations but are confronted with a multiplicity of obstacles such as those mentioned above.

A BIT OF A ROADMAP FOR THIS BOOK

The book is organized in roughly two sections. In the first one we have grouped chapters that address dilemmas encountered when "doing things as usual" or when we follow what is standard practice in a particular field.

The chapters unveil ethical dilemmas that confronted contributors as they did what was expected of them while engaging in human rights work – in other words, when they followed the dos and don'ts. Sandy and Jen had their students go through the standard security training offered by a provincial jail prior to attending class inside the jail; Shayna respected the evaluation criteria established to select and fund contributions for a documentary; Christina abided by the standard procedure in addressing the Canadian parliamentary Standing Committee on Citizenship and Immigration; Jason respected his non-governmental organization's stance of limiting its engagement in Moria to distance itself from the harms produced by the European Union and the Greek government; Neil relied on his social worker ethical code when confronted with a problematic situation in the Kakuma refugee camp; and I followed the guidelines provided by a funding agency when budgeting for conducting research in the Democratic Republic of Congo.

In the second section we have grouped the chapters that reflect on dilemmas encountered when challenging the "normal way of doing things," when authors leave the beaten path while engaging in human rights work. Kristi grappled with the principle of interviewees' right to refuse to be anonymized when deciding whether or not to name HIV activists in Uganda in her publications; Katsi'tsí:io, Cougar, and Sarah abandoned colonial research recruitment processes and, instead, embraced Indigenous worldviews and relationality to build relationships with the community, co-researchers, participants, and potential participants; Myrto transformed her practices of photojournalism with sex workers in Cyprus and Greece; Claudyne spoke out of turn and took up space when she gave a Ted Talk on sex work activism despite not being a sex worker; Nick subverted his role as a government employee and human rights educator to advocate for social justice; Yuriko invited members of the Rohingya community she had conducted research with, and for, to attend and actively participate in the oral defence of her PhD thesis; and, finally, Lara resisted conventional academic pressures to distance herself from the relationships she established with her participants and their political project of community rebuilding.

By structuring the book in this way, we are showing that ethical dilemmas emerge when engaging in human rights work whether we follow common or standard practices or explore alternative paths. In the first case, the ethical dilemma is harder to notice or, at least, harder for others to see precisely because engaging with the normative practice makes it harder to see that choices were made at all. We tend to believe that if these practices were problematic someone would have already pointed it out. They are ethical by virtue of their continuity through time and, in some instances, through space. Once we see the ethical dilemma that emerges from a particular practice, attempting to address it is challenged by the weight of tradition. The institutions, organizations, associations, or groups that have produced said practices have a vested interest in maintaining the status quo, as there is a natural inertia to change. Furthermore, in order to convince institutions and those working within them to change, we tend to rely on the experience, opinions, and expertise of those outside the institution whose opinions are considered less legitimate precisely because of their condition as outsiders.

In the second case, when human rights workers step off the beaten path, the ethical dilemma might be easier to see, and people will be more readily convinced there is, in fact, an ethical dilemma given that we have already proceeded differently than expected. We will then almost be held responsible for the dilemma, assumed to be the result of us knowingly and purposefully straying from the "way we do things." In such instances it is difficult to obtain institutional support that allows us to work through the dilemma without being pressured to get back onto the beaten path. That is why this book is so important. As we engage in human rights work, we are tied to some form of institution, organization, association, or group, and any formal structure tends to restrict ethical exploration and reflexivity. However, as a community of people committed to human rights work we can create and hold space to encourage and accompany ethical exploration and reflexivity through open and genuine conversations.

A BIRD'S EYE VIEW OF THE MANY ISSUES RAISED IN THE BOOK

Because we want you, the reader, to engage with each chapter in your own way, we do not want to impose the main "takeaway" on you or on the contributors. We are, therefore, breaking away from tradition and will not present each chapter as is usually done in academic texts. We will instead point to broader issues touched upon by multiple chapters. One commonality that comes across multiple chapters is how the broader institutional context itself structured, created, or was the underlying source of the dilemma. Some chapters discuss the way the institutions (prison, academia, international non-governmental organizations, government, funding agencies, professional orders) imposed criteria or conditions that contributors thought of as ethically problematic. The contributors also address the way these institutions limited their options for handling the situations they were encountering by establishing proper practices or by creating a hierarchy of ethical principles or values to guide their action. Finally, contributors also felt complicit in instances where the institutions they were attached to are part of a colonial system based on harms and power imbalance; they felt as though they were unintentionally contributing to the perpetuation of coloniality, whiteness, patriarchy, nationalism, ageism, classism, and other systems of oppression.

Contributors discuss how being or acting ethically requires us to work on ourselves and take the necessary time to do it genuinely. This means embarking on a learning journey of self-growth with a commitment to decolonize the mind and the world and a disposition to question our own practices. It also means practising self-care, meaning we ensure that we are kind and compassionate with ourselves (our limitations, our mistakes, our oversights), as well as recognize the need to tend to our own wounds and heal our experiences of trauma while renewing our commitment to those whose dignity is continuously undermined. Many contributors address struggling with our own privilege, history, subjectivities, emotions, assumptions, vulnerabilities, self-interests while figuring out our place in each situation and our place in the constellation of power relations within that specific situation as well as within the broader structural context. They describe the challenges of coming to terms with the fact that we are not in control of the situation and what will happen or will be done with our words and actions. Consequently, although exhausting, we remain vigilant and mindful of the potential for harm we are generating by speaking, writing, or doing. This process forced many of us to become humble about what we know and about our limitations and fallibility as human beings and forced us to learn to look beyond ourselves – or those in traditional positions of power – for answers.

Throughout this edited volume, contributors alert us to unethical attitudes we face when engaging in human rights work. Across chapters we see contributors being erased, silenced, delegitimized on grounds of who we are or the work we do, or with claims that how we do our work is not valid, valuable, or relevant. Contributors also describe attempts at being co-opted, used, or taken advantage of by institutions and actors seeking to preserve current social orderings.

Finally, contributors speak of the issues encountered when attempting to be and act ethically toward the people and communities we are working with, for, and toward. How can we be accountable to them? How can we become aware of the unintended consequences of our actions? How can we work toward honouring and supporting all forms of knowledge and recognizing a community's and individual's contribution to knowledge creation and dissemination? How can we contribute to the creation of space for others to speak and be heard and how can we support others in their effort to speak and be heard? This involved for many of us challenging the grounds on which legitimacy and expertise is granted or refused. It also meant acknowledging that the colonial languages we use to communicate are, in and of themselves, tools of oppression; thus this meant trying to develop ways to communicate that are empowering and liberating. It also meant working toward recognizing, valuing, fostering, and maintaining relationships, reciprocity, autonomy, agency, dignity, privacy, trust in a way that is context-specific or culturally relevant. Other challenges we encountered were respecting the self-care that communities and individuals engage in; negotiating safety, security, vulnerability, and access with and for those who are collaborating with us or for whom we are working, given that the local or global politico-economic contexts produce different and shifting risks and dangers; knowing when, how, why, and what to say in what circumstances (advocacy, knowledge dissemination, for example). We all had to work toward expanding our ethical gaze. In other words, we had to consider practices, relations, situations, contexts, and so on as being part of the realm of ethics despite too often being told they should not be thought of through an ethical lens.

The issues listed above transcend particular modes of engagement in human rights work. They might come up in different ways and people might encounter them, experience them, and deal with them differently, but they will resonate with artists, activists, journalists, policy-makers, practitioners, scholars, and volunteers doing human rights work. We hope that reading our stories contributes to your own ethical journey. We encourage you to share that journey with others by opening up about your own experiences, practices, emotions, and doubts. Let's keep paying it forward!

NOTE

1 At the 2018 Canadian Association for Forced Migration Studies (CARFMS) conference and the Social Practice of Human Rights (SPHR) conference in 2019, for instance. See Bilotta et al. (2018, 2019), Plaut et al. (2018), and Taha et al. (2018).

REFERENCES

Abdelnour, S., and M.A. Moghli. 2021. "Researching Violent Contexts: A Call for Political Reflexivity." *Organization* 0 (0): 1–24. https://doi.org/10.1177/13505084211030646.

Armbruster, H., and A. Laerke. 2010. *Taking Sides: Ethics, Politics and Fieldwork in Anthropology.* New York: Berghahn.

Baarts, C. 2009. "Stuck in the Middle: Research Ethics Caught between Science and Politics." *Qualitative Research* 9, 4: 423–39.

Baker, R. 2022. "Principles and Duties: A Critique of Common Morality Theory." *Cambridge Quarterly of Healthcare Ethics* 31, 2: 199–211.

Bauman, Z. 1993. "Introduction: Morality in Modern and Postmodern Perspective." In *Postmodern Ethics,* 1–15. Cambridge: Blackwell.

Bell, A.D., and J.M. Coicod. 2006. *Ethics in Action: The Ethical Challenges of International Human Rights Nongovernmental Organizations.* Cambridge: Cambridge University Press.

Bilotta, N., C. Clark-Kazak, M. Felices-Luna, S. Plaut, and L. Rosenoff Gauvin. 2019. Panel: Ethics and Methods in Human Rights Work. Social Practice of Human Rights Conference, University of Dayton, Dayton, OH, October 1–4.

Bilotta, N., C. Clark-Kazak, D. Taha, S. Plaut, L. Rosenoff Gauvin, and M. Felices-Luna. 2018. Panel: Researching Forced Migration – Ethics. Canadian Association of Refugee and Forced Migration Studies Conference, Ottawa, May 22–25.

Bouwer, J. 2019. "Ethical Dilemmas and Decision-Making (Models)." In *Ethical Dilemmas in the Creative, Cultural and Service Industries,* 77–96. London: Routledge.

Brayboy, B.M.J., H.R. Gough, B. Leonard, R.F. Roehl II, and J.A. Solyom. 2012. "Reclaiming Scholarship: Critical Indigenous Research Methodologies." In *Qualitative Research,* edited by S.D. Lapan, M.T. Quartaroli, and F.J. Riemer, 423–50. San Francisco: Jossey-Bass/Wiley.

Bulley, D. 2009. *Ethics as Foreign Policy: Britain, the EU and the Other.* Abingdon, UK: Routledge. https://doi.org/10.4324/9780203878859.

Caine, V., S. Chung, P. Steeves, and J.D. Clandinin. 2020. "The Necessity of a Relational Ethics alongside Noddings' Ethics of Care in Narrative Inquiry." *Qualitative Research* 20, 3: 265–76.

Chakrabarti, G., and T. Chatterjea. 2020. *Ethics and Deviations in Decision-Making: An Applied Study.* Singapore: Palgrave Macmillan.

de Sousa Santos, B. 2016. *Epistemologies of the South: Justice against Epistemicide.* New York: Routledge.

Dzidic, P., and B. Bishop. 2017. "How Do Our Values Inform Ethical Research? A Narrative of Recognizing Colonizing Practices." *American Journal of Community Psychology* 60: 346–52.

Ehrich, L., M. Kimber, J. Millwater, and N. Cranston. 2011. "Ethical Dilemmas: A Model to Understand Teacher Practice." *Teachers and Teaching: Theory and Practice* 17, 2: 173–85.

Ellis, C. 2007. "Telling Secrets, Revealing Lives: Relational Ethics in Research with Intimate Others." *Qualitative Inquiry* 13, 1: 3–29.

Ellsberg, M., and L. Heise. 2002. "Bearing Witness: Ethics in Domestic Violence Research." *Lancet* 359: 1599–604.

Garlinton, S.B., and M.E. Collins. 2021. "Addressing Environmental Justice: Virtue Ethics, Social Work, and Social Welfare." *International Journal of Social Welfare* 30: 353–63.

Goode, E. 2001. "The Ethics of Deception in Social Research: A Case Study." In *Extreme Methods*, edited by M. Miller and R. Tewksbury, 239–57. Toronto: Allyn and Bacon.

Grant, A.D, K. Swan, K. Wu, R. Plenty Sweetgrass-She Kills, S. Hill, and A. Kinch. 2022. "A Research Publication and Grant Preparation Program for Native American Faculty in STEM: Implementation of the Six R's Indigenous Framework." *Frontiers in Psychology* 12. https://doi.org/10.3389/fpsyg.2021.734290.

Grosfoguel, R. 2007. "The Epistemic Decolonial Turn." *Cultural Studies* 21, 2–3: 211–23.

Haggerty, K. 2004. "Ethics Creep: Governing Social Science Research in the Name of Ethics."

Holland, S. 2009. "Public Health Ethics: What It Is and How to Do It." In *Public Health Ethics and Practice,* edited by Stephen Peckham and Alison Hann, 33–48. Bristol: Policy Press. https://doi.org/10.1332/policypress/9781847421029.003.0003

Hopgood, S. 2006. *Keepers of the Flame: Understanding Amnesty International.* Ithaca, NY: Cornell University Press.

Indaimo, J. 2015. *The Self, Ethics and Human Rights: Lacan, Levinas & Alterity*. Abingdon, UK: Routledge.

Iphofen, R. 2011. *Ethical Decision-Making in Social Research: A Practical Guide.* London: Palgrave Macmillan. https://doi.org/10.1057/9780230233768.

Juhila, K., J. Ranta, S. Raitakari, and S. Banks. 2021. "Relational Autonomy and Service Choices in Social Worker–Client Conversations in an Outpatient Clinic for People Using Drugs." *British Journal of Social Work* 51: 170–86.

Kirkness, V.J., and R. Barnhardt. 1991. "First Nations and Higher Education: The Four R's–Respect, Relevance, Reciprocity, Responsibility." *Journal of American Indian Education* 30, 3: 1–15.

Mackenzie, C., C. McDowell, and E. Pittaway. 2007. "Beyond 'Do No Harm': The Challenge of Constructing Ethical Relationships in Refugee Research." *Journal of Refugee Studies* 20, 2: 299–319.

Mattison, M. 2000. "Ethical Decision Making: The Person in the Process." *Social Work* 45, 3: 202–12.

Matusek, J.A., and M. O'Dougherty Wright. 2010. "Ethical Dilemmas in Treating Clients with Eating Disorders: A Review and Application of an Integrative Ethical Decision-Making Model." *European Eating Disorders Review* 18: 434–52.

Meara, N.M., L.D. Schmidt, and J.D. Day. 1996. "Principles and Virtues: A Foundation for Ethical Decisions, Policies and Character." *Counselling Psychologist* 24, 1: 4–77.

Mignolo, W. 2001. "Géopolitique de la connaissance, colonialité du pouvoir et différence colonial." *Multitudes* 3, 6: 56–57.

Monteiro, A.R. 2014. *Ethics of Human Rights*. Cham, Switzerland: Springer.

Morgan, M. 2020. *Care Ethics and the Refugee Crisis Emotions, Contestation, and Agency.* New York: Routledge.

Motilal, S. 2010. *Applied Ethics and Human Rights: Conceptual Analysis and Contextual Applications*. Cham, Switzerland: Springer.

Ndlovu-Gatsheni, S.J. 2021. "Internationalisation of Higher Education for Pluriversity: A Decolonial Reflection." *Journal of the British Academy* 9, 1: 77–98.

Noddings, N. 1984. *Caring: A Feminine Approach to Ethics and Moral Education*. Berkeley: University of California Press.

Parent, A. 2011. "Keep Us Coming Back for More": Aboriginal Youth Speak about Indigenous Knowledge and Wholistic Education. *Canadian Journal of Native Education* 34, 1: 28–48.

Plaut, S., C. Clark-Kazak, D. Taha, N. Bilotta, L. Rosenoff-Gauvin, and M. Felices-Luna. 2018. Roundtable: Researching Forced Migration – Transcending Disciplinary Borders. Canadian Association of Refugee and Forced Migration Studies Conference, Ottawa, May 22–25.

Ross, F.C. 2005. "Codes and Dignity: Thinking about Ethics in Relation to Research on Violence." *Anthropology South Africa* 28: 99–107.

Shotton, H.J. 2018. "Reciprocity and Nation Building in Native Women's Doctoral Education." *American Indian Quarterly* 42, 4: 488–507.

Smith, L.T. 2012. *Decolonizing Methodologies: Research and Indigenous peoples*. London, UK: Zed Books.

Taha, D., C. Clark-Kazak, S. Plaut, N. Bilotta, L. Rosenoff Gauvin, and M. Felices-Luna. 2018. Panel: Researching Forced Migration – Decolonizing Refugee Research. Canadian Association of Refugee and Forced Migration Studies Conference, Ottawa, May 22–25.

Tamale, S. 2020. *Decolonization and Afro-feminism*. Ottawa: Daraja Press.

Tapper, A., and S. Millett. 2014. "Is Professional Ethics Grounded in General Ethical Principles?" *Theoretical and Applied Ethics* 3, 1: 61–80.

Wadds, P., N. Apoifis, N., S. Schmeidl, and K. Spurway. 2020. *Navigating Fieldwork in the Social Sciences: Stories of Danger, Risk and Reward*. Cham, Switzerland: Palgrave Macmillan.

Witte Jr, J., and F.S. Alexander, eds. 2010. *Christianity and Human Rights: An Introduction*. Cambridge: Cambridge University Press.

PART 1

Ethical Dilemmas When Following the Rules or Doing Business as Usual

1

The Ethical Quagmire of Carceral Tours for Prison Education Programs

ARE COMPROMISED ETHICS AN ACCEPTABLE EDUCATIONAL TOOL?

Sandra Lehalle and Jennifer M. Kilty

While we consider access to education to be a fundamental human right, it is perhaps safe to say that professors teaching post-secondary courses in Canada are rarely able to secure, or contribute to, this right for some of our most vulnerable populations. For this reason, despite being university professors[1] with more than fifteen years of teaching experience each, we were exceptionally privileged to embark upon the Walls to Bridges (W2B) journey. W2B is a program that brings together "inside" (currently incarcerated) and "outside" (university-based) students in a prison classroom context. This means that the classroom for the semester-long course is located inside a carceral facility, not on a university campus, and that the outside students and professor travel to attend classes with the incarcerated students in that space each week. One requirement outlined in our memorandum of understanding (MOU[2]) with the institution where we hold classes is that the first week of class be for the outside students alone, who are required to attend a security lecture that correctional staff decided to couple with a tour of the institution. The opportunities we were given to teach W2B courses certainly came with their fair share of "ethically important moments" (Guillemin and Gillam 2004), one of which this chapter endeavours to unpack – *the carceral tour*. Notably, carceral tours are not required aspects of the W2B program.

While we know that ethical dilemmas are both unavoidable and unanticipated in field research (de Laine 2000), we learned that they are similarly unavoidable and unanticipated in pedagogical practice, especially in a carceral setting. Teaching in a carceral setting requires constant reflection and critical consideration of a variety of small as well as more burdensome or "heavy" ethical issues. While many of these ethical issues were discussed during our W2B facilitator training,[3] nothing could have truly prepared us for the lived experience of the ethical dilemma of the carceral tour in real time. As professors, we glimpsed some of the ethical questions that carceral tours engender during our site visits to recruit inside students to participate in our class. During these visits, we addressed groups of prisoners in open space–common rooms and at the entries to particular security ranges. On one of our first recruitment visits we witnessed a man showering in plain sight about ten feet away, shielded by only a half-wall. Although this initial encounter signalled one of the major points of contention about carceral tours – non-consensual voyeurism and the invasion of privacy – this was only a preview of the ethically questionable experiences we would have as a result of participating in tours of the facility with small groups of university students.

ONCE UPON A TIME IN PRISON: OUR SHARED VIGNETTE OF A CARCERAL TOUR

The first year we taught the course, only one of the six outside students selected to participate in the class had ever set foot inside a carceral institution. The first part of the admissions process required that the institution perform a criminal record check for all outside students.[4] And while we asked students to think about how they might feel about "going inside," none admitted to any apprehensions about spending three hours of class time each week for a semester inside a prison or being subject to the security search that was a mandatory part of gaining entry to the institution. At least, that was their mantra at the time of the interview, at which point we would often lock eyes, speaking without words that we thought the students were somewhat naive about the ways they anticipated the experience might affect them.

The day of the security lecture and tour was cold and blustery but bright, a typical January day in Canada. We instructed the students to meet us in the external perimeter parking lot of the detention centre fifteen minutes before the security lecture was to begin; this was a mandatory component of the legally binding memorandum of understanding between the university and the institution. We wanted to pass through the security gate as a group to avoid bothering the correctional staff that operated the cameras and intercom with multiple requests for entry. The students were more visibly nervous today; they fidgeted a lot and as the fence gate with barbed wire began to roll open to allow us entry, a hush fell over our group.

The security lecture touched upon a number of things, beginning with a history of the institution and the changes it witnessed over the years.

The officer spoke about once housing young offenders and how the second level was repurposed to house adult women. "You'll see," he said, referencing the tour to come. He outlined policies and protocols to follow, such as flattening yourself against the wall should you hear an alarm bell in order to make way for staff who would be running to the source of the emergency.

He spoke of appropriate clothing to wear – "business casual" – and ran through a list of what not to wear, notably referencing prohibited clothing items without noticing that most of them were specific to women. "No sandals, open-toed shoes, or high heels. No tank tops, spaghetti straps, or shorts. No midriff shirts or anything low-cut. These guys don't see a lot of women and would be glad to see you *girls,* so it's important to present yourself professionally." He also instructed us not to look at or speak to the prisoners, whom he referred to as "inmates."[5] "We do have guys in here who are violent and dangerous. You have to keep your distance. They will call at you, try to talk to you as you walk by. Don't engage with them."

This was followed by a show and tell of confiscated contraband items. He passed around a box full of shivs and shanks fashioned out of toothbrushes and pens so students would see the hidden dangers that could be lurking among them at any time. The emphasis was clearly on the dangers the prisoners posed to us and the need to take extra precautions about our safety. As one student described in their class journal:

> Our security lecture consisted mostly of the two white shirts recounting tales of the most dangerous situations that have happened to guards at the institution in their time and warning us about how dangerous the prisoners are, reminding us to keep our guards up at all times. They even went as far to mention to me that the ring I was wearing should not be worn next time, as the small stone that was in the ring could be used as a weapon if it had fallen out. (outside student journal[6])

The officer also made a point to tell us that "physical contact is prohibited. Don't shake their hands, don't hug them. A lot of them have AIDS and it's safer if you don't have contact." After the security lecture ended, our instructor pointed out a blue button on the wall that was encased in a small Plexiglas box. "Should something happen in your class, there will be a button on the wall just like this. Press it and we will come running."

Coming out of the administration wing we passed by the kitchens and laundry. The smell was unwelcoming, not clean or hearty; it was institutional, sour, and at least one student tried to mitigate the stench by breathing into their shirt. Turning down the first corridor, after being told of an old murder happening in this specific spot, we were led past the room where our class would be held and walked toward the "pod" area, where men are housed in two-person cells, with up to forty men sharing the common space demarcated by a series of octagon shaped metal picnic tables that are bolted to the floor and by a shared television and a shower stall, with only a half-wall so the individual remains visible to the guards stationed in the communication tower that sits at the centre of the pod unit. The five pods sprawl outward from the tower like slices of concrete pie.

Prisoners were dressed in orange jumpsuits and many stopped what they were doing to stare at our group. Some smiled or waved. Some called out. Few ignored us. We gazed at their faces and bodies through a barred and Plexiglas wall, divided by space, attire, and circumstance. Our guide said it was important not to linger because "seeing visitors gets them riled up and we don't want to cause problems for the guards manning this unit." Some of the students looked at the men and then quickly away, back to our tour guide or to the floor. Others smiled awkwardly and seemed unsure about it, given what was said during the security lecture. We would discuss this experience later as a group: outside students expressed feelings of insecurity and discomfort with the way they were instructed not to communicate or "look" at prisoners and the simultaneous use of the tour, which they interpreted as voyeuristic and dehumanizing, while inside students expressed agonism over what for them is a routine practice.

We walked through the minimum-security unit, where one student commented, "I thought only American prisons would have bunkbeds and rooms where so many guys (thirty-six) lived." Others nodded, wide-eyed at the revelation that this occurs in Canada. We passed through a narrow corridor where we had to walk in single file. There were narrow rectangular windows with Velcro window dressings on either side. "These are the solitary units that lead to the max-security wing." The officer lifted a few of the window coverings until he found one that was unoccupied and invited the students to peek inside. Their jaws dropped as they witnessed the sparse conditions of confinement – a narrow cot, metal sink, and toilet. Nothing else. We were not allowed to walk down the maximum-security or segregation ranges because "it will agitate the inmates and they may harm themselves or others. The guys in there are violent, and we don't want you getting too close to them."

As our group walked through the various parts of the institution, the students were quiet – a few of them asking the odd question or making a comment as we walked through the dreary concrete hallways. "I didn't realize the 'yard' would look like that. It's an actual cage. Did you see the mesh roof?" "How can they not give them winter clothes so they can go outside during the winter?" "I can't believe he was making jokes about the cells in that one wing being so cold that there was frost on the wall." "Is it normal to call prisoners 'clients'?" Despite their earlier protestations that they held no apprehension about spending time in a prison each week for a semester, they were nervous, perhaps even a little afraid.

Once the hour-long tour was over we returned to the administration wing to collect our things. We thanked our guide and told him that we would see him next week. Making our way outside, we asked the students if they had questions. Going into a carceral space is an embodied experience, and we encouraged them to reflect upon it with the use of all of their senses. It was minus fifteen degrees Celsius, yet we stood in the parking lot talking for fifteen to twenty minutes. The students had a lot to say and many unanticipated questions. Four years of studying critical criminology had, in a way, made them feel invulnerable to commonly held fears of criminalized Others. They had been educated about the ways that criminalization and imprisonment dehumanize citizens who are disproportionately poor and racialized. Still, the security lecture and tour challenged those critical learnings and fostered a sense of unease, apprehension, and fear among the students. Leaving the parking lot that day, we realized that the tour had shifted the way the outside students felt about entering a carceral space. It was no longer something they studied and felt they knew; it was an institutional monolith whose inhabitants they were being encouraged to be afraid of.

THE ETHICAL DILEMMA OF THE CARCERAL TOUR

As criminologists, the ethical predicaments that carceral tours pose were not a new discovery for us on that January day. We had discussed them with experienced W2B members who, during our facilitator training, shared their negative lived experiences of tours, which was also why we did not tour the prison where we completed the training. We are also familiar with the literature on the issue, some of the most critical work having been written by a colleague (Ferguson, Piché, and Walby 2015; Kleuskens et al. 2016; Piché and Walby 2010; Walby and Piché 2011, 2015). The novelty came from experiencing the tour with and for our students, and through their eyes. In this sense, we simultaneously lived through an ethical conundrum as individuals and as a group. By our presence, our movement, and our gaze, we were invading the intimacy, privacy, and personal space of incarcerated people without them being able to prepare, refuse, or consent. We were entering without announcement and observing without explanation the forced residence of these persons in positions of subjugation and vulnerability. The time we spent inside doing brief presentations about W2B in order to recruit inside students, perhaps because it was purposeful and operational, did not generate the same feelings of unease that the tour did. In those instances, it was just the two of us, and we were permitted to speak directly and freely with small groups of prisoners about the program. In contrast, on the tour we were instructed not to engage, speak, or even make eye contact with prisoners – a direct instruction that dehumanizes and firmly situates them as objects of voyeuristic fascination.

Both professors and students experienced ethical anxieties about denying the dignity of those we witnessed on tour that day. It was obvious that the students were uncertain about how to behave in order to respect the people inside. Our collective anxiety about participating in a carceral tour speaks to Jonathan Darling's (2014, 202–3) point regarding the ethics of encounters in fieldwork, which "demands the development of situated judgments which exceed procedural models of ethics." More than recognizing the limits of procedural ethics in helping us think through the tour as a field site in and of itself, we had to remember that "being responsive to this context of ethical expectations and practices thus demanded a recognition of the compromises of 'the field' and of how such compromises could challenge the politics and views that one carries into 'the field'" (Darling 2014, 210). As Bryan McCann writes, "The bodies of the incarcerated, the bodies of prison staff, the bodies of students, my own body, mediated representations of criminalized bodies and prisons, as well as the ghosts that haunt the prison engage in a co-constitutive choreography of ambivalence" (McCann 2019, 96).

In this haunting ambivalence, diverse emotions emerged during the tour and lingered well after its completion. Feelings of discomfort, doubt, and shame resulting from participating in carceral tours were similarly identified in the literature (Smith, Koons-Witt, and Meade 2010) and by many of our students, as documented in their journals.

> As we walked through rows of cells, I felt confused. Was it better for me to try and respect the little bit of privacy people inside already don't have, or was it worse to walk past them as if they don't exist? All of the sudden the anxieties seemed to hit. (outside student journal)

> It felt like we were gazing at animals at the zoo behind plexiglass barriers, placing an emphasis on the division between us and them on the inside. I struggled with where to look; I didn't want to stare at them through the glass like zoo animals, however I also did not want to completely ignore them, as they are human beings and I didn't want to make it seem like I was afraid to make eye contact. (outside student journal)

How should we deal with the tension between our moral principles (e.g., our respect for incarcerated folks and students) and our behavioural transgressions (e.g., lifting the curtains on the isolation cell windows)? The procedures imposed by the institution clearly went against the interests of incarcerated people, for whom human rights work is aimed. We went inside with the good intentions of providing education and opening up a closed institution to the outside world. Even so, we had to navigate the tension of doing harm (to all the people we crossed paths with during the tour) in order to do good (education for ourselves and a small group of students). With each step, we embodied the controversy around carceral tours: wanting to see the conditions of confinement in the institution with our own eyes, yet without the ability to prevent our engagement in a practice that inherently denies certain human rights and disregards the humane and moral treatment of our fellow citizens.

THE CONSEQUENCES OF PARTICIPATING IN THE CARCERAL TOUR

There were many consequences of our tour, some of which we will never be wholly conscious of. We will never grasp the short- and long-term impact of our gazes upon the prisoners we viewed that day. We discussed our thoughts and feelings about the tour as a group during the third week of class, and our students wrote about it for one of their reflexive journal entries, which made things more palpable and thought-provoking for the group. As the outside students confided to us, the tour made them nervous, anxious, and, in some cases, scared of entering the institution again and participating in the class. Despite spending years studying criminology, the security lecture and carceral tour raised concerns about the individuals who would become their classmates.

> As a criminology student, I am taught to critically analyze all information that is presented to me, so I took everything they said with a grain of salt. Understanding that the context in which this information is being shared is based in bias, in hopes of furthering the divide between

> themselves and the prisoners for the sake of their own personal safety. (outside student journal)

The process and content of the security lecture and tour contributed to a division between the two groups of students by emphasizing the dangers that the prisoners could potentially pose. It reified the cleavage between students rather than encouraging the connectedness that W2B pedagogy relies upon and promotes. Leaving the parking lot that day, we realized that the first class, to be held the following week, was going to require a lot of ice breakers to help facilitate rapport and trust between the two groups of students, who were likely to be cautious about what to say and how to act in front of one another. Would the outside students clam up and be too anxious to participate? Would the inside students stay quiet out of fear of being judged or evaluated? In that sense, the lecture and tour were counterproductive to course goals, especially as course content aimed to unpack the Othering processes at play in the criminal justice system.

If the goal of the tour was to give students a chance to better understand the reality of prison, the tour partially missed its mark. During this tour, we were provided "an institutionally friendly view of incarceration" (Piché and Walby 2010), the narrative of which focused more on the building and its history than on its inhabitants, who were largely mentioned to facilitate security warnings and sensationalism.

> If I wasn't a criminology student I think I might have interpreted our tour [as] somewhat of a reliable way of knowing the prison and its operations. (outside student journal)

On its own, the tour does not allow students to critically engage with penality (Kleuskens et al. 2016). The tour script does not reveal the ways in which the prison inflicts harm on incarcerated people or on the racialized, classed, and gendered inequities and structures that shore up mass incarceration (Piché and Walby 2010). Even if carceral tours were organized via a consultative process that would shift prisoners' voices from the margins to the centre (Minogue 2009), we agree with Justin Piché and Kevin Walby (2010) that grasping the relational dynamics and complexities of prisoners' experiences requires more than the limited time spent on a tour.

This means that our participation in the tour contributed to misrepresenting penality, an obvious shortcoming for a criminology program. By accepting the tour without objection, we also contributed to its normalization and legitimation through the eyes of the institution and its employees. We unwillingly maintained, reproduced, and encouraged a zoo-like atmosphere for prisoners (Huckelbury 2009; Minogue 2009; Wacquant 2002).

OUR EXCUSES AND JUSTIFICATIONS FOR PARTICIPATING IN THE TOUR

How did we rationalize and justify the negative consequences of our participation in a carceral tour? After much thought and discussion, we could no longer ignore the irony reflected in our reasoning to "live with it": what Gresham Sykes and David Matza originally (1957) identified as the methods used by delinquents to justify their illegitimate actions. We had, perhaps unconsciously, adopted three of these justifications: denial of responsibility, denial of injury, and appeal to higher loyalties.

Denial of Responsibility

Our main line of defence was an easy one: *The tour was imposed on us as a mandatory component of the MOU – we had no choice.* We rationalized our participation because it was offered as part of the mandatory security lecture. Our lack of power was also a shield with regard to the content of the tour: *It was not our fault if the tour was scripted a certain way – we had no power to dictate tour content.* We were convinced (or maybe we convinced ourselves) that we had no choice, no power to say no without putting the whole program in jeopardy. Certainly, now that the program has been running for over three years, we are left with the unanswered question of what would have happened if we had opposed the tour from the beginning. We assumed that refusing the tour for ethical reasons could trigger a difficult conversation with correctional staff that could create tension in our burgeoning relationship with institutional authorities. Of course, this might not have been the case, and some staff might have felt relieved of the burden and risks they associated with the tour.

Denial of Injury

Our second excuse consisted of minimizing the harm caused by our participation in the tour. As we could not directly assess the harm caused by our presence, it was relatively easy to downplay its existence: *The prisoners barely noticed us and if they did, they are subject to many tours. At least we did it without voyeuristic intention.* Some scholars argue that a prison tour with students is different from prison tourism because you can set required readings to educate students about the ethical concerns[7] and critical reflection assignments for them to process their experiences (Smith 2013). We even tried to justify the tour by saying that we participated in the most respectful way possible: *We did not look too much or too long. We did not ignore the prisoners; we looked at them to acknowledge them; we even made some gestures such as an eye contact, a smile, or a nod of the head.* Both of us found relief in Hayden P. Smith's (2013, 61) paraphrasing of Craig Minogue's work (2009) that "it is not looking per se that is pedagogically unethical but rather it is how one looks." There was comfort to be found in the fact that not all carceral tours are voyeuristic in nature; reformers, writers, and concerned members of the public often take part in these tours in order to educate and inform (Casella and Fennelly 2016) – which were, likewise, our main motivations.

Appeal to Higher Loyalties

Of all the possible justifications, our conviction of and focus on the greater good of the educational program we were implementing was our driving force. We did not want to jeopardize a program that supported a fundamental human right too often denied to prisoners: education. The Walls to Bridges teaching and learning experience has a number of benefits for the university and for corrections, as well as for the facilitators and students. It contributes to the production of a stronger relationship between the prison and the community and is a unique way to invest in a particularly marginalized segment of the population who are often unable to secure post-secondary education (Pollack 2014, 2016). Walls to Bridges courses also aim to build bridges between inside and outside students and between the prison and university communities and contexts. As many of the outside students are future professionals in this field, having humanizing connections with incarcerated people may contribute to building a safer, more humane correctional environment in the long term. A bridge is also fostered by encouraging incarcerated people to see their value as post-secondary students, which opens the door to future educational possibilities. For example, the authors are currently supervising a doctoral student that they met during their W2B training and who was, at that time, incarcerated in a federal prison for women. These points aside, we cannot ignore the inherent power dynamics or different socio-political, economic, and cultural materialities that exist between the inside and outside students.

In addition to the education that Walls to Bridges courses provide, the program also supports a broader interpretation of human rights (e.g., access to education, humane treatment) that is enacted through respectful and non-judgmental socialization, a rare commodity inside carceral spaces. With a collective will to share knowledge, but also respect, dignity, and equality, we later learned that some of the inside students referred to our course as "humanity Tuesdays" (Kilty, Lehalle, and Fayter 2020). Given the many positive effects of the W2B program (Pollack 2014, 2016), it certainly makes sense to think that these outweigh the discomfort or harm created by a prison tour. Yet, we both regret our failure to confront the guard who gave the security lecture and tour about some of his language, notably how he warned us not to touch the prisoners or shake hands with them "because they might have AIDS." We did not approach him about this both because we doubted it would change anything and because we did not want to seem confrontational.

We also felt justified doing the tour because we were inside the facility for thirteen weeks and were not one-time voyeurs; the tour marked the first line of communication and long-term collaboration with the institution that permits us to engage in education and sustained human contact with prisoners. Over the thirty-nine hours of class held inside the detention centre, we initiated a continuous and deep dialogue about a variety of different issues and topics with the inside students that was far from the silent, detached "penal gaze" denounced by Smith (2013, 61): "When dialogue does not occur between students and inmates, the social exchange becomes uncomfortable with students left holding the 'penal gaze.'" It was our role as professors "to direct this 'gaze' towards critical socio-cultural, historical, and political perspectives, in lieu of simply being conduits and testers of knowledge." Carceral tours require educators to facilitate "an educated or critical gaze and dialogue" among their students, including prisoners and, if possible, staff, which only comes from direct interaction (Smith 2013, 61; see also Calaway, Callais, and Lightner 2016).

Taking up this point, we framed the tour as a way to build compassion and to help outside students see what the conditions of confinement are like for their fellow classmates so as to offer perspective about what it is like to live and study in such an environment. This decision meant that we prioritized the gains accorded to a handful of students (and the positive impact on their future life and career) against the perhaps incalculable harms caused by our voyeurism on the tour that day.

COMPROMISING IN AN UNETHICAL SITUATION: DEVELOPING AN EXPERIENTIAL LEARNING OPPORTUNITY

Given the tenuous and skeptical relationship that corrections has with external researchers and educators (Duguid 1997, 2000; Laverick 2010; Wacquant 2002), when we finally found ourselves on the precipice of teaching the first course, we were especially reticent to challenge or question correctional protocols out of fear of jeopardizing the opportunity and long-term viability of the program. This meant that we had to accept working within rather than against the logic of risk management that structures correctional decision making (Piché and Walby 2010; Wacquant 2002), regardless of our personal and intellectual views on the problems this particular governing logic creates – such as chronically overestimating risk, especially for women and prisoners of colour, which leads to their over-representation in the more austere forms of holding, including maximum-security and segregation units (SSCHR 2019).

Subsequently, when our primary contact at the institution indicated that the first week of the course would contain a mandatory security lecture for the outside students followed by a tour of the facility, we agreed and avoided initiating a conversation about why we felt uncomfortable about participating in a tour. After all, we had visited the institution on several occasions as we drafted the MOU and had been escorted through the different areas of the institution to make short presentations to the prisoners about the W2B program and the content of the specific course we were going to be teaching, to facilitate inside student recruitment. Would a more formal tour be different? Would it *feel* different? Would the men and women incarcerated at this institution experience the tour differently from when we came to speak to them about the W2B program and the specific course we were going to facilitate? There was so much riding on the opportunity we were being given to create and teach this course, emotionally, politically and pedagogically, that we prioritized the unprecedented access we were being given above some of the larger ethical questions that the carceral tour presented for us.

Our decision to remain silent about our concerns pertaining to the ethics of the carceral tour was difficult and intimately bound up in and by our emotions and our professional and pedagogical desire to ensure the viability of the program. Did we prioritize our academic identities and the scholastic rewards we would receive – including praise from colleagues and the university for organizing such a unique experiential learning opportunity – over the humanity of the incarcerated men and women we would be viewing while on the tour? What other possible courses of action could or should we have tried to mobilize? For critical scholars whose research aims to speak truth to power, we felt unease and shame at our failure to do so in this particular context.

Given that only half of our students participated in the tour (i.e., the inside students are not permitted to participate), we made the decision to address our concerns directly with the students in class. We chose to embrace our emotions and use them as both a jumping-off point and a structuring mechanism for discussion, effectively turning this ethical issue into a *teachable moment* (Kilty, Lehalle, and Fayter 2020). To do this, we took care to adapt our syllabus to include critical literature on carceral tours, which we assigned for the third week of class.[8] Students read articles that spoke to the scripted and staged nature of carceral tours, the problematic memorialization of punishment, the nature of our collective cultural engagement in penal spectatorship, and the pleasure that punishment provides to penal spectators.

Beyond assigning critical literature to read, we drew from our W2B training to think through how to mobilize circle pedagogy in a way that would foster critical thinking, discussion, and dialogue about this issue among the students. W2B teachings draw from Indigenous and circle pedagogy (Graveline 1998; Hart 2002; Palmer 2004), emphasizing the need to learn from each person's whole self – spiritually, physically, mentally, and emotionally – and from one another's personal experiences and histories (Pollack 2014, 2016). To facilitate this in relation to the carceral tour, we wanted the inside and outside students to get to the point that they were comfortable not only examining the content of this literature in a traditional academic debate and discussion format, but also critically self-reflecting based upon their personal experiences as tour participants and thus voyeurs and as the focal points or objects of the tour exhibition and thus performative. Our approach dovetails with the view that mobilizing a prison tour as an experiential learning opportunity requires "focus[ing] on the social construction of knowledge rather than the acquisition and repetition of information" and "full pre-briefing and debriefing by the professors" (Smith, Koons-Witt and Meade 2010, 3, 8–9; see also McCann 2019; Smith 2013).

To facilitate these discussions and reflections, we set up poster boards in the four corners of the classroom, at the top of which we wrote discussion questions based on the assigned literature. We divided the class into mixed inside/outside student breakout groups to tackle the discussion questions together. Questions included: *What kind of witnessing do scripted representations of penal space and practice allow you to engage in? What does it mean to think of carceral tours as a performance? What are the pros and cons of using carceral tours as an experiential learning and pedagogical opportunity? Do carceral tours objectify prisoners, and if so, how? Do carceral tours increase the pains, indignities, and degradation of prisoners, and if so, how? Do/can cultural representations of punishment realistically capture the pains of imprisonment? Reflect on your position as a consumer of penal spectatorship. What do we gain emotionally from watching or witnessing human suffering?*

Once the breakout groups finished brainstorming responses, the class returned to the full circle to share them. After a lengthy discussion, we opened the floor for a more self-reflexive exercise. We began by asking the inside students to share their personal feelings about having experienced carceral tours while inside, and then asked the outside students to reflect upon how they felt while participating in the tour three weeks earlier and how they felt about it now, in hindsight. What we have learned from teaching this course five times is that the carceral tour discussion consistently marks a significant turning point in the class where the inside and outside students commune, find strength in their shared reflections, and it is during this week that mutual rapport and trust seem to emerge. In this sense, carceral tours are more than a point of academic debate. These discussions seem to break open the class by allowing the two groups of students to find common ground and understanding from their different experiential vantage points in relation to the same event.

It is important to note that the inside students very clearly understood the academic critiques of carceral tours and were particularly upset to learn that some tours are heavily scripted and are thus more performative than authentic (Piché and Walby 2010; Walby and Piché 2015). While some students situated all tours as voyeuristic, overall, the inside students also identified that there are differences between tours that can be informative to an ignorant public and those that are more akin to "dark tourism" and voyeuristic fascination (Walby and Piché 2011); many noted that they felt comfortable with W2B students participating in a tour because it would help to sensitize them to the conditions in which their fellow classmates are forced to live, learn, and complete their coursework. These skeptical but more supportive attitudes toward W2B students participating in a tour were markedly different from what inside students who participated in our facilitator training had to say about tours. This difference of opinion could be the result of the very different carceral spaces in which these groups of students were living; our training took place at a federal women's prison with inside students who had participated in W2B courses, while our class is offered in a provincial detention centre where the conditions of confinement are much worse.

The apprehension that the outside students felt about going into the prison "largely stemmed from the image of prisoners that the security lecture and tour conjured for them (i.e., that they are all dangerous and manipulative)" (Kilty, Lehalle, and Fayter 2020, 102). Hearing the personal views and experiences of their inside classmates calmed those fears and allowed us "to refocus the carceral tour discussion around what it means to come in to look at prisoners where they live and what it means to be looked at" (Kilty, Lehalle, and Fayter 2020, 102–3). We addressed issues of privacy, trust, and what it feels like to experience dehumanization by way of carceral voyeurism. As the students empathized with one another they learned by reflecting on our shared sense of humanity (Helfgott 2003; McCann 2019; Wilson, Spina, and Canaan 2011). This exercise allowed us to critically examine the value of carceral tours and how this practice, while often the only way for citizens to see inside a prison setting, can skew the public's perception of criminalized people and problematically reinforce views of a need to invoke more punitive management strategies in carceral settings. When asked to produce group projects that documented the material realities of incarceration, most students try to push back against institutional power and the unethical practices they experienced or witnessed or that were discussed in the course – including the tour. A few examples of these projects[9] included creating a map of the institution and drafting an accompanying tour script from the perspective of prisoners; writing and acting out a scene that satirized the intake process; and producing a time capsule that included different institutional items (e.g., toothbrush, deodorant, golf pencil) to signify a more truthful representation of carceral life than what is typically presented on prison museum tours (Ferguson, Piché, and Walby 2015; Klueskens et al. 2016; Walby and Piché 2011, 2015).

Our collaborative teaching experiences reflect Wendy Calaway, Todd Callais, and Robin Lightner's (2016, 434) contact hypothesis, which suggests that direct contact with criminalized people may be a pathway toward combatting myths and stereotypes, as well as developing less prejudicial views and an "openness to more productive criminal justice strategies." These are certainly positive outcomes, and they helped us and the students to better "recognise and respect the differential social power" between incarcerated and free citizens (Campbell, Dalke, and Toews 2020, 106), but at what cost? Did our participation in the tour threaten, complicate, or even deny outright the dignity of the incarcerated men and women we viewed?

AN INCONCLUSIVE CONCLUSION

> *Carceral tours as they physically affect prisoners ... maybe those should be ended.* (outside student journal)

It is hard, if not impossible, to deny that carceral tours compromise the dignity of incarcerated people, regardless of our benevolent intent and the value of the experiential learning opportunities the tour provides. In this way, we (the professors and outside students) benefited from a process that has a negative effect on incarcerated people. We knew this prior to the tour and feel it emotionally each time we take the tour (as well as in the months and years that follow); in effect, this means that we set aside or bracket our emotions in order to participate in a process that, at least without the consent of every incarcerated person at that institution, is inherently unethical. That we view carceral tours as unethical does not discount the value they have in terms of experiential learning.

In order to address the ethics of this practice and better contend with the institutional practices to which we were subject as guests inside this particular prison facility, we incorporated this ethical quagmire into course content, using it as a teachable moment to foster connection and compassion among inside and outside students. We instituted the practice of having a debriefing session with outside students directly following the security lecture and tour, at which point we begin to deconstruct the language and content of the tour – to get them thinking critically right away rather than leaving them afraid of the coming weeks. We built this discussion about carceral tours into the course syllabus in order to give us the opportunity to gain insight into the felt/embodied experiences of students on both sides. As the tour became part of the whole experience, it emerged as an innovative learning opportunity that has been especially enriching for students who envision a career working in, or in partnership with, corrections (Pollack 2014, 2016). Students gain first-hand experiential and observational knowledge about an environment where concerns about risk and safety are prioritized over the mental, emotional, and physical well-being of incarcerated people.

That said, we suggest that educators must weigh the harms the tour inflicts against the benefits it provides as a teaching tool when deciding whether to include this as part of their curriculum. This kind of analysis stands outside normative ethics and is more inclined to the feminist tradition of an ethics of care (Tronto 2005), which we tried to take responsibility for and address by way of class content, discussion, and assignments and by working to develop a sense of reciprocity and respect among students. Care ethics overlap with W2B principles in that they both seek to incorporate the value of care as a guiding principle and emphasize the importance of how we think of and respond to individuals. In this sense, both models problematize normative ethics for stressing generalizable standards and impartiality and, instead, situate ethics as an interpersonal phenomenon that requires us to ask not only what is just, but also what is a just response (Gilligan 2008). We mobilized these teachings to be able to embrace and make the best of a situation that we were ethically uncomfortable with.

Ultimately, we each experience different levels of discomfort in response to such ethical quagmires, and the decision to include the tour as part of pedagogical practice is a matter of personal choice. In fact, the two of us actually feel differently about using the tour in the future. One of us intends to continue participating in the tour because she feels the prolonged engagement with the site that the specific W2B experience brings offsets some of the harm it creates, with the caveat that they will not walk down ranges or peer into any occupied cell spaces. The tour also provides the outside students with a better understanding of the living and study conditions of their fellow classmates and creates the opportunity for critical self-reflection about a shared experience from very different vantage points that fosters familiarity, respect, understanding, and solidarity between students. That said, she intends to gauge student reactions closely, and should they – especially the inside students – begin to say they do not support the use of this teaching tool, she will re-evaluate and is open to cancelling it. In this way, she is adopting a consequentialist stance and utilitarian ethics that prioritize achieving a greater good and that is supported by her feminist care ethics efforts. The other of us intends to refuse future participation in the carceral tour[10] because she sees such tours as attacks on the human rights of prisoners and is willing to take a leap of faith, trusting that students will be able to build understanding and empathy without the use of such tours. In this way, she is adopting a deontological ethical position that prioritizes her responsibility to protect, respect, and promote the dignity of prisoners over the perceived pedagogical benefits gleaned from the tour exercise.

In closing, we suggest that discussions of *in situ* ethical quandaries do not result in one decidedly correct course of action. Instead, these discussions highlight the degree to which our own personal morals, values, and life experiences come to shape our ethical decision making in the field, and as this conclusion attests, even long after the initial experience that gave rise to the issue occurred. One thing is certain, however, and that is the importance of continued critical self-reflection and discussion about the benefits and harms that are generated by the ethical dilemma in question, so as to remain open to changing one's course of action in the future.

NOTES

1 Both authors identify as white women, one of whom is Francophone, the other Anglophone.

2 We teach in a provincial detention and remand centre in the province of Ontario; the MOU prevents us from disclosing the name of the institution. Detention and remand centres are maximum-security, although they house people in the full complement of security designations – minimum-, medium-, and maximum-security and segregation.

3 Our week-long intensive W2B facilitator training took place at Grand Valley Institution for Women – a federal penitentiary located in Kitchener, Ontario.

4 The first time we taught the course, it was listed as a fourth-year criminology seminar where all the outside students were majoring in criminology: five identified as female and one as male; two identified as visible minorities (one Black, one other); and all were Canadian. We have since worked to have the course listed as a faculty-wide "field research course" valued at six rather than three course credits and have subsequently opened outside student recruitment to the wider faculty of social sciences and thus to students majoring in a variety of different programs of study (e.g., political studies, feminist and gender studies, conflict studies, sociology, social work, and psychology). We have had a few international students participate as well. While outside student recruitment remains disproportionately female, we have been able to recruit students from diverse ethnic and racial backgrounds, with 25–50 percent of outside students per course identifying as non-white.

5 The term "inmate" reflects how penal language can become sanitized by corrections, which further dehumanizes criminalized individuals. Following convict criminology, we use the term "prisoner" to more accurately reflect the prison context and experience.

6 Outside students consented via email to our use of their journals (anonymized) for publication purposes. Unfortunately, we cannot use the inside student journals for two reasons: (1) we return the journals at the end of term; and (2) we cannot easily communicate with the inside students once the course is over – meaning we lose touch with many, especially when they are transferred to other institutions or are released.

7 We elaborate on the course activities dedicated to these discussions in greater detail later in the chapter. Notably, we provide readings on both circle and Indigenous pedagogy and carceral tours, as well as critical material on other topical course content. While we have not (as of yet!) provided traditional readings on ethics, the selected course material provides students with a way of thinking critically about the topical issues as they are experienced across the intersection of various social identity locations (e.g., race, Indigeneity, gender, class, sexuality, etc.) that dovetails with the teachings of Indigenous pedagogy (Graveline 1998; Hart 2002) and feminist care ethics (Gilligan 2008; Tronto 2005).

8 For the first two classes, we assigned reading material about the Indigenous and circle pedagogical approaches employed in W2B courses to familiarize students with this style of teaching. During these two classes, the students also discussed and decided collectively the rules ("dos and don'ts") of the class.

9 At the end of the term, all projects are presented in front of representatives from both the university and the institution during a closing ceremony.

10 She also plans to use her established relationships with the institutional authorities to communicate that the MOU requires a security lecture but does not specifically require a tour to be a part of this effort.

REFERENCES

Calaway, W.R., T. Callais, and R. Lightner. 2016. "Going to Prison: The Effect of a Prison Tour on Students' Attitudes toward Punitiveness." *Journal of Criminal Justice Education* 27, 3: 432–48.

Campbell, M., A. Dalke, and B. Toews. 2020. "Naming and Sharing Power in Prison Workshop Settings." *Ethics and Social Welfare*, 14, 1: 105–17.

Casella, E.C., and K. Fennelly. 2016. "Ghosts of Sorrow, Sin and Crime: Dark Tourism and Convict Heritage in Van Diemen's Land, Australia." *International Journal of Historical Archaeology* 20: 506–20.

Darling, J. 2014. "Emotions, Encounters and Expectations: The Uncertain Ethics of 'The Field.'" *Journal of Human Rights Practice* 6, 2: 201–12.

de Laine, M. 2000. *Fieldwork, Participation and Practice: Ethics and Dilemmas in Qualitative Research.* Thousand Oaks, CA: Sage.

Duguid, S. 1997. "Cognitive Dissidents Bite the Dust: The Demise of University Education in Canada's Prisons." *Journal of Correctional Education* 48, 2: 56–68.

–. 2000. *Can Prisons Work? The Prisoner as Object and Subject in Modern Corrections.* Toronto: University of Toronto Press.

Ferguson, M., J. Piché, and K. Walby. 2015. "Bridging or Fostering Social Distance? An Analysis of Penal Spectator Comments on Canadian Penal History Museums." *Crime Media Culture* 11, 3: 357–74.

Gilligan, C. 2008. "Moral Orientation and Moral Development." In *The Feminist Philosophy Reader*, edited by A. Bailey and C.J. Cuomo, 467–77. Boston: McGraw-Hill.

Graveline, F.J. 1998. *Circle Works: Transforming Eurocentric Consciousness.* Halifax: Fernwood Publishing.

Guillemin, M., and L. Gillam. 2004. "Ethics, Reflexivity, and 'Ethically Important Moments' in Research." *Qualitative Inquiry* 10, 2: 261–80.

Hart, M. 2002. "Deepening Our Understanding: Talking with Conductors of Sharing Circles." In *Seeking Mino-Pimatisiwin: An Aboriginal Approach to Helping*, 61–103. Halifax: Fernwood Publishing.

Helfgott, J.B. 2003. The Prison Tour as a Pedagogical Tool in Undergraduate Criminal Justice Courses." *Corrections Compendium* 28, 8: 1–12.

Huckelbury, C. 2009. "Tour de Farce." *Journal of Prisoners on Prisons* 18, 1–2: 126–28.

Kilty, J.M., S. Lehalle, and R. Fayter. 2020. "Collaborative Teaching and Learning: The Emotional Journey of UOttawa's First Walls to Bridges Class." In *Contemporary Criminological Issues: Moving beyond Insecurity and Exclusion*, edited by C. Côté-Lussier, D. Moffette, and J. Piché, 93–118. Ottawa: University of Ottawa Press.

Kleuskens, S., J. Piché, K. Walby, and A. Chen. 2016. "Reconsidering the Boundaries of the Shadow Carceral State: An Analysis of the Symbiosis between Punishment and Its Memorialization." *Theoretical Criminology* 20, 4: 566–91.

Laverick, W. 2010. "Accessing Inside: Ethical Dilemmas and Pragmatic Compromises." In *Ethnography in Social Science Practice,* edited by J. Scott-Jones and S. Watt, 89–104. London: Routledge.

McCann, B.J. 2019. "Live, Virtual, and Spectral: Being Present at the Prison (Tour)." *Text and Performance Quarterly* 39, 2: 95–115.

Minogue, C. 2009. "The Engaged Specific Intellectual: Resisting Unethical Prison Tourism and the Hubris of the Objectifying Modality of the Universal Intellectual." *Journal of Prisoners on Prisons* 18, 1–2: 129–42.

Palmer, P. 2004. *A Hidden Wholeness: The Journey toward an Undivided Life*. San Francisco: Jossey-Bass.

Piché, J., and K. Walby. 2010. "Problematizing Carceral Tours." *British Journal of Criminology* 50, 3: 570–81.

Pollack, S. 2014. "Rattling Assumptions and Building Bridges: Community-Engaged Education and Action in a Women's Prison." In *Criminalizing Women: Gender and (In)justice in Neo-liberal Times*, edited by G. Balfour and E. Comack, 290–302. Winnipeg: Fernwood Publishing.

–. 2016. "Building Bridges: Experiential and Integrative Learning in a Canadian Women's Prison." *Journal of Teaching in Social Work* 36, 5: 503–18.

Smith, H.P. 2013. "Reinforcing Experiential Learning in Criminology: Definitions, Rationales, and Missed Opportunities concerning Prison Tours in the United States." *Journal of Criminal Justice Education* 24, 1: 50–67.

Smith, H.P., B.A. Koons-Witt, and B. Meade. 2010. "Demystifying Prisons through the Use of Experiential Learning." *Corrections Compendium* 35, 2: 1–12.

SSCHR (Standing Senate Committee on Human Rights). 2019. *Interim Report of the Standing Senate Committee on Human Rights.* Ottawa: Government of Canada.

Sykes, G.M., and D. Matza. 1957. "Techniques of Neutralization: A Theory of Delinquency." *American Sociological Review* 22, 6: 664–70.

Tronto, J.C. 2005. "An Ethic of Care." In *Feminist Theory: A Philosophical Anthology*, edited by A.E. Cudd and R.O. Andreasen, 251–63. Oxford: Blackwell Publishing.

Wacquant, L. 2002. "The Curious Eclipse of Prison Ethnography in the Age of Mass Incarceration." *Ethnography* 3, 4: 371–97.

Walby, K., and J. Piché. 2011. "The Polysemy of Punishment Memorialization: Dark Tourism and Ontario's Penal History Museums." *Punishment and Society* 13, 4: 451–72.

–. 2015. "Staged Authenticity in Penal History Sites across Canada." *Tourist Studies* 15, 3: 231–47.

Wilson, D., R. Spina, and J.E. Canaan. 2011. "In Praise of the Carceral Tour: Learning from the Grendon Experience." *Howard Journal* 50, 4: 343–55.

2

Fascist Logic

EXPOSÉ OR PROPAGANDA?

Shayna Plaut

In 2013, Peter Klein, a multiple Emmy–award winning journalist, and I started working on an anthology documentary project focusing on the rise of the political and cultural "right" throughout Europe. We felt that the English language coverage in the West was too simplistic – recycling a narrative of "1938 all over again"[1] – and wanted to understand why people were feeling like strangers in their own homes, and thus we called this project *Strangers at Home*.[2]

This was a project of "empowerment journalism," which is the cornerstone of the Global Reporting Centre (GRC).[3] Empowerment journalism brings together the technical skills and equipment of the GRC with stories and storytellers in communities that are often silenced or marginalized and is an alternative to traditional "parachute journalism," where journalists from the Global North come to a "foreign land" or "exotic location" and tell the story that they see, or that they want to see, and then share it with the rest of the world as "their" (singular) story. When done well, "empowerment journalism" enables people to shape, and share, their own narratives but do it in a way that will be "attractive" to Western audiences and media outlets. Peter is the founder and director of the GRC and I am a research manager. Our projects have won worldwide recognition and awards in journalistic and academic circles.

Peter is the son of Hungarian Holocaust survivors and my grandparents fled Europe because of anti-Semitic violence. As a journalist, academic, and activist, I have been involved in human rights advocacy for nearly twenty-five years – working in the field of refugee and migration rights, as well as that of Roma (Gypsy) advocacy. Both of us are Jewish with deep ties to Europe and a strong commitment to the rights of those who are often unseen or marginalized.

After years of working in journalism and human rights, neither of us are strangers to complicated or uncomfortable stories, but unlike the hundreds of stories we have worked on previously, this project was deeply personal and brought up two ethical dilemmas: (1) How do we, as the curators and engine of this project, bring in a plurality of voices when one of those voices is a perspective with which we profoundly disagree? and (2) By choosing to institutionally and financially support such stories, what is our responsibility if the project is used – or misused – to recruit others into this fascist cause?

THE ETHICAL DILEMMA: A GOOD AND DANGEROUS STORY

Through personal contacts, social media, and professional associations we approached some storytellers as well as put out a wide call for people to "pitch" us stories about "feeling like a stranger at home" in Europe. We received more than sixty entries and, having a few people already in mind and wanting no more than nine total, we had to choose only three or four for the project. Our standards had to be very high.

One of the most intriguing came from a joint collaboration between an Italian fascist (Davide Di Stefano) and an American, a Columbia Graduate School of Journalism–trained stringer (Chris Livesay). The story was Davide's, a man in his late twenties to early thirties, who ran one of the larger neo-fascist groups in Italy that both opposed migration and provided material support to poor, ethnic Italians. There was no question that the story, told from Davide's eyes, would be sympathetic to him and his perspective. It was also clear that Chris (the American journalist) would have the skill and craft to make an aesthetically pleasing piece of journalism.

As a partnership between Davide, Chris, and the GRC, it was a perfect example of what "empowerment journalism" could do. It also brought to light the perspective – indeed the logic – behind the rise of the right in Italy, which was the point of *Strangers at Home*. What was clear was the logic to their vitriol: by handing out pasta to the poor and seeking to be the voice of those who are hungry and unemployed, the fascists were reframing what it meant to be the outsider, the victim. No longer was it the immigrant or refugee, but rather working-class, ethnic Italians were becoming strangers in Italy. But in choosing, funding, and promoting this piece, the project also had the potential to give racism and fascism legitimacy – and this is something that both Peter and I, on a professional, personal, and familial level, found both dangerous and disgusting.

However, based on the compelling story, unique character angle, and technical skill, we knew Davide and Chris's story had the potential to be compelling and, indeed, attractive.

We bit. The pitch went into the "yes" pile.

Then, as we were drafting the congratulations email, we stopped and looked at each other, and I said to Peter, "Wait. Do we want to give five hundred Euros to fascists? You are the son of Holocaust survivors; I am a Jew who has spent the past quarter of a century working professionally in the world of human rights. We have both a personal and professional connection to the consequences of fascism; do we want to be the ones providing a video platform for fascists to spread their hatred?"

To be clear: it was not the money that gave us pause; it was the fact that we were providing Davide a *platform* and thus, in a way, *validating* his fascist party and ideals. At the same time, we are journalists and academics. We are worried about censorship – not only in terms of denying a voice or a platform but also in terms of actually skewing the story by *not* including this perspective: we wanted to show the reasons *behind* the increasing attractiveness of fascism. Failing to do so presented an incomplete truth, which is also dangerous.[4]

We had to think. Really think.

In the end we decided to go with it.

It is a short beautiful piece, and we titled it "Fascist Logic."

CONTEXT(S)

People in various countries, cultures, and contexts are feeling alienated and not at home in their land. Why? Why are these similar feelings of alienation in such diverse places eliciting shockingly similar responses: populism, nativism, and fascism. Our hope that presenting a more nuanced picture of people and stories would provide a better understanding of the *motivations behind the rise of the right*. Why are people feeling like strangers in their homes?

To be clear, in our initial outreach to specific storytellers as well as in our open call, we made no secret of the fact that we found the rise of nativism and fascism problematic. However, we found the stories about the rise of the right in Europe as told in the English language were far too sweeping and simplistic, often "painting Europe as an un-nuanced monolith of intolerance," as we wrote in our call for stories and storytellers:

Casa Pound rally, 2015 | *Film footage: Chris Livesay*

> Extremist voices are resonating with people throughout Europe – but what this extremism looks like and who it targets varies from country to country. We've all seen the coverage and we know that when journalists come from abroad, they often get it wrong. The stories that are told and the stories that are sold are too thin and simplistic, painting Europe as an un-nuanced monolith of intolerance. Not only is this inaccurate, it's dangerous. That's why we want YOU to tell your stories.
>
> What are YOU seeing in your country? What are the underlying reasons for the rise of neo-Nazi political parties, vigilante groups and racist violence? What do people really talk about at polite dinner parties or after a few drinks at the bar? When do people clutch their purse or lock up their daughters? Why? And perhaps, more importantly, in what way are people in your country resisting?

Each accepted story would receive five hundred euros to make a short – a sixty- to ninety-second video piece – with the goal of eventually creating a longer anthology documentary weaving these different stories together.[5] These shorter pieces would get the conversation going and hopefully attract funding for the larger project.

Years of teaching human rights has led me to believe that as long as an environment of trust and mutual respect with the facilitator (be it a journalist or professor or artist) is cultivated and maintained, openness and growth often comes from a place of *discomfort*. This is the cornerstone of co-constructed learning and engagement for purposes of social and political change. Facing things that are outside ourselves – our world view, our comfort zone, if you will – pushes us into a place of questioning and reflexivity. In other words, we wanted to make people a little uncomfortable so that they would be open to listening and perhaps to hearing something new.

My role was to organize the project itself, including working directly with the storytellers so that they could tell the best possible story in the best possible (most compelling) way. Way before COVID-19 and Zoom calls – through phone calls, email, and Skype – I worked remotely with people across many time zones, helping them craft their story. They would make the video in their own country, with their own equipment and crew, and send the file via WeTransfer.

Peter and I would review the draft videos in Vancouver, where the GRC was based, and make editing suggestions, both in terms of content and technique.[6] This process would go back and forth for as long as it took – and sometimes it took many months. In some cases, with the storytellers' permission or request, we would do the editing "in house" and send it to them for final approval, but this was rare.[7] In keeping with the GRC's commitment to empowerment journalism, it was always a collaborative process with the understanding that it was *their* story to tell.

THE IMPORTANCE OF UNDERSTANDING THE PROBLEM TO BETTER IDENTIFY POSSIBLE SOLUTIONS

We wanted the final film, *Strangers at Home,* to comprise a variety of perspectives, geographies, and feelings of estrangement and alienation and the ways these manifest in the socio-political sphere. We were not looking for coherence or agreement but rather for a wide and varied pastiche of what it means to be a stranger at home. And all the shorts needed to be good.

When telling a story as a journalist or an advocate, it is tempting to make things black and white – an angelic victim, a vicious perpetrator. It is easy. But it is lazy. And it is rarely an accurate representation of reality. Human beings are complex, and the shifting contexts of the world restructure priorities and motivations; the impetus behind *Strangers at Home* was to counter the simplistic and sensationalistic perspective we saw in the English language media's coverage of the rise of the right in Europe. Starting in 2012, we saw headlines blaring "It's 1938 All Over Again!" to explain the rise of the Golden Dawn in Greece, Jobbik in Hungary, and

Film footage and translation: Chris Livesay

KKK-look-alikes in Finland. This was not only inaccurate, it was also dangerous. Rather than trying to *understand* how the political and social right was galvanizing in different places in Europe, the story became the West's *fear* of fascism in Europe. As Edward Said ([1979] 1994) so clearly explained (and predicted) in the pivotal text *Orientalism,* once again the West becomes the lens of knowledge and the star of the (media) show.

In addition, increasingly it seems that we, the news consuming public, continue to seek out and hear only those things for which we already are sympathetic. This is also evident in those who create and produce such news. As media theorist Todd Gitlin pointed out in his 1998 essay (way before Facebook and Twitter), "the public sphere is subdividing into *sphericals* owing to the proliferation of media outlets and the splintering of the mass audience. This is facilitating social succession and exclusion" (Gitlin in Curran and Liebes 1998, 13; emphasis added). The effect is that we choose to not engage with and, thus, neither learn nor understand the perspectives of those with whom we disagree. This may feel more comfortable but without that engagement we lack an understanding of *why* people believe or behave in certain ways. And then when faced with the results – be it the increasing frequency of democratically elected right-wing populist politicians; the exploding growth of xenophobic media; or the increased acceptability of racism in mainstream discourse – we tend to disregard the people themselves (they are dismissed as "stupid," "provincial," "uneducated") rather than address the root concerns or fears that led to these responses. *Strangers at Home* is rooted in the belief that in order to combat nativism and the rise of the socio-political right, we need to understand *why* and thus *listen* to those uncomfortable truths.

In the spirit of director Joshua Oppenheimer's *The Act of Killing* (2012) and the sequel *The Look of Silence* (2014), both Peter and I were driven to ask *why*? Although this both humanized and complexified the perpetrators (Anderson and Jessee 2020; Plaut 2014), Peter and I *did not* see this as *validating* their ideas, but rather as a way to better *understand* why the fascists believed they had become strangers in "their own" land, and thus how to combat the potentially dangerous consequences of such alienation.

ASSUMING THE AUDIENCE(S) OF THE PROJECT

Given that *Strangers at Home* looks to expose the reasons behind the rise of nativism in Europe, there is already a context to the film – an assumed audience of either (a) journalists with an interest in narrative storytelling, (b) people who want a better understanding of the way to use storytelling as a form of advocacy and vice versa, or (c) people who are well aware of the rise of the social, political, and cultural right in Europe and want to better understand why this is happening. Often the audiences were a mixture of all the above – journalists, activists, community educators, academics – and these were the people we thought of when we selected the films to include. The audiences, like the films themselves, were part of a greater gestalt.

The videos are the storytellers' way of *explaining* what is happening in their own countries – why they feel like strangers in their homes – and of creating empathy for their feelings of estrangement so that those underlying reasons can be addressed. As I said repeatedly when screening *Strangers at Home,* too often the problem is diagnosed by people in English-speaking North America, not by people in their own country and context; thus the solutions and problems are mismatched. In Davide's case he felt like a stranger at home because of poverty, unemployment, the feeling of the working class and the poor being overlooked by their governments, and thus a loss of dignity. Therefore, the easy solution becomes a populist nativism, scapegoating "them" – the real strangers. It is an ugly logic – a sick logic. But it is a logic, and that is what we wanted to show.

As *Strangers at Home* unfolded, it became clear that if we wanted to focus on *why* the rise of the right in Europe, we needed to understand a multiplicity of perspectives, including, or perhaps especially, those with whom we very much disagreed.[8] We both felt it was important to engage with people who were *not* sympathetic victims, but rather are often seen as perpetrators and vilified and dismissed in order to better expose, engage, and combat this kind of nationalism and fascism. We did not want confirmation bias. We were not interested in cherry-picking perspectives we agreed with, recognizing that this was *not* going to bring about change but, rather, risked the project becoming a narrowing, easily dismissed echo chamber (Adichie 2009/2014; Gitlin 1980).[9] We also were concerned that by silencing such views they would only grow stronger. The same ideas undergirded another popular piece in *Strangers at Home:* "Hate Poetry" covers a movement in Germany where people who receive hate mail – in this case journalists with Arab, Muslim, and/or Kurdish last names – read their mail out loud to a public audience. As one of the journalists and organizers in the film explains simply, "We send this shit that we receive privately back out into the public sphere" in order to take away the threat and expose it.[10]

THE PRACTICALITIES OF EVALUATING THE VARIOUS PIECES

When evaluating the various pitches, we created yes, no, and maybe piles. Our way to determine which pitch went on what pile was based on a careful alchemy of geographic diversity, a strong character that created a "pull," and a unique story that would get people to think. This last point is especially important because we were quite concerned that this project could easily become "just one more" human rights film – with a swelling score and a clear victim or hero that leaves the viewer rooting for the causes they already believe in. The audience feels good and validated and learns very little and the film feels both trite and ineffective. We were guided by the larger goal of the project, which was to really explore *why* there were people feeling like they were strangers in their own homeland.

And we are also journalists. We want complexity. We want controversy. As journalists we see our role as unearthing the stories that would not normally be seen and, as narrative journalists, providing the platform to explore *who, what, where, when,* and most importantly *why?*

"Fascist Logic" clearly had the potential to fulfill these criteria and, given the partnership with the journalist, it also had the potential to be done in an aesthetically pleasing way: well-paced with nice camera angles, good lighting, and tight shots.

About six weeks after we put out the original call for pitches, we made our final decisions and contacted the storytellers to let them know the results. If they were selected, we then scheduled calls with them to go over their idea and offer advice in terms of framing the story in the most compelling way. After they completed their filming and sent in their piece, we went over any edits or technical changes that were needed. As expected, because of the clear storyline, compelling character, and skilled craftmanship, "Fascist Logic" was, by these standards, one of the best pieces.

WHAT UNINTENDED CONSEQUENCES MIGHT EMERGE?

At the Global Reporting Centre, we never had a conversation regarding the "rights" to the film. This was for a few reasons. First, the GRC is founded on the idea of collaborative journalism and empowerment journalism (Lefkowich, Dennison, and Klein 2019) and is deeply committed to the idea that the *stories* belong to the storytellers; the GRC's role is to offer the technical skills and platform to get those stories out to larger, more diverse, and perhaps more powerful audiences. Second, the way the films were made – the fact that they were filmed in the home country with local crews and equipment and, for the most part, edited there, meant that for the most part the storytellers were the "owners" of the film.

When we *were* directly approached regarding rights to a film, it was by the storytellers for whom we were sympathetic. For example, "Educating Racism" is a piece profiling a Romani educator who is combatting systemic racism and the "tracking" of Romani children into special education programs in the Czech Republic. After having their story selected but prior to agreeing to participate in the project, they asked the GRC to sign a memorandum of understanding that they would be able to use the film in their own campaigns to combat racism against Roma in the education system in central Europe. We signed the memorandum without hesitation, asking only that GRC be given credit in the film, thus creating a precedent of creative ownership with the storytellers.[11] We were never directly approached by Davide or Chris regarding the rights for "Fascist Logic"; thus we have no idea how it is being used.

We were so taken by the idea that by better understanding the multiple, context-laden reasons *undergirding* the rise of nativism throughout Europe, we – as activists, journalists, thinkers, and doers – could better confront and change it, we failed to see that this project could actually *support* what we were trying to combat. We simply never considered that Davide could easily use the film as a form of propaganda – to rally the masses of the fascist organization or introduce them to the public or to sympathetic local governments by showing the "good work" the fascists were doing (e.g., handing out food to the poor). Of course, in addition to Davide using the film for his own purposes, it could easily be downloaded or screened on its own by others who hold xenophobic and nationalist views. And given that I am not connected to the world of Italian fascists (or any other fascists for that matter) I have no idea how this piece may be circulating in those circles.

As the person who was most often the public face of this project, I travelled throughout Europe, Canada, and the US presenting *Strangers at Home* to audiences of journalists, students, advocates – I even presented clips of the film, and the story behind making it, to the United Nations Office for the High Commission for Human Rights and the United Nations High Commissioner for Refugees.[12] Depending on time, my presentations involved screening three to four films, and "Fascist Logic" was always the second film. I would give a bit of context before each short; for "Fascist Logic" I explained that we hesitated to include this film because it was inherently giving space and a platform to a fascist, but in the end, we decided that we could not include only the perspectives of those with whom we agreed but, rather, we needed to create a space to engage with and listen to those with whom we did not agree. In this way we would be better able to understand the reasoning and combat it – hence why we titled the film "Fascist Logic." It was not a logic we agreed with, but there was a logic. I was often asked questions about the film – about why we included it and the risks of including it.

After a number of presentations a pattern in the questions regarding "Fascist Logic" emerged: Whereas in the US and, to a lesser extent, Canada, audiences seemed to agree with the idea of providing a forum for conflicting ideas, European audiences seemed to fear that screening the film was, in some way, validating the content. I welcomed these questions. There is an old adage in journalism (and in art and academia for that matter) that you can work as hard as you can on a piece but once you release it to the public, you no longer have any control over how it is understood or (mis)interpreted. It is true; believing in control is folly, but I still fell for the myth: I always screened the films as part of a larger – usually ninety-minute – presentation that included a bit of my own history (Jewish; works with Roma people in central/eastern Europe since 2001; background in human rights) as well as the context of the project (silence or the oversimplified reporting of the rise of the right in Europe in the English language press) and the theories that helped shape the larger project. Thus, I always assumed that I would be able to frame the way the films were shown and, to some extent, how they were seen. Plus, I always ensured there were at least twenty minutes to field questions or clean up misconceptions. But there was a problem. Within the context of the *Strangers at Home* project, the contemplative message regarding fascism made sense, but it simply never occurred to me that these films were anything other than a part of *our* larger project. This reflects a deeply troubling self-centredness that we were attempting to counter through the project.

IF HINDSIGHT IS 20/20 ...

I still think it was the right decision to include the film in *Strangers at Home*. It is a good piece of journalism. It has a good story, a compelling character, a swelling music score, and even a dramatic flag waving scene. And although a bit outdated (much has changed in the world since 2013–15, when we put together the pieces, including the fact that, as of publication, a follower of Mussolini is the current prime minister of Italy), "Fascist Logic" contributes a lot to the larger conversation about why people may feel like a stranger at home and how this manifests in politics and culture. And, of course, given the time and skill and equipment that went into the making of the piece, the storytellers had a right to their five hundred euro honorarium. So, yes, I would still give five hundred euros to a fascist to make a film, and given the structure of the GRC and its commitment to collaborative journalism, the storytellers – including Davide and Chris – would still have the rights to the film.

But I kick myself for my own narrow thinking. In my journalism, research, and teaching, I constantly harp on the fact that we need to see who is *not* in the room, *not* in the story, *not* being quoted, and to think about a piece from that person's perspective. By not seeing how this piece could be used by fascists to promote their own ideals, I have failed to recognize their agency; and it is always dangerous to underestimate people's agency. As my mother always says, you cannot unscramble eggs, nor can you put toothpaste back in a toothpaste tube. So the best question may be, Where do we go from here?

After the same questions arose again and again at the Q&As following my presentations – some about the larger project but many centred on "Fascist Logic" specifically, it became evident that we needed to have a video contextualizing *Strangers at Home*. This introduction could either be a mini version of the presentation I usually give, or one that included interviews with some of the storytellers themselves.[13] In this way, people could then present the project on their own, in their own communities, classrooms, or non-governmental organizations, for example, which is one of the main goals of the project. But while still putting the project out into the world (it is freely accessible on the web), we could retain some of the power by framing the larger story. In this way we, at the GRC, would be guiding the audiences watching the videos on their own to see them as part of a larger conversation on nativism in Europe.

In 2021 we received funding to produce an introductory video to upload on the website and also perhaps link to all the smaller stories. So if someone downloads any one video (there are nine in total), they will automatically see the contextualizing video (like those annoying ads on webpages). Or at least they will get a pop-up that says "Do you want to watch this video for context?" to which they can click "yes" or "no" (like those annoying pop-ups asking if you want to take a "tour" of the new updated software/interface).

In addition, if we do this project again, I would include a statement in the contract that requires the storytellers to notify us anytime they screen the film themselves. In that way we can (1) keep track of circulation and audiences, which is important for our own records and marketing, and (2) respond (either publicly or privately) if the film is being used in a way that is counter to the messaging of *Strangers at Home*.

But I am not sure if that is enough. In the end it is mostly benefiting us, the creators of the project.

Perhaps the best I can do is recognize that my own passion and commitment could easily obfuscate the consequences of my decisions and try to mitigate that the next time I am in a position to solicit and curate others' stories.

NOTES

1 For example, see J. Gotlieb, "Was 2016 Just 1938 All Over Again?" (Gotlieb 2016) and "The Central Question, Is It 1938? (Fallows 2015).
2 https://globalreportingcentre.org/strangers/.
3 For more information on "empowerment journalism," please see Lefkowich, Dennison, and Klein (2019).
4 See Chimamande Ngozi Adichie's (2009/2014) "The Danger of a Single Story" as well as discussions of contextual objectivity put forward by El-Nawawy and Iskandar (2002).
5 There are many different kinds of anthology documentaries; some of the most well-known are *Freakonomics* (2010) and *11'09"01* (2002), eleven shorts from around

the world that are nine minutes long about the effects of the September 11, 2001, terrorist attacks.

6 Although Peter and I were the main contacts, we also put together a board of journalists, filmmakers, and academics (see the team on the Global Reporting Centre website, https://globalreportingcentre.org/strangers/team/index.html) with expertise in Europe who helped us review the initial pitches and narrow them down to the final nine.

7 Given that the GRC is also housed within the UBC Graduate School of Journalism, it was often the journalism students, many of whom had professional journalistic backgrounds, who would be doing the editing work.

8 This was not the first time that Peter and I engaged in this process. On December 10, 2014 (Human Rights Day) I published an interview with Peter in *Praxis Center* exploring why, as the son of Holocaust survivors, he chose to interview a variety of torturers throughout his journalistic career.

9 "Fascist Logic" was not the only piece that focused on the perspective of a nationalist but it was by far the most engaging in terms of the charisma of Davide's character and of the piece's sophisticated cinematic style and its populist appeal. "Defending Russia," which profiles a lawyer who trains a vigilante militia to "defend Russia" from the "foreigners," also highlights fear and nativism, but the main character is a bit of a caricature, and it is more difficult to engage with him or take him seriously. "Queen of the Gypsies," one of the last interviews done with Esma Redzepova, the world-famous Romani singer, also has a (nostalgic, Yugoslavian) nationalist undertone that denies and belies the notion of systemic racism against Roma people but is much more nuanced.

10 The notion that racist and fascist ideas should be publicly exposed (and thus shamed) is *not* universally agreed upon, as can be seen from the different reactions to lone-gunman terrorist attacks in Norway (2011) and New Zealand (2019), respectively. Whereas literally hundreds of profiles were written about Anders Behring Breivik, as well as the trial (most notably *One of Us* by Åsne Seierstad [2016]), the prime minister of New Zealand was adamant in response to the attack in her country, stating "You will not hear me speak his name," and the media followed suit.

11 We are aware of one other film, "Identification," which explores how the Slovak government only recognizes the sex of a person on their birth certificate for the purpose of issuing state ID and other state records. Thus, if a person wants the gender of their choice to be recognized by their government, they *must* undergo full surgery. There were plans for "Identification" to be used by Transfuzia, a trans-rights group profiled in the film.

12 The website of the Office of the High Commissioner for Human Rights includes a link to the PowerPoint presentation at https://www.ohchr.org/EN/Issues/Migration/Pages/Shapingthepublicnarrativeonmigration.aspx.

13 The full presentation, which was also the Canadian premiere screening, is available at Simon Fraser University's Institute for the Humanities, https://www.youtube.com/watch?v=RlOqfswhATc.

REFERENCES

11'09"01. 2002. Produced by Alain Brigard. https://www.imdb.com/title/tt0328802/.

Adichie, C.N. 2009/2014. "The Danger of a Single Story." TED Talk, March 10. https://www.ted.com/talks/chimamanda_ngozi_adichie_the_danger_of_a_single_story.

Anderson, K., and E. Jessee. 2020. *Researching Perpetrators of Genocide*. Madison: University of Wisconsin Press.

El-Nawawy, M., and A. Iskandar. 2002. *Al Jazeera: The Story of the Network That Is Rattling Governments and Redefining Modern Journalism*. Cambridge, MA: Westview Press.

Fallows, J. 2015. "The Central Question, Is It 1938?" *The Atlantic*, March 3, 2015. https://www.theatlantic.com/international/archive/2015/03/the-central-question-is-it-1938/386716/.

Gitlin, T. 1980. *The Whole World Is Watching: The Making and the Unmaking of the New Left*. Berkeley: University of California Press.

–. 1998. "Minisphericals." In *Media, Ritual and Identity*, edited by J. Curran and T. Liebes, 168–74. London, UK: Routledge.

Gotlieb, J. 2016. "Was 2016 Just 1938 All Over Again?" *The Conversation*, December 30, 2016. https://theconversation.com/was-2016-just-1938-all-over-again-70728.

Lefkowich, M., B. Dennison, and P. Klein. 2019. "Empowerment Journalism – Commentary for Special Issue of Journalism Studies." *Journalism Studies* 20, 12: 1803–09. doi:10.1080/1461670X.2019.1638294.

Oppenheimer, J., dir. 2012. *The Act of Killing*. DVD. Denmark: Final Cut for Real.

–. (2014). *The Look of Silence*. DVD. Denmark: Drafthouse Films and a Final Cut for Real.

Plaut, S. 2014. "What Does It Take to Have an Open and Honest Conversation about Torture?" Praxis Center, December 10, 2014. https://portside.org/2014-12-11/what-does-it-take-have-open-and-honest-conversation-about-torture.

Said, E. (1979) 1994. *Orientalism*. New York: Vintage Press.

Seierstad, A. 2016. *One of Us: The Story of a Massacre in Norway – and Its Aftermath*. Translated by Sarah Death. New York: Farrar, Straus and Giroux.

3

The Politics of Representation and Allyship in Human Rights Policy Work

Christina Clark-Kazak

There is a well-repeated adage that the closer one is to policy making, the further one is from the problem. In this chapter, I use the example of "expert testimony" at the Canadian parliamentary Standing Committee on Citizenship and Immigration to highlight ethical dilemmas related to human rights research and advocacy work in politicized policy spaces. This chapter draws on the intersectional worlds of gender, nationality, race, age, and class to critically analyze how positionality affects not only the way I engage reflexively in human rights advocacy, but also the way different knowledge is valued and framed in policy spaces. Popularized by Kimberlé Crenshaw (1989) as a metaphor to describe how systems of oppression overlap, intersectionality has been widely used in feminist research to highlight complex, multilayered power relations (Sen, Iyer, and Mukherjee 2009). Reflexivity requires human rights researchers and activists to recognize our own positionality within these intersecting power relations (England 1994), the way these positions impact our work, and how we are perceived. As Linda Alcoff (2009, 121) argues, "Who is speaking to whom turns out to be as important for meaning and truth as what is said; in fact what is said turns out to change according to who is speaking and who is listening."

I am a white settler Anglophone Canadian who has not personally experienced forced migration. As a researcher whose work focuses on migration in Canada and globally, and as a former Canadian federal public servant, I am regularly invited to contribute to policy-making processes. In contrast to empirical data collection, such policy work does not require formal ethics approval from my university. However, any policy change could have significant impacts on the lives of people seeking refugee protection in Canada. This chapter highlights the procedural and relational ethical gaps that can arise in high-level policy work that seeks to effect practical change, with no formal requirement to consider standard ethical principles, such as voluntary, informed consent, confidentiality, and minimizing harm. It also considers the ways power relations at individual, community, and institutional levels intersect to determine access to policy space, as well as the politics of representation and "bias." Drawing on transcripts from a specific meeting of the parliamentary committee on "Migration Challenges and Opportunities for Canada in the 21st Century," in which I participated, this chapter highlights ethical dilemmas related to representation and to co-option into exclusionary discourses and decision-making processes. I conclude with some ideas about allyship through a perspective of the radical ethics of care.

VIGNETTE

In November 2018, I was invited as an "expert witness" to the Canadian parliamentary Standing Committee on Citizenship and Immigration. The committee was considering the Global Compacts on Migration and Refugees, which were subsequently adopted by the United Nations (UN) General Assembly in December 2018. As international political statements – similar to the UN Declaration on Human Rights and the UN Sustainable Development Goals – the Global Compacts set important international norms for protection of migration rights but are not legally binding. Moreover, individual countries do not sign and ratify them, because they are UN declarations, not treaties or conventions. However, at the time of the committee meeting, several countries had expressed reservations about the Global Compacts impinging on their sovereignty, a claim that had been publicly expressed by then-leader of the opposition Conservative Party, Andrew Scheer (Zimonjic 2018).

The Standing Committee on Citizenship and Immigration is a standing committee of Parliament and is governed by established Standing Orders (Canada, House of Commons, n.d.). The composition of the committee is based on the standings of recognized parties in the House of Commons. On this particular committee, the majority Liberal party was represented by the chair and members, while the Conservatives, NDP, and Bloc were represented by members only. The committee meeting follows a formal, established protocol, including how the meeting is physically set up and how much time each witness is accorded, as well as speaking times of each member. The chair sometimes allows extra time at their discretion.

The committee meeting I attended was divided into two sessions, both on the Global Compacts. In the session before me, a white settler male academic from a leading Canadian university and a white male non-Canadian representative of the UN Refugee Agency (UNHCR) office in Canada were questioned, mostly on the legal status of the Global Compacts. In my session, I, a white settler female academic, provided my intervention, followed by testimony from two representatives of the non-governmental organization One Free World International (OFWI), which advocates on behalf of persecuted religious minorities. The primary OFWI intervention was given by a volunteer: a Yazidi Canadian woman who shared very personal details of sexual violence and mental illness caused by family separation through the resettlement process. The founder and director of OFWI – who is described on the organization's website as "a human rights advocate ... [whose] human rights journey started in his native Egypt that he was later forced to flee after he was severely tortured and sentenced to death for his conversion to Christianity" (OFWI, n.d.) – briefly outlined the OFWI's work but mostly intervened in the question period in response to questions specifically addressed to him.

Several aspects of this scenario unsettled me. First, the politics of representation were blatantly manifest. The chair and participants did not treat all testimony equally, nor give equal time to each "witness." Intersecting power relations meant that our "expertise" was valued differently depending on our subject positions and our assumed authority on the issue. The Yazidi woman was expected to share intimate personal traumas of rape and mental health, while the white academics and UNHCR representative were asked questions by members of Parliament (MPs) about process and, at some points, to confirm points made by One Free World International. The male academic in the first session did not have his PhD at the time of the meeting, but committee members always referred to him as "Professor," and the chair gave him extra time for his testimony. Committee members addressed me as "Ms.," and the chair cut off my testimony before the allocated seven-minute mark. It was clear that issues of gender, nationality, and class were at play here.

Second, the lines of questioning made me feel like all of us "expert witnesses" were being co-opted into "policy-based evidence-making" (Mythen, Walklate, and Peatfield 2017; Strassheim and Kettunen 2014). For example, committee members questioned the UNHCR representative and the academics several times over the legal implications of the Global Compacts. As mentioned above, this was a politicized issue at the time. Factually speaking, the Global Compacts are not legally binding.

However, by repeating this fact over and over (albeit in response to politically charged questions), our responses discursively undermined the importance of the collective commitments in the Global Compacts to, for example, more equitable responsibility sharing. To be fair, we did emphasize the Global Compacts' normative value and encouraged the Canadian government to respect the principles in the Global Compacts, but the overwhelming message was that Canada is not legally bound to respect them.

Another clear example of this co-option was a line of questioning to the OFWI representative: "Do you think it's fair that illegal border crossers are allowed to bring extended family members into the country when Yazidi refugees are not allowed to do so?" (Larry Maguire, Conservative MP). Here, the premise of the question pitted resettled refugees – such as those represented by OFWI as "legitimate" refugees – against "illegal" border crossers, highly politicized and inaccurate language for refugee claimants exercising their right to seek asylum under international and Canadian law. While this discussion could have been an opportunity to open up questions about definitions of family across immigration categories, some committee members instead used their questions to score political points against refugee claimants. The OFWI representatives did not address the issue of refugee claimants, but instead focused on the psychosocial effects of family separation for Yazidis, which was their purpose in appearing as witnesses. While I felt a moral obligation to correct the myth of illegal border crossers, this question was not posed to me, and I could not – within the confines of the committee structure – intervene unless the chair called upon me. In response to the next question that *was* posed to me, I was tempted to return to this issue, but I did not do so for two reasons. First, the moment had passed and I wanted to have the time to address the question that was directed at me. Second, communications research has shown that mythbusting exercises sometimes end up reinforcing the negative message (Geiger and Meuelemann 2016). However, I still felt like I was complicit in this politicized discussion because I did not directly challenge the polarizing and erroneous language of "illegal border crossers."

While procedural ethics, as manifested in institutional research ethics boards, focus solely on data collection with human subjects,[1] in this chapter, I argue, similarly to Felices-Luna (this volume), for a more relational approach to radical care ethics that takes into account power relations in all interactions. To be clear, I am not advocating for research ethics board oversight over all policy and advocacy activities. Rather, I suggest that researchers and advocates have an *ethical responsibility* to think deeply about dilemmas related to representation, politicized policy making, and allyship. This chapter reflects on two recurring ethical dilemmas in human rights policy work: first, what Alcoff (2009) has summarized as "the problem of speaking for others"; and, second, the co-option of advocates and allies into policy-based evidence making.

WHO SPEAKS FOR WHOM? REPRESENTATION, REPRESENTIVITY, AND TESTIMONY

> "I'd like to thank all the witnesses. Particularly, I'd like to acknowledge and say thank you to you, Adiba, for coming forward as a witness. It's extremely difficult and I think courageous for you to come to share your story with us and to be that advocate and voice for change. I want to acknowledge that."
>
> – JENNY KWAN (VANCOUVER–MOUNT PLEASANT NDP)

I put the term "expert witness" in scare quotes in this chapter to underscore that this is the name the parliamentary committee uses to describe us, and not one I would have chosen to describe myself. In this section, I would like to unpack some ethical questions related to both expertise and testimony.

As the International Association for the Study of Forced Migration code of ethics states, "We acknowledge that too often forced migration researchers are positioned as 'experts' on other people's lives and experiences, and too often speak for, or in the name of, people in forced migration" (2018, n.p.). Expertise is intimately linked to power inequalities in the production of knowledge. Who is identified as an expert, and the extent of their expertise, is tied to real and perceived hierarchies of knowing. As Stehr and Grundmann argue, "Experts are persons of whom it is assumed that, based on their routine contact with specific topics, they have accumulated experience in contexts relevant for taking action, and thus enjoy both trust and social respect" (Stehr and Grundmann 2011, x). Academics are sought out as "experts" often because of positivist notions of objective science – the idea that we can be "unbiased" because our knowledge is based on "facts" and data. In contrast, those with direct experience of forced migration are invited to "share their story," thereby circumscribing the limits of their expertise to their personal circumstances. There needs to be critical reflection about the way "universalized and standardized identities of suffering are established through personal testimony about international human rights violations" (McQuaid 2016, 51).

The parliamentary committee also uses the notions of "witness" and "testimony" both in their formal procedures and in the everyday language of the committee, as demonstrated in the quote from Jenny Kwan, NDP member, above. This quasi-judicial language begs questions about the way the "truth" is constructed during these committee meetings and in other similar policy spaces (Cameron 2018; Lawrance and Ruffer 2015). Grundmann (2017, 27) emphasizes the relational idea of expertise: "Experts mediate between the production of knowledge and its application; they define and interpret situations; and they set priorities for action. Experts are primarily judged by clients, not necessarily by peers (professional or scientific); and they rely on trust by their clients."

Underlying the "expert witness" label are important ethical questions around representation and representivity. In the scenario above, the academics appeared as individuals, while the other people attended as UNHCR and OFWI representatives, respectively. The UNHCR representative was clearly restricted in his ability to speak to issues, at several points deferring the committee to the other academic witness, to Canadian government departments, or to the International Organization for Migration. Similarly, as Nick Catalano explains in their chapter (this volume), public servants represent the government and are thus formally and informally restricted in what they can say publicly. As mentioned above, OFWI was represented by the founder and director, as well as by a volunteer. The organization aims to be "a voice for the voiceless," particularly "persecuted religious minorities" (OFWI, n.d.). It was in this context that the volunteer was invited to share her story of persecution as a Yazidi woman.

While OFWI thus provided an opportunity for a first-hand account of persecution and forced migration, the idea of *giving* "a voice for the voiceless" is not without ethical tensions. Indeed, non-governmental organizations often act as gatekeepers, controlling access to knowledge and policy making (Steimel 2016). Most of the questions for the OFWI representatives were posed to the director, even though he is not Yazidi. To his credit, he often deferred to the volunteer, but the fact that MPs first sought the "official" position highlights questions around representation and credibility. Moreover, at one point, the director shared details about the volunteer's "meltdown" and subsequent hospitalization. While this incident was linked to the volunteer's own testimony and was intended to expose lack of cultural sensitivity in mental health interventions, the fact remains that this was not his story to tell. The Yazidi woman was present and had a voice. By telling her story, the director not only breached confidentiality but also reinforced the power inequities which made MPs more likely to pose questions to him than his colleague.

It is important to question "the very notion of 'the voiceless'" often evoked by human rights advocates and researchers (McQuaid 2016, 58). Speaking for others and presenting oneself as "'the voice of the voiceless' ... paradoxically replicat[es] the anonymity and invisibility generated by structures of oppression" (McQuaid 2016, 58). While procedural ethics privilege anonymity as a way of protecting confidentiality, such standard "ethical" practices can lead to charges of "stealing our stories" (Pittaway, Bartolomei, and Hugman 2010; see also Clark-Kazak 2009). Similarly, even when well-intentioned, sharing other people's stories or speaking for them can be tantamount to appropriation.

In contrast to the UN and non-governmental organization representatives, the other academic and I, appearing as individuals, did not represent our universities or any other institution. I was invited directly by public servants who act as clerks to the standing committee based on my academic research. No one had to pre-read or approve my text or talking points. Technically speaking, the academics are only accountable to ourselves. While this leeway opens up possibilities for advocacy, it also creates a potentially dangerous ethical void. We have a platform, but there are no checks and balances on using this platform responsibly or in the best way possible to amplify the messages of those who do not have opportunities to appear before the committee. I will return to this point in the penultimate section.

The question of representation also begs questions of representivity, especially in relation to intersecting positionalities and power inequalities. In the context of discussions of immigration, citizenship and immigration status are important. In the standing committee meeting described here, only one of the four[2] testimony slots was given to people with direct experience of forced migration. As members of Parliament, all committee members are Canadian citizens, accountable to their constituencies, while the UN representative is a citizen of a different country. In this politicized context, the testimony of those perceived to be Canadians by birth – who also were "neutral" academics – was sometimes used to corroborate information provided by recent citizens or "outsiders." For example, both the other academic and I had to reiterate points made by the UNHCR representative about the non-legal nature of the Global Compacts, while I was asked on two occasions to comment on the Yazidi resettlement question – an area where I have limited knowledge.

In terms of socially constructed race, we as witnesses were not as diverse as the MPs or the Canadian population. Only the OFWI representatives were visible minorities. In the context of explicit and implicit racism in Canadian immigration policy, the fact that the racialized witnesses were also newcomers reinforces racialized understandings of citizenship and belonging (Thobani 2007).

Gender also factors into intersecting power relations. As mentioned above, the male academic was addressed as "Professor," while I was called "Ms." Normally, I ask students and non-academic colleagues to use my first name, rather than my academic title. However, in this context, I had a visceral, angry reaction at this differential, gendered treatment. I felt undermined and discredited. This was exacerbated by the chair's discretionary use of the time allocated. Each "witness" was supposed to have seven minutes to make our original remarks. At the beginning of his intervention, my male colleague started speaking quickly. The chair interrupted him: "I'll just ask the witness to slow down one notch for the interpreter. I'll give you a little extra time for their benefit, not yours" (Open Parliament, n.d.). In contrast, I had timed my prepared remarks carefully to be able to convey all of my ideas clearly within the allocated time. However, at the five-minute mark, I was told, "Okay. I need you to wind up quickly" (Open Parliament, n.d.). These examples of gender discrimination may perhaps seem trivial. But they have an impact on the way committee members, other witnesses, and I perceived the value of our testimonies. As such, I became focused on these micro injustices and felt less empowered and articulate in my subsequent interventions.

Mumilaaq Qaqqaq, member of Parliament for Nunavut, has spoken out publicly about the mental health toll of being constantly discredited in public policy spaces because of intersectional power inequalities (CBC News 2021). Although she was a democratically elected leader of the largest electoral riding in the world, her views and the rights of her constituents were regularly ignored. As a young Inuit woman, she had to constantly assert her right to be in Parliament:

> So many of these systems in place are not built for Indigenous people, are not built for racialized individuals, are not built for women. So I spend a lot of my time [reminding myself], 'I belong here. I belong here. I belong here.' I know my truth. I know my history. I know the truths and history for my constituents. (Qaqqaq, quoted in TakingITGlobal 2020)

Qaqqaq's experiences demonstrate the degree to which systemic racism and patriarchy explicitly and implicitly impact the value attached to an individual's testimony in official government spaces.

The kinds of questions posed to each witness also varied depending on our subject positions, the value attached to our testimony, and who we were perceived to "represent." For example, the issue of family reunification was raised by the female Yazidi representative of OFWI, but the question was posed to the male director. Similarly, the white settler academics – perceived to be "objective" – were often asked to confirm or corroborate information provided by other witnesses.

EVIDENCE-BASED POLICY MAKING OR POLICY-BASED EVIDENCE MAKING?

> "I think we all agree that we should or want to reduce migration, whether it is forced or driven by economic necessity."
>
> – SALMA ZAHID (SCARBOROUGH CENTRE, LIBERAL)

Participation in policy-making spaces, such as the one described in this chapter, can provide important opportunities to engage in advocacy and to influence the way issues are discussed and decisions are taken. However, in politicized contexts, especially partisan spaces like parliamentary committees, and on politicized issues such as migration, testimony can be manipulated or taken out of context. Human rights researchers and advocates have an ethical obligation to reduce the risks of the latter, but also to be aware of ways they may be co-opted through the process.

As the quote above by MP Salma Zahid, on an assumed common goal "to reduce migration," and as the previous example about "illegal border crossers" illustrate, witnesses may be confronted by normative statements and underlying assumptions with which they do not agree. This poses an ethical dilemma: Do they use their limited time to register their disagreement? By not contradicting such statements, are they tacitly endorsing them? In these particular examples, the question was not directed at me and by the time I was given an opportunity to intervene, the moment had passed. However, as mentioned above, I still felt ethically responsible for not publicly contradicting these narratives.

In a less dramatic but no less ethically fraught way, human rights researchers and advocates may find themselves co-opted into an exercise of policy-based evidence making, whereby a policy has already been decided and witnesses are used to confirm and legitimate a pre-established decision. Here, I would like to focus on the example of Yazidi resettlement to Canada. In contrast to the rather divisive politicized discussion on the Global Compacts, questions to the OFWI representatives appeared to demonstrate a consensus across the political parties that Canada could and should resettle Yazidis facing religious persecution. Therefore, the discussion focused more on the numbers. Both a Liberal (Whalen) and New Democratic (Kwan) MP asked me how many should be resettled. In the first instance, I deferred to the OFWI colleagues, who proposed a figure of four thousand. MP Kwan then asked me to confirm that.

I did not have in-depth knowledge of the circumstances of Yazidis, or sufficient information at that moment to endorse a specific number. Here, I was caught between, on the one hand, my desire to amplify the experiences of those who had direct experience and knowledge of the context and, on the other hand, an ethical obligation to only comment publicly on issues that I knew well enough to have an informed opinion. In response to MP Kwan's question about the four thousand figure, I said, "I would support the resettlement of as many Yazidis as necessary to resolve that long-standing and entrenched issue. I think this is where Canada has shown leadership in the past and this is where Canada can show leadership now." This is, admittedly, a non-answer that could be interpreted and used in contradictory ways.

As Timothy Kuhn and Michele Jackson (2008, 474) argue, "Knowledge, or that which is taken to be knowledge, is communicatively constructed." In the vignette above, the testimonies we gave to the committee – however imperfect – discursively constructed "evidence" that is part of the permanent public record. It is ethically incumbent upon those of us who are given opportunities to participate in such knowledge- and policy-production processes to think carefully about what we say and how we say it.

UNINTENDED CONSEQUENCES OF TESTIMONY AND POLICY

This point leads to a final ethical dilemma about the unintended consequences of both testimony and policy. While most human rights researchers and advocates are well-intentioned, we need to think carefully about the potential negative implications of our work. First, we may be quoted out of context. Academics often make nuanced arguments about complicated issues. We often acknowledge the opposite point of view before rebutting it. Few of us are trained in effective communications strategies. As a former public servant, I think very carefully about the "front page" test (Baker 1997), that is, asking ourselves how we would feel if our spoken or written words or actions were published on the front page of a major international newspaper. However, this is not standard practice in academia.

Second, even when our work is accurately represented, there can be potentially negative implications of the policies for which we are advocating. For example, I work on age discrimination within migration law and policy. My conceptual framework is based on the notion of social age – the idea that age, like gender, is both a biological reality and a social construct. I argue that chronological age is itself socially constructed – a product of context-specific ideas of human development as a time-bound process that can be measured chronologically through particular biomedical approaches. I advocate for a more holistic understanding of age that is not solely based on chronological age. However, many human rights colleagues have pointed out to me the potential misuse of the social age framework to deny unaccompanied minors access to specialized services and protection because they come from cultures where they may be socially considered as adults because of other markers, such as marriage or education or puberty. In other words, a potential negative consequence of what is intended to be a progressive approach to age could actually backfire by taking away specific rights and protections to under-eighteen refugee claimants who "present" as adults.

TOWARD ALLYSHIP?
FROM PROCEDURAL ETHICS TO A RADICAL ETHICS OF CARE

So, how do we deal with these multiple layers of ethical dilemmas? It could be easy to default to paralysis by analysis – to do nothing so that we do not have to navigate this ethically fraught context. However, doing nothing is also a decision – our silence or inaction can be filled by others with different agendas and less reflexive approaches. As Alcoff argues (2009, 125), "We certainly want to encourage a more receptive listening on the part of the discursively privileged and to discourage presumptuous and oppressive practices of speaking for ... But a retreat from speaking for will not result in receptive listening in all cases."

One potential way forward is to rethink approaches to ethics. In most institutional settings, including universities, the focus is on procedural ethics. "Procedural ethics encompasses research ethics approval processes such as developing research protocols, participant information sheets, informed consent forms, and other procedural documentation supporting research. These procedural ethical processes are different from ethics-in-practice: the day-to-day ethical issues that arise during research conduct" (Chiumento, Rahman, and Frith 2020, 1). A procedural approach is limiting precisely because it does not address the ethical dilemmas that arise in the everyday messiness of research and advocacy (see also Felices-Luna, this volume). Moreover, as mentioned above, some of this work – including policy interventions – is not subject to research ethics board approval.

While I am not advocating for an expansion of board oversight into policy work, I do think that human rights researchers and practitioners need to reflexively consider key ethical questions before and during our participation in policy making. We cannot assume that good intentions are enough. We also cannot assume that our intentions are inherently good. All of us are motivated by multiple drivers, including career advancement and external validation. If I honestly reflect on the anger I felt at the Professor/Ms. dichotomy highlighted above, it was partially related to my own sense of pride, rather than solely linked to gender discrimination. In fact, when I went back through the transcripts, I noted that the male academic *was* sometimes referred to as "Mr.," and on one occasion the chair addressed me as "Professor." The fact that I did not tune into this nuance at the time and misremembered the scenario demonstrates that I have become accustomed to the power accorded to me as a privileged, white academic.

To help me come to terms with this privilege, I have benefited from the work of colleagues who propose a radical ethics of care: "Theorized as an affective connective tissue between an inner self and an outer world, care constitutes a feeling with, rather than a feeling for, others. When mobilized, it offers visceral, material, and emotional heft to acts of preservation that span a breadth of localities: selves, communities, and social worlds" (Hobart and Kneese 2020, 1). Radical care ethics are characterized by relational social ontology, underscoring the mutual and interdependent ways in which people are connected, but within asymmetric power relations (Lawson 2007). Applying this relational approach to the ethical dilemmas of representation and representivity highlighted above, it is incumbent upon us to engage in critical reflexivity throughout policy-making processes. Who are we and how are we connected to others through personal and institutional relationships? How are these relationships embedded in intersecting but unequal power relations? To whom are we accountable and responsible? As Lawson (2007, 6) argues, this approach "asks us to take seriously the ways in which our work is '*for* others' and to build connection and responsibility as key values."

How can we build this connection and responsibility in policy work? As Grundmann (2017, 27–28) argues, "Experts are not only characterised by their embodiment of skills and experience. What matters is their performance." Our policy praxis needs to embody care.

Engaging in allyship is one way forward. As research on LGBTQ+ (Russell and Bohan 2016), anti-racism (Brown and Ostrove 2013; Erskine and Bilimoria 2019), and Indigenous (Smith et al. 2015) advocacy has shown, in some cases allyship can reinforce existing power relationships (Kluttz, Walker, and Walter 2020). However, allyship from a critical care ethics perspective is rooted in connection and responsibility. It means "establishing a meaningful relationship with and ensuring accountability to those with whom individuals are seeking to ally themselves" (Brown and Ostrove 2013, 2212). It challenges human rights activities and researchers to carefully consider their positionality within these power inequalities and how they can use this to effect change (Smith, Puckett, and Simon 2015). Building on notions of reciprocity and respect, allyship is earned – no one has a right to self-identify as an ally.

One way to practically engage in meaningful relationship building is to defer to other colleagues whose perspectives would diversify the conversation. For example, Share the Platform (2020) is "a group of practitioners and scholars from refugee and non-refugee backgrounds who call upon their refugee colleagues to deliver their expertise on the unique needs and experiences of refugee populations in a wide variety of fields." Another example is a male colleague who acknowledges the lack of female perspectives in mainstream media and provides a list of female "experts" when contacted for interviews (Vucetic, n.d.). The idea here is to move from tokenistic invitations to "share your story" to meaningful ways to shape policy making. When transferring access to policy spaces to others is not possible, human rights activists and researchers should work with those most affected by policies to craft and amplify key messages and positions. It is also our responsibility to proactively reflect on our own positionality and the potential unintended consequences of our actions and positions. Human rights researchers should use our privileged platforms to raise issues that others cannot address – because of their precarious legal status, limited access, or institutional affiliation. As "independent" witnesses, academics are well placed to speak truth to power in policy-making contexts. It is our responsibility to maximize the change-making potential of our policy-making opportunities.

Reflecting back on the dilemmas raised by the vignette, there are a few changes to the way I will engage in this kind of institutionalized, politicized policy-making in future. First, I will make more efforts to ensure that I find out who else will be testifying and reach out to them in advance to gain insights into their key messages and positions. For example, had I been aware that OFWI would be advocating for Yazidi resettlement to Canada, I could have taken time in advance to gain more knowledge of the situation and formulate a better-informed position on this issue. I should also have coordinated more closely with my academic colleague to strategize on our messaging and decide who was best placed – given the intersectional power relations mentioned above – to highlight which issues. Second, I should have done a better job of anticipating the types of politically charged, partisan questions that would be asked. When I was a public servant, one of the tasks early in my career was to prepare speaking points for the minister during parliamentary question period. I should have used this training to get a better sense of the way both the parties and the individual members had recently intervened on the topic of the Global Compacts, so that I could better position myself within the politics of policy-based evidence making. Finally, I should have better used my opening statement to front-end issues that are most important to the people whose lives are affected by the discussion. Though I did consult broadly while preparing my remarks, I did not adequately prioritize the most important issues for the communities with whom I work, especially as I was cut off before my allocated time. I therefore "wasted" time on admittedly self-serving points about the Global Academic Network provided for in the Global Compact on Refugees and consequently did not have time to address other key issues, such as internal displacement being absent from the Global Compacts. I would also have had prepared better "speaking points" with my key messages to use during the question period.

CONCLUSION: THE POWER OF PRIVILEGE IN POLICY MAKING

How do – and should – we use this privileged access to policy spaces? In this chapter, I have highlighted some of the ethical dilemmas that arise in politicized policy-making contexts in an attempt to underscore the responsibility of those of us who are invited into these spaces, to reflect carefully on this question in the context of intersecting power relations. We need to honestly and reflexively evaluate our own privilege and motivations and better amplify the work of under-represented individuals, organizations, and issues. Radical care ethics extend beyond the procedural ethical imperative of "doing no harm" to "include a reasonably limited commitment to actively working for the *prevention of* harm" (Pettersen

2011, 54; my emphasis). We cannot possibly anticipate and mitigate every risk that may arise through our research and advocacy work. But we do have an ethical obligation to *care:* about the people whose lives may be impacted by policies and about our role in (inadvertently) reinforcing or dismantling oppressive structures as a result of decisions made in policy-making spaces.

NOTES

1 I use the term "human subjects" because that is the terminology used by research ethics boards.

2 The One Free World International representatives co-presented in one testimony slot.

REFERENCES

Alcoff, L.M. 2009. "The Problem of Speaking for Others." In *Voice in Qualitative Inquiry: Challenging Conventional, Interpretive, and Critical Conceptions in Qualitative Research,* edited by A.Y. Jackson and L.A. Mazzei, 117–35. Abingdon, UK: Routledge.

Baker, S. 1997. "Applying Kidder's Ethical Decision-Making Checklist to Media Ethics." *Journal of Mass Media Ethics* 12, 4: 197–210.

Brown, K.T., and J.M. Ostrove. 2013. "What Does It Mean to Be an Ally? The Perception of Allies from the Perspective of People of Color." *Journal of Applied Social Psychology* 43, 11: 2211–22.

Cameron, H.E. 2018. *Refugee Law's Fact-Finding Crisis: Truth, Risk, and the Wrong Mistake*. Cambridge: Cambridge University Press.

Canada, House of Commons. n.d. Committees. Accessed March 3, 2021. https://www.ourcommons.ca/about/OurProcedure/Committees/c_g_committees-e.htm.

CBC News. 2021. "Nunavut MP Speaks about Return to Parliament after Extended Leave." February 28, 2021. https://www.cbc.ca/news/canada/north/nunavut-mp-return-mumilaaq-qaqqaq-1.5931320. For the full radio interview, see Mumilaaq Qaqqaq, interviewed by Piya Chattopadhyay, *Sunday Magazine,* CBC, 28 February. https://www.cbc.ca/listen/live-radio/1-57-the-sunday-magazine/clip/15827261-the-sunday-magazine-february-28-2021.

Chiumento, A., A. Rahman, and L. Frith. 2020. "Writing to Template: Researchers' Negotiation of Procedural Research Ethics." *Social Science and Medicine* 255: 112980. doi: 10.1016/j.socscimed.2020.112980.

Crenshaw, K. 1989. "Demarginalizing the Intersection of Race and Sex: A Black Feminist Critique of Antidiscrimination Doctrine, Feminist Theory and Antiracist Politics." *University of Chicago Legal Forum* vol. 1989, article 8: 139. https://chicagounbound.uchicago.edu/uclf/vol1989/iss1/8.

England, K.V.L. 1994. "Getting Personal: Reflexivity, Positionality, and Feminist Research." *Professional Geographer* 46, 1: 80–89. doi:10.1111/j.0033-0124.1994.00080.x.

Erskine, S.E., and D. Bilimoria. 2019. "White Allyship of Afro-diasporic Women in the Workplace: A Transformative Strategy for Organizational Change." *Journal of Leadership and Organizational Studies* 26, 3: 319–38.

Geiger, B.B., and B. Meueleman. 2016. "Beyond 'Mythbusting': How to Respond to Myths and Perceived Undeservingness in the British Benefits System." *Journal of Poverty and Social Justice* 24, 3: 291–306.

Grundmann, R. 2017. "The Problem of Expertise in Knowledge Societies." *Minerva* 55, 1: 25–48.

Hobart, H.J.K., and T. Kneese. 2020. "Radical Care: Survival Strategies for Uncertain Times." *Social Text* 38, 1: 1–16. doi:10.1215/01642472-7971067.

International Association for the Study of Forced Migration. 2018. Code of Ethics: Critical Reflections on Research Ethics in Situations of Forced Migration. http://iasfm.org/wp-content/uploads/2018/11/IASFM-Research-Code-of-Ethics-2018.pdf.

Kluttz, J., J. Walker, and P. Walter. 2020. "Unsettling Allyship, Unlearning and Learning towards Decolonising Solidarity." *Studies in the Education of Adults* 52, 1: 49–66.

Kuhn, T., and M.H. Jackson. 2008. "Accomplishing Knowledge: A Framework for Investigating Knowing in Organizations." *Management Communication Quarterly* 21, 4: 454–85.

Lawrance, B.N., and G. Ruffer, eds. 2015. *Adjudicating Refugee and Asylum Status.* New York: Cambridge University Press.

Lawson, V. 2007. "Geographies of Care and Responsibility." *Annals of the Association of American Geographers* 97, 1: 1–11.

McQuaid, K.R.V. 2016. "'We Raise Up the Voice of the Voiceless': Voice, Rights, and Resistance amongst Congolese Human Rights Defenders in Uganda." *Refuge: Canada's Journal on Refugees* 32, 1: 50–59.

Mythen, G., S. Walklate, and E.-J. Peatfield. 2017. "Assembling and Deconstructing Radicalisation in PREVENT: A Case of Policy-Based Evidence Making?" *Critical Social Policy* 37, 2: 180–201.

OFWI (One Free World International). n.d. Last accessed October 29, 2020. https://ofwi.org/.

Open Parliament. (Transcripts of Parliamentary Standing Committee on Immigration and Citizenship). https://openparliament.ca/committees/immigration/42-1/136/.

Pettersen, T. 2011. "The Ethics of Care: Normative Structures and Empirical Implications." *Health Care Analysis* 19, 1: 51–64. https://doi.org/10.1007/s10728-010-0163-7.

Pittaway, E., L. Bartolomei, and R. Hugman. 2010. "'Stop Stealing Our Stories': The Ethics of Research with Vulnerable Groups." *Journal of Human Rights Practice* 2, 2: 229–51.

Russell, G.M., and J.S. Bohan. 2016. "Institutional Allyship for LGBT Equality: Underlying Processes and Potentials for Change." *Journal of Social Issues* 72, 2: 335–54.

Sen, G., A. Iyer, and C. Mukherjee. 2009. "A Methodology to Analyse the Intersections of Social Inequalities in Health." *Journal of Human Development and Capabilities* 10, 3: 397–415.

Share the Platform. n.d. https://www.sharetheplatform.org/.

Smith, J., C. Puckett, and W. Simon. 2015. *Indigenous Allyship: An Overview*. Waterloo, ON: Office of Aboriginal Initiatives, Wilfrid Laurier University.

Stehr, N., and R. Grundmann. 2011. *Experts: The Knowledge and Power of Expertise*. Abingdon, UK: Routledge.

Steimel, S., and C. Alvares. 2016. "Negotiating Knowledges and Expertise in Refugee Resettlement Organizations." *Cogent Social Sciences* 2, 1: article 1162990. https://doi.org/10.1080/23311886.2016.1162990.

Strassheim, H., and P. Kettunen. 2014. "When Does Evidence-Based Policy Turn into Policy-Based Evidence? Configurations, Contexts and Mechanisms." *Evidence and Policy: A Journal of Research, Debate and Practice* 10, 2: 259–77.

TakingITGlobal. 2020. "Politics with Mumilaaq Qaqqaq." Future Pathways Fireside Chats, July 9, 2020. https://medium.com/future-pathways-fireside-chats/politics-with-mumilaaq-qaqqaq-aacaf3c4ace3.

Vucetic, Srdjan. n.d. "Media." Last accessed December 20, 2022. https://srdjanvucetic.wordpress.com/media/.

Zimonjic, P. 2018. "Ex-Harper Immigration Minister Calls Out Scheer over 'Factually Incorrect' Statements on UN Migration Pact." CBC News, December 4, 2018. https://www.cbc.ca/news/politics/alexander-scheer-trudeau-un-compact-1.4932698.

4

Navigating the Ethical Challenges of Work with Detained Migrants and Asylum Seekers in Greece

Jason Phillips

A CAMP BURNS …

On September 8, 2020, Moria camp on the Greek island of Lesbos burned to the ground. In the span of a few hours approximately twelve thousand asylum seekers, including about four thousand children, were rendered homeless, forced to sleep on tombstones and in parking lots (Stevis-Gridneff 2020). It is reported that some of Moria's residents deliberately set the fire, an act of desperate self-harm allegedly triggered by the Greek authority's imposition of a quarantine on the camp in the wake of several residents testing positive for the coronavirus (New York Times 2020). To those of us familiar with Moria, it may have been public health measures that lit the spark, but it was years of degrading treatment and a lack of hope that were the kindling upon which it burned. As Mahbube Ahzani, age fifteen, who had been in the camp with her family for ten months, so aptly put it, "I think sleeping on the street is bad, but Moria is bad-bad" (Stevis-Gridneff 2020).

Operating in situations that are "bad-bad" is the hallmark of humanitarian action. Driven by what many refer to as an "imperative" to save life and preserve human dignity, humanitarians regularly foray into the most extreme situations of conflict, destitution, and rights deprivation to attempt to provide succour and protection. Doing so, however, is fraught with the potential that one's efforts to do good can inadvertently contribute to harm. Two manifestations of this persistent ethical problem (Slim 2015) are the risk that aid givers can become complicit in the harms they seek to ameliorate or that they may legitimize oppressive structures, policies, or actors at the root of the suffering of those being served. Both manifestations raised their heads for humanitarian agencies that considered if and how to work in Moria. While not unique in themselves, the specific political context in which Moria was embedded provoked and exacerbated these ethical problems. The International Rescue Committee's (IRC) reluctance to engage in Moria was closely linked to the role that it played within the European Union's (EU) 2016 migration management agreement with Turkey, which was seen as harmful to asylum seekers' rights and well-being. This tension played out such that IRC kept its work with Moria's residents to a small portion of the country's program portfolio relative to its work with other needy populations.

As a senior manager at IRC, I visited Moria several times between 2017 and 2018 to support the organization's programs in Greece.[1] In 2019, IRC and Stichting Vluchteling (the Dutch Refugee Foundation) engaged me as an independent researcher to evaluate the ethical tensions that arose in IRC's work with detained asylum seekers in both Greece and Libya (Phillips 2019). The shift in role from aid practitioner to external aid evaluator was accompanied by a shift in my understanding of and stance toward complicity. This moral evolution had two dimensions. I discovered a more nuanced and, in retrospect, more empirically (and emotionally) accurate way to understand the way I and IRC were grappling with the concept of complicity in relation to Moria: as moral taint, or pollution, rather than as actual contribution to harm. My ethical stance also evolved from what might be considered an almost deontological fetishism to a grudging consequentialism. During my time at IRC, I staunchly believed that the agency should desist from all forms of engagement with Moria in order to keep its hands clean from harms being perpetrated by the EU's flawed asylum policies. But in the course of my research, I developed a greater appreciation of the potential for aid to mitigate the worst harms that Moria's residents were suffering and IRC's ability to bring a modicum of humanity into a space characterized by its inhumanity.

SETTING THE STAGE FOR ETHICAL TENSION: MORIA, THE "WORLD'S WORST REFUGEE FACILITY"

Greece has long served as a principal entry point for refugees, asylum seekers, and migrants to the EU.[2] Fleeing war in Syria and other conflicts, they arrived in numbers that increased exponentially in 2015, when approximately 850,000 of the one million people who arrived in the EU entered through Greece. Most entered from Turkey via proximate Greek islands such as Lesbos. Greece was largely a transit point for these new arrivals, who quickly made their way out of the country along the "Balkan route" to northern European countries such as Germany and Sweden.

Under then extant EU asylum framework provisions, responsibility for the processing of all asylum claims, as well as for the long-term hosting and eventual return of failed claimants, fell on states of first arrival. Yet due to the rapid movements of such large numbers of people, Greece's asylum system was unable to keep pace, leading to the failure to identify and register people moving onward through Europe. EU member states responded unilaterally by erecting border fences, reintroducing border checks, and instituting caps on the number of people who could claim asylum. Political and public backlash against the surge in arrivals, compounded by frequent graphic reporting on the fatally dangerous crossings of the Aegean Sea, led the EU to undertake concerted efforts to stem arrivals to the European mainland.

The cornerstone of the approach adopted to address this situation was the agreement reached between the EU and Turkey in March 2016, commonly referred to as the EU-Turkey deal (hereafter, the Deal; European Commission 2016). The Deal had two mutually supportive elements. It was an initiative to help front-line states, i.e., Greece and Italy, fulfill their duties to quickly identify, register, and fingerprint incoming migrants with support provided by EU agencies. It was also a package of relocation measures that aimed to take pressure off front-line states by allowing for the orderly and equitable hosting of accepted asylum claimants throughout member states. Under the agreement's terms, all migrants and asylum seekers who arrived on the Greek islands after March 20, 2016, were liable to be returned to Turkey. In exchange for each return, the EU promised to resettle one Syrian from Turkey. The EU also offered Turkey six billion euros, the lifting of visa requirements for its nationals, and the resumption of Turkey's EU accession process.

The EU's plan to manage the massive increase in migrant and asylum-seeker arrivals included the establishment of ten facilities across Greece and Italy known as "hotspots," or Reception and Identification Centres.[3] On Greece they were established on the islands of Lesbos, Chios, Samos, Leros, and Kos. Set up between October 2015 and March 2016, they originally functioned as open facilities to register, screen, and help arriving migrants and asylum seekers before their transfer to the Greek mainland (Majcher 2018).[4]

After the Deal, however, the role of Reception and Identification Centres changed such that they became the centrepiece of the enforcement of the Deal (Majcher 2018). Under a Greek law adopted in April 2016, the Reception and Identification Centres were converted into "closed" facilities wherein newly arrived asylum seekers were prevented from leaving the premises for up to twenty-five days while they were being registered. Reception and Identification Centres like Moria also became spaces for pre-removal detention for those receiving a decision of return to Turkey as well as those asylum seekers with low recognition rates. Due to civil society pressure, overcrowding brought about by excessive delays in processing asylum claims, the failure of the intra-European relocation scheme to gain traction with member states, and limited returns to Turkey, the "closed" nature of the centres was eased in practice, if not in law. Residents of Moria not explicitly held in the "detention" enclosure were permitted to enter and exit the facility during the day (Majcher 2018).[5]

An additional feature of the hotspot approach in Greece is what is referred to as the "geographic restriction." Pursuant to this measure, asylum seekers were no longer transferred to the Greek mainland unless they met specific vulnerability criteria.[6] They were forced to remain on the island where they were originally registered and were made to undergo a fast-track border procedure to determine whether Turkey was a safe country to which they could return. Due to excessive administrative delays many found themselves, in effect, stranded on islands like Lesbos for months, if not years.

Substandard living conditions have characterized Moria since 2016. Extreme overcrowding, lack of basic services and appropriate shelter, high degrees of violence, and poor hygiene have been constants.[7] In September 2018, a *Guardian* headline referred to Moria as "the world's worst refugee facility" (Leape 2018). Since that time efforts were made by the Greek authorities, in partnership with the United Nations High Commissioner for Refugees to decongest Moria, moving more people to the Greek mainland and other more hospitable locations on the island. Yet by the time fire razed the camp in September 2020, its population had surged again to over twelve thousand, almost four times its capacity (Stevis-Gridneff 2020).

FEELING CONNECTED TO HARM: A VIGNETTE OF A TOUR OF MORIA

In February 2017, I travelled to Greece to support the IRC's work with migrants, refugees, and asylum seekers. The trip had two components: participation in a regional meeting and project oversight. IRC's European management team invited me to attend their meeting in Athens to facilitate a reflection on humanitarian ethics and a critical examination of live ethical challenges IRC faced in its work, in what was the latest in a series of IRC leadership forums where I had led similar exercises. The two closely linked moral conundrums that my colleagues identified as the most pressing for discussion were how to respond to EU humanitarian and development assistance funding opportunities that instrumentalized aid for the purpose of restricting migration to Europe, and whether the provision of assistance to residents of Moria could render IRC complicit in the harms that Greece's and the EU's asylum policies were inflicting on them.

The other part of my mission entailed visiting IRC programs in and around Athens and on Lesbos and meeting with partner organizations, recipients of IRC services, and representatives of the government of Greece. It was during my trip to Lesbos that IRC's country director and other members of the IRC Greece team gave me my first tour of Moria. Having already facilitated the reflection session at the regional meeting, I commenced the tour with my ethical radar on high alert, hypersensitive to the perceived harms that the camp and asylum policy were inflicting on its residents.

Entering the camp, a confusing paradox immediately struck me. I considered myself a fairly seasoned humanitarian, having worked in the sector for twenty years. Yet the prison-like infrastructure of Moria caught me off guard. It seemed oddly different and more sinister, more repressive, than other refugee or displaced persons camps in Asia, Africa, or the Middle East that I had visited or in which I had worked. The facility was surrounded by chain-link fence and topped with barbed wire. It had the look and feel of a site of detention, which, of course, it was. I had not visited other prisons or immigration detention facilities, as these were not typical spaces in which IRC worked. Snaking through various stanchions was a line of people waiting to receive a food distribution that reminded me of cattle. I am still not sure why witnessing countless food distribution exercises in African refugee camps that utilized similar mechanisms of control did not provoke the same response, but something about my understanding of Moria as a prison seems to have been at play.

Juxtaposed with the optics and feeling of extreme deprivation of liberty was the reality that Moria's residents were, in fact, allowed to leave. As we approached the camp entrance and showed our IDs to the Greek authorities, people were milling about and walking into and out of the camp without obstruction. The "inside" and "outside" of the camp were also difficult to demarcate. A small tent city called the "Olive Grove," home to predominantly African asylum seekers with little expected chance of gaining refugee status, had been haphazardly and spontaneously built all around the fenced enclosure without any formal services or infrastructure.

There were holes in the fences, and people moved in and out of them between the Olive Grove and Moria "proper." The practical "openness" of the camp contrasted with its architecture, which conveyed incarceration, problematizing my preconceived notions of Moria as a space of fundamentally greater restrictions on residents' freedom of movement than other locations where IRC worked on Lesbos, such as Kara Tepe camp.

IRC's work – or should I say absence of it – in Moria also discomfited me. The needs were great and visible, the humanitarian imperative crying out for engagement. My colleagues showed me the camp's toilet and showering facilities, overflowing with feces, floors covered with stagnant water. A water and sanitation colleague accompanying me opined that as one of the leading environmental health agencies on the island, IRC had the wherewithal to fix the facilities relatively quickly but had resisted impulses doing so. For a minute I was inclined to advocate for IRC taking on a role improving the camp's sanitation facilities, willing to reconsider IRC's current stance opposed to the rebuilding of the camp's infrastructure. But as I walked through lanes of tents that thousands called their homes, I felt a visceral sense of embarrassment and twinge of remorse when I saw IRC's logo, bright yellow and black, emblazoned on several of the shelters. The best way to describe how I felt was dirty: sullied by any visible expression of a relationship with a place, and system, so inimical to the dignity and rights of those who were forced to be there. Further discussion with the IRC team led to the erasure of our agency's logo from those shelters. I left Moria conflicted: I wanted IRC to help alleviate the suffering of Moria's residents, but I did not want IRC to be a part of Moria, and I did not want anyone to see whatever help we provided.

AMBIVALENT ENGAGEMENT: THE HUMANITARIAN IMPERATIVE TRUMPS THE PURITY OF PRINCIPLE IN MORIA

IRC began work in Greece in July 2015 at the northern end of Lesbos, closest to where most of the boats from Turkey were landing. Based on its assessment that there were larger needs on other parts of the island and that other non-governmental organizations were already working in Moria, IRC opted to focus its attention elsewhere. Moria was a "non-issue" at this pre-Deal time. In the first nine months after IRC commenced operations in the country, it provided ad hoc support in Moria including non-food item distributions when another camp, Kara Tepe, temporarily closed and residents were relocated; followed up on the protection of clients who transited to Moria from other places where IRC was providing assistance;

supported garbage collection in the site via a service contract with the municipality of Mytilene; and periodically improved the water, sanitation, and shelter infrastructure when overcrowding was deemed to create public health risks. IRC also launched a digital information platform, Refugee.info, available to any Moria resident who had a smartphone, to help new arrivals identify and access services across the island and, eventually, all of Greece. IRC's one sustained touch point with the camp was its transportation program. In response to the hardships newly arriving asylum seekers faced in their fifty-kilometre journey on foot from their arrival point on the north of the island to Mytilene, coupled with the criminalization of unregistered migrants procuring transport, IRC began a large-scale busing operation from the north to Mytilene, including to Moria (International Rescue Committee Greece 2016).[8]

The announcement of the Deal upended humanitarian operations in Greece. Wide sections of the human rights and humanitarian community, including IRC, met the Deal with immediate vocal criticism on multiple grounds. To some it represented an abandonment of Europe's ostensibly humane values toward the world's most downtrodden. To others it undermined international, EU, and member state asylum laws, further externalizing Europe's borders and shirking the EU's, and Greece's, responsibilities for protection and care of asylum seekers. Many held up the "return to Turkey" provision as harbouring the potential to cause direct harm to already traumatized people by returning them to a location that was deemed to be unsafe.[9] Médecins Sans Frontières (MSF) went so far as to refuse to accept future funding from any EU member state in protest (Kingsley 2016). In addition to denouncing the Deal, IRC suspended its transportation program to Moria, issuing a press release stating, "The International Rescue Committee will not transport refugees to the closed facility at Moria ... We cannot knowingly participate in the transportation of some of the world's most vulnerable to a place where their freedom of movement is in question" (International Rescue Committee 2016b).

Sitting in my office in Den Haag in the weeks following IRC's decision to denounce the Deal and cease its transportation program, I remember feeling three things. First, my organization's principled, public stance in defence of the rights of asylum seekers in Greece, in opposition to what I believed was a deeply flawed and dangerous retreat from humane asylum policy in the EU, made me very proud. Second, I was secretly envious of the lengths to which MSF was willing – and able – to go to protest the Deal, even though I knew it would not be possible given the differences between IRC's and MSF's funding models.[10] Finally, I was struck by what appeared to be the tenuous and inconsistent ethical logic underpinning my organization's stance toward the Deal and Moria. IRC works in contexts around the world where the freedom of movement of those it serves is heavily constrained, whether in refugee camps in Thailand or Kenya, in camps for internally displaced persons housing family members and alleged affiliates of the Islamic State in both Iraq and Syria, or with interned Rohingya in Myanmar. Yet in none of those situations had the deprivation of liberty led to such a vocal outcry and a cessation of programming. By contrast, it was often one of the foundations on which engagement was justified. So, while it pleased me to be a part of an agency that was "standing on principle" in Greece, I was immediately confronted with a slippery slope that left me unsettled: What felt right in relation to Moria may, if taken to its logical extreme and adopted as an organizational precept, be institutionally untenable. A humanitarian agency that opts to refrain from working in all situations where displaced persons' freedom of movement is constrained would not only be abdicating its fundamental responsibilities but would also quickly find itself obsolete.

The abstention from work in Moria more or less guided IRC's thinking from March 2016 to mid-2019, although it was not dogmatically enforced. Between March 2016 and October 2017, IRC provided various forms of one-off material assistance in Moria in response to sudden onset emergencies. In September 2016, tents, mattresses, and blankets were provided in the aftermath of a fire. In November 2016, one hundred more tents and non-food items were donated after another fire killed two residents. In January 2017, IRC donated and installed forty-eight life shelters – a form of temporary accommodation able to withstand the elements better than tents – in the midst of winter.[11] IRC received a request from the Greek authorities for additional life shelters in October 2017 to prepare for the ensuing winter, but the donation never took place.

In each of these instances, IRC went to great lengths, both internally and externally, to justify these donations as exceptional, temporary, reluctantly pursued actions taken only for their immediate effect of reducing suffering, and to depict them as representative of the failure of duty bearers to uphold their responsibilities to provide dignified living conditions. Illustrative of this is the IRC's press release issued in November 2016 that accompanied its tent donation:

> Earlier this week the IRC warned that unless immediate steps are taken to improve the response for refugees stranded in Greece, lives would be lost. It gives us absolutely no pleasure to be shown correct ...

> As a humanitarian it is soul crushing to see events like this happen within the European Union. It is an abdication of our responsibility as global leaders that we, in Europe, refuse to do better for some of the world's most vulnerable. (International Rescue Committee 2016c)

IRC's intermittent interventions in Moria in the name of the humanitarian imperative frustrated me. I felt it was more important, and would be more powerful from an advocacy perspective, to maintain strict fidelity to our position of abstinence, to be able to oppose European and Greek policy with fully clean hands. Besides, the one-off, in-kind nature of the aid struck me as little more than band-aids, which multiple agencies other than IRC could provide. While they offered some, albeit limited, redress of an acute immediate need, and may have temporarily fostered more positive relationships with Greek authorities, I viewed them as coming at the cost of IRC being a partner in a system of structural repression of asylee rights.

By the time IRC embarked on a strategic planning exercise for Greece in September 2017, its thinking about engagement in Moria had begun to change. On the one hand, it became less inclined to accede to ad hoc requests for "emergency" infrastructure support.[12] On the other hand, it became increasingly concerned about the evidently harmful effects that camp conditions and continued restrictions to the islands were having on Moria's residents. Specifically, IRC and other actors began to identify the acute mental health needs of residents of Reception and Identification Centres as a hidden and unaddressed crisis. Prolonged stagnation in poor camp conditions was seen to exacerbate, if not actually provoke, severe psychosocial distress among its residents (MSF Greece 2017). In response, IRC commenced operations, in January 2018, to meet the mental health needs of Reception and Identification Centre residents and bring those needs to a wider audience through advocacy. IRC started a Mental Health and Psychosocial Support program targeting clients in both Moria and Vial, the Reception and Identification Centre on the island of Chios. Through December 2018, IRC provided 285 clients with individual and group counselling sessions.[13] The program consisted of case management support, patient referrals to hospital and psychiatrist care, training on Mental Health and Psychosocial Support care for non-medical staff from other agencies at the Reception and Identification Centres, and transportation to and from the Reception and Identification Centres to IRC counselling centres established outside them. In keeping with concerns about

Moria and Vial's roles as part of the Deal and taking advantage of their continued "open" nature, IRC structured the program such that there would be no sustained physical presence or direct client services provided inside them.

UNPACKING COMPLICITY

How can one's efforts to alleviate suffering contribute, directly or indirectly, to a perpetuation of that suffering? How can a humanitarian agency operate in the midst of, or in proximity to, actors or systems that deprive people of their rights, that treat them inhumanely, without perpetuating or legitimizing them? How does one navigate between ameliorating the harms of systems that one opposes without becoming a part of those systems themselves?

Behind these questions lurks the spectre of complicity. It was a fear of complicity with the EU's and Greece's pernicious asylum and detention systems, so visibly manifest in the suffering of Moria's residents, that provoked my visceral repulsion at the sight of IRC's logo attached to the camp's infrastructure. But how should we understand complicity in a humanitarian context like Moria? How did it rear its head and cause consternation for IRC in Greece? How useful a lens is it, really, through which to view IRC's operational decisions and my revulsion at working in Moria? Thanks to the opportunity I was given to examine the ethics of IRC's decision making vis-à-vis Moria from the external vantage point of an independent researcher, I was able to better reflect on the nuances of complicity and, in turn, to recalibrate my understanding of the conditions under which abstention of aid provision in defence of principle is an appropriate way to mitigate the perceived participation in harm.

IRC stakeholders interviewed as part of the ethical evaluation of the agency's work in Greece articulated concerns about moral responsibility as a pervasive fear that engagement in Moria and, by extension, association with the Greek authorities that controlled the Reception and Identification Centres and the EU institutions that supported them, would indirectly contribute to the harms caused by Europe's flawed approach to migration management. "Complicity" was the term IRC stakeholders, and I, used to capture these fears. Indeed, the mini-case study that I prepared to guide ethical reflection at the Athens regional conference was entitled "The Risk of Complicity – Hotspots in Greece." I drew on humanitarian ethicist Hugo Slim's (2015, 18) definition as "the act of cooperating in serious wrongdoing that brings or exacerbates harm instead of relieving it. In its most extreme form, the risk is that acts of kindness can enable or obscure concurrent acts of atrocity." I assumed, without much reflection, that this was the phenomenon that I and IRC were grappling with, the ethical reference point that IRC's operational and advocacy decisions were to be judged against.

IRC's and my own concerns about complicity were articulated in a variety of ways. At the most macro level, the association with, and provision of, support in Moria led to fears that IRC's actions were contributing to the legitimization of the EU's migration management that further externalized its borders. Such efforts were deemed to undermine European, international, and EU–member state asylum laws, represent an abdication of European values, and support a global proliferation of migration laws that criminalized migrants and migration. Too close an association with Moria ran the risk of legitimizing the Deal along with its problematic collective expulsions, refoulement, and commodification of asylum seekers. Europe's migration management approach, of which Moria was an integral component, was not an attempt to find a solution to the problem of migration but, rather, "an extreme defeat for human rights" (Phillips 2019).

There was also perceived risk in the potential legitimization of authorities in control of Moria, or the approach to asylum being taken in Greece. These concerns surfaced due to the fact that unlike other camps for asylum seekers on Lesbos which were under the management of the municipality of Lesbos, it was the Greek Ministry of Migration Policy that administered Moria, local and EU security actors were on site, and it was a place where vulnerable asylum seekers such as unaccompanied children were detained. IRC association with that facility and such actors was feared to be conferring approval for or endorsement of the way the space was being administered.

Beyond questions about legitimization of policies and actors deemed to be causing harm, concerns about complicity embodied the fear that engagement could contribute to the expansion or institutionalization of the detention regime in the country. This led to restrictions placed upon the programs IRC chose to implement such that they did not support the infrastructure of detention.[14] Since the introduction of the Deal, IRC desisted from intervening in ways that could expand, or beautify, the physical spaces of detention. Yet like many other humanitarian actors, IRC eventually came around to the position, with which I concurred, that the provision of services to people that could be directly consumed (i.e., mental health care) were at the boundary of what was acceptable without crossing into direct support for the workings of the Reception and Identification Centres themselves. The provision of mental health support or legal aid was aimed at "helping people to be informed about their rights, helping them to have the best chance to get the protection they need," as opposed to being "part of the system supporting the functioning of the facilities of detention" (Phillips 2019).

Concerns about complicity were intertwined with an awareness that humanitarian action in Moria could inadvertently substitute for, or absolve, principal duty bearers from their responsibilities. Several IRC staff expressed wariness that the organization's actions could inappropriately subsidize the failures of state or multilateral actors that bore the first and foremost accountability for providing dignified asylum in accordance with national and international law. The involvement of non-state actors in immigration detention "can complicate the accountability and responsibility" of state authorities, putting humanitarian non-governmental organizations (NGOs) in a problematic position of deflecting criticism away from duty bearers. Put more bluntly, the "involvement of NGOs in detention service provision risks providing the state with normative cover for its detention activities" (Flynn 2017, 595). Frustration that those perceived as holding the principal duty to offer humane protection and assistance were unable, or unwilling, to live up to those obligations was a dominant undercurrent in IRC's programming decisions and advocacy messaging around Moria.

Sentiments about Greek governmental responsibility for the situation in Moria, however, shifted over time. At the outset of its response in 2015, IRC depicted Greece, beset by a crippling financial crisis and forced to shoulder the responsibility for the massive inflow of over eight hundred thousand migrants and asylum seekers almost on its own, given common EU asylum system breakdown, with great sympathy. IRC and other NGOs directed their initial calls for increased accountability at the EU. As one IRC staff initially described the situation, it was not a "refugee crisis" but an EU-"manufactured humanitarian crisis" that produced the "shameful situation on the [Greek] islands" (Phillips 2019). IRC's messaging consistently called upon the EU to help Greece uphold Europe's responsibilities to protect asylum seekers and migrants on their territory. Appropriate support entailed, among other things, redistributing successful asylum seekers throughout EU member states so that Greece did not have to shoulder the burden all by itself; provision of financial assistance to manage and improve the asylum process; and deployment of technical assistance and labour from specialized EU agencies to Greece to expedite and professionalize all aspects of asylum claim processing.

As the years wore on, conditions in Moria did not get better, they got demonstrably worse. Yet in the intervening period huge sums of money and technical resources from the EU were poured into Greece. What was previously perceived as an excusable lack of capacity began to slide into questions about how much longer it was appropriate to consider the lack of winterized housing in Moria an "emergency" to which an NGO response was warranted. Lack of preparedness for known seasonal weather variations had become the status quo. Under such conditions, it became harder and harder to justify involvement in what was considered a core duty of the responsible authorities, the provision of safe, appropriately weather resistant accommodation. Reflecting on the history of IRC's donations of shelter supplies to Moria, one IRC leader noted that with each one, IRC "needed to be careful about crossing the line in fixing what should be fixed by the Greek or EU authorities" (Phillips 2019). When IRC's concerns about inadequate housing continued to go unheeded, and deaths ensued one winter, IRC took to Twitter, denouncing the EU and Greek authorities. IRC hoped such an approach would instill a greater sense of responsibility in the Greek authorities, but it "didn't really work," as requests for similar and even more direct assistance followed (Phillips 2019). IRC's rebuff of such requests, however, was not without consequence: its staff were berated by Greek government officials at a public forum in September 2018, accused of complaining about substandard conditions in Moria but being unwilling to do anything to help improve them.

Only once I began to research the concept of complicity during the evaluation of IRC's work in Greece and Libya did I begin to question whether it was, in fact, the ethical concept best suited to explain how I felt about IRC's stance toward Moria. The more I read about complicity, the more I sensed I had bought into what Slim calls the "myth of humanitarian responsibility." Complicity sits at the centre of this myth:

> Humanitarian agencies can seem especially morally responsible in situations which are not of their making and in which primary responsibility belongs to others ... [As such,] the charge of 'complicity' is the laziest moral label that is used to over-emphasize humanitarian responsibility in situations that are ruthlessly controlled by others ... When working in

> the midst of wrongs it is an ethical requirement to have a good sense of one's place and rationale within them, and set appropriate strategies of prevention, mitigation, and remedy to one's contributions. It is, however, foolish to overstate one's contribution because it allows the parties who are truly responsible to take cover behind a smokescreen of blame that circulates around humanitarian scapegoats rather than themselves. (Slim 2015, 186, 206)

Rather than being a binary distinction in which one simply is or is not complicit (in retrospect, to a large degree the way I was thinking about things when I was with IRC), Slim, philosophy professor Gregory Mellema, MSF physican Chiara Lepora, and political philosopher Robert E. Goodin approach the concept as a continuum with gradations of moral responsibility increasing or decreasing depending on factors such as the degree of shared intent to cause harm, the centrality of one's contributing acts to the actual causing of the harm, the efforts one takes to denounce the harm, and the capacity one has to prevent or obstruct the harm from happening or continuing. These frameworks for assessing moral responsibility also account for the possibility that one may knowingly contribute to wrongdoing in the pursuit of a different or greater good or that one can be coerced into contributing to harm (Lepora and Goodin 2013; Mellema 2016; Slim 2015). Complicity has further been shown to be of limited decision-making value for humanitarian agencies facing strategic decisions such as whether to enter or exit an operation.[15]

When reflecting on IRC's operational and advocacy work in Greece and my experience visiting Moria from these vantage points, I gravitated toward Mellema's concept of "moral taint" and Slim's notion of moral "pollution" as more helpful ways to describe the ethical discomfort that IRC and I were experiencing. According to Mellema, moral taint can be brought about when one's proximity to, or association with, a principal actor causing harm rubs off on them to damage their moral reputation and sense of moral self-worth, even when one is not directly or indirectly contributing to that harm (Mellema 2016). As further explained by Slim (2015, 196), "One could lose one's innocence by being polluted or tainted due to being associated with something that is bad or wrong, and yet in which one is not even complicit ... In many situations, it seems to be a sense of pollution rather than a strict ethical logic of association that influences people's attitudes to humanitarian agencies' association with political powers of various kinds."

IRC's cautious, highly circumscribed interventions coupled with its denunciatory advocacy demonstrated the types of preventative and mitigating efforts Slim (2015) identifies as essential to reducing the degree of moral responsibility that a humanitarian agency should be ascribed for the wrongs perpetrated by others. I prioritized my fear of damage to IRC's moral reputation and, in turn, to my own sense of moral self-worth over the alleviation of Moria's residents' suffering. By inadvertently imbibing the myth of humanitarian responsibility, I perceived IRC to be at greater risk of complicity in the harming of Moria's residents than it may actually have been.[16]

CONCLUSION: BRINGING HUMANITY TO HELL

When working in contexts that deny the humanity of those one is attempting to serve, how does one find the sustenance to continue "humanitarian" action? Immigration detention has been described as "a system that inherently limits efforts to alleviate suffering" (Kotsioni 2016, 41). At its foundation, its practices are based on an assault on the dignity of those detained, a "negation of their most fundamental identity, that of a human" (Kotsioni 2016, 49). It is thus no coincidence that one of the most frequently used terms to describe the conditions and abuses detained migrants and asylum seekers face is "inhumane." Moria, according to one IRC staff member, was "an ongoing traumatization" (Phillips 2019).

It can be extremely stressful and demoralizing to work under such conditions. In response, IRC staff found moral sustenance in small victories that signalled their work made a difference in individual lives. There was transformational power in the most mundane acts under conditions of such extreme dehumanization: as one IRC staff member reflected, "We are friendly and professional in our dealings with our mental health clients ... our clinic is 'a small heaven' for them" (Phillips 2019, 40).

While not phrased in such terms, it was evident from IRC staff that the desire to uphold the dignity of detainees was a basis on which they justified working in detention spaces; was an implicit objective of that work; and was one of the most important ways some individuals motivated themselves to continue with it in the face of repeated challenges. None of the IRC staff interviewed for the 2019 evaluation ever used the term *témoignage* per se,[17] but some of its constituent principles clearly resonated throughout the agency. IRC considered it necessary to be present among, within, and alongside this oppressed group to enable the agency to speak convincingly and authentically about their plight and to advocate for solutions, no matter how unlikely they might come to fruition. This physical proximity, the demonstration of solidarity with those most in need wherever they happen to be, is one of the truest forms of expression of the principle of humanity. Feedback from IRC clients in Moria receiving mental health services suggests proximity and presence were valued. "We [the humanitarian community] are probably the only ones seeing them as human beings," one IRC staff member observed. "Maybe this is the most important part of the intervention" (Phillips 2019, 41).

But as much as solidarity brought some relief to those who were detained, it also had beneficial impact on IRC staff, expanding their sense of humanity. For one employee, the residents of Moria were "very vulnerable people, but they are very resilient and strong. You see very fast results which usually takes a long time. This feels really good." For another "seeing how they try and fight ... they don't give up ... is changing my view of life. It makes me want to help them more and more. I am like a student and they are my teachers" (Phillips 2019, 41).

It may be impossible to quantify, but the importation of small doses of dignity into these most inhumane of environments should be treated as a critically important result of IRC's work in Moria. The advancement of human dignity sits at the heart of the principle of humanity, yet this essential component of humanitarian action is often overlooked or avoided in the quest to deliver life-saving services (Fast 2016).

Assessing the value of a humanitarian intervention with greater emphasis on how it may advance human dignity in addition to simply saving a bare life can change the ethical calculus within which concerns about complicity are weighed. Before I left IRC and conducted the review of my former agency's actions in Moria, I prioritized clean hands and the abstinence of assistance because I felt that an absolutist fidelity to the principle of "do no harm" was in the best interests of the long-term rights of all asylum seekers in Greece. But as I came to better appreciate the nuances inherent in the concept of complicity, I found that I was more accurately experiencing anguish at the prospect of moral taint, a lesser but by no means immaterial form of moral responsibility for harm. Interviews with former colleagues on the front lines of service delivery helped me to see how IRC's engagement promoted dignity and a sense of shared humanity. The combination of these two realizations altered my ethical outlook on humanitarian engagement in Moria: the risk of pollution to my moral reputation by association with structural harm became less important than the dignity and improved well-being that could accrue from interventions addressing the greatest needs of Moria's residents.

NOTES

1 I was the International Rescue Committee's vice-president for International Strategy and Partnerships, based in Den Haag, Netherlands, during this period.

2 The ensuing analysis is largely based on Global Detention Project (2019); Maiani (2018); and Majcher (2018).

3 Another overlooked aspect of global detention practice worth highlighting is misleading labelling by those instituting liberty restricting–practices. Grange's (2013) study of the language of immigration detention highlights the prevalent use of euphemisms often associated with the hospitality sector – such as accommodation, reception centres and temporary homes – to describe what is, in fact, the deprivation of migrant or asylum-seeker liberties in conditions that equate to, or approximate, detention.

4 Moria, for example, was a former military base that had previously been repurposed in September 2013 as a reception camp for migrants.

5 The de facto limited "openness" of Moria was also confirmed via an interview with IRC staff.

6 Examples of vulnerability criteria include people over sixty-five years of age, unaccompanied minors, people with a serious illness, or victims of human trafficking. For a regularly updated list, refer to "Vulnerability Assessment on the Greek Islands," Refugee.info, https://www.refugee.info/greece/vulnerable-people-linked-on-faq-page-only--greece/vulnerability-assessment-on-the-greek-islands?language=en.

7 See, for just one example, International Rescue Committee (2017).

8 From the inception to suspension of its busing operation in March 2016, IRC provided transportation assistance to almost 128,000 asylum seekers.

9 See, for example, International Rescue Committee (2016a).

10 Unlike MSF, whose institutional funding model is grounded in private, unrestricted resources, IRC relies upon grants from governments, including the EU and its member states, to implement its programs.

11 It was these life shelters I saw during my February 2017 visit to the camp.

12 In May 2018, for example, the Greek authorities asked IRC for another donation of forty to fifty tents. While IRC considered the potential temporary good that such a donation could have had and acknowledged the tents were readily available in storage, IRC ultimately decided against the donation. The tents were part of an emergency stockpile that needed to be preserved for a "real emergency," whereas replacing damaged tents in Moria could no longer be considered as such. It was felt, furthermore, that the Greek authorities had a fundamental responsibility to maintain adequate shelter in the camp.

13 IRC annual report to donor funding this work, February 2019, shared with author.

14 In Greece, the reluctance to engage in infrastructure-related interventions in Moria after the Deal was also driven by concerns that adding more facilities in an already extremely overcrowded space would further reduce the quality of life for its residents.

15 MSF, *He Who Helps the Guilty Shares the Crime? INGOs, Moral Narcissism and Complicity in Wrongdoing*. Draft circulated as part of the KUNO (Dutch Humanitarian Knowledge Network) meeting with Hugo Slim, February 2019, shared with author, March 2019.

16 Re-characterizing the discussion of complicity as moral taint, or pollution, in no way diminishes the discomfort that IRC staff felt about being associated with an asylum system deemed wrong and harmful. Nor does it insulate the organization from potential negative repercussions that can accompany a tarnished moral reputation brought about by association with these systems and its controlling actors. It also does not remove the need for IRC to continuously examine and design its work to guard against the risk that its actions and words (or silence) move up the scale of moral responsibility into the realm of complicity.

17 This concept of témoignage is most frequently associated with the practice of bearing witness, as articulated and developed by MSF (see https://www.doctorswithoutborders.org/who-we-are/principles/bearing-witness).

REFERENCES

European Commission. 2016. *EU-Turkey Statement: Questions and Answers.* Memo 16/963, March 19, 2016. http://europa.eu/rapid/press-release_MEMO-16-963_en.htm.

Fast, L. 2016. Unpacking the Principle of Humanity: Tensions and Implications. *International Review of the Red Cross* 97, 897–98: 111–31.

Flynn, M. 2017. Kidnapped, Trafficked, Detained? The Implications of Non-state Actor Involvement in Immigration Detention. *Journal on Migration and Human Security* 5, 3: 593–613.

Global Detention Project. 2019. *Country Report: Greece Immigration Detention.* https://www.globaldetentionproject.org/countries/europe/greece#country-report.

Grange, M. 2013. "Smoke Screens: Is There a Correlation between Migration Euphemisms and the Language of Detention?" Global Detention Project, September 17, 2013. https://www.globaldetentionproject.org/smoke-screens-is-there-a-correlation-between-migration-euphemisms-and-the-language-of-detention.

International Rescue Committee. 2016a. "'Illogical and Unethical'–The EU-Turkey Deal Will Mean More Indignity, More Disorder, More Illegal Journeys and More Lives Lost." Press release, March 19, 2016. https://www.rescue.org/press-release/international-rescue-committee-illogical-and-unethical-eu-turkey-deal-will-mean-more.

–. 2016b. "The International Rescue Committee Will Not Transport Refugees to Closed Facility at Moria, Lesbos." Press release, March 23, 2016. https://www.rescue.org/press-release/international-rescue-committee-will-not-transport-refugees-closed-facility-moria.

–. 2016c. "Moria Deaths a 'Damning Indictment' of European Leaders' Response to Refugee Crisis." Press release, November 25, 2016. https://www.rescue.org/press-release/moria-deaths-damning-indictment-european-leaders-response-refugee-crisis.

–. 2017. "Asylum Seekers in Abysmal Conditions on Islands." Press release, October 23, 2017. https://www.rescue-uk.org/press-release/greece-asylum-seekers-abysmal-conditions-islands.

International Rescue Committee Greece. 2016. *Results, Achievements and Contributions to Date.* Internal, unpublished report. Copy on file with the author.

Kingsley, P. 2016. "MSF Rejects EU Funding in Protest at Refugee Deal." *Guardian*, June 17, 2016. https://www.theguardian.com/world/2016/jun/17/refugee-crisis-medecins-sans-frontieres-rejects-eu-funding-protest.

Kotsioni, I. 2016. "Detention of Migrants and Asylum-Seekers: The Challenge for Humanitarian Actors." *Refugee Survey Quarterly* 35, 2: 41–55.

Leape, S. 2018. "Greece Has the Means to Help Refugees on Lesbos – But Does It Have the Will?" *Guardian*, September 13, 2018. https://www.theguardian.com/global-development/2018/sep/13/greece-refugees-lesbos-moria-camp-funding-will.

Lepora, C., and R.E. Goodin. 2013. *On Complicity and Compromise*. New York: Oxford University Press.

Maiani, F. 2018. "Hotspots and Relocation Schemes: The Right Therapy for the Common European Asylum System?" RefLaw.org, University of Michigan Law School. https://perma.cc/WTL2-6PZC.

Majcher, I. 2018. "The EU Hotspot Approach: Blurred Lines between Restriction on and Deprivation of Liberty (PART II)." *Border Criminologies* (blog), *Faculty of Law Blogs, University of Oxford*, April 5, 2018. https://www.law.ox.ac.uk/research-subject-groups/centre-criminology/centreborder-criminologies/blog/2018/04/eu-hotspot-0.

May, L. 2013. "Innocence and Complicity." Paper presented to the ICRC Conference on Complicity and Humanitarian Action, November 4–5, Geneva.

Mellema, G. 2016. *Complicity and Moral Accountability*. Notre Dame, IN: University of Notre Dame Press.

MSF Greece. 2017. *Confronting the Mental Health Emergency on Samos and Lesbos.* Médecins sans Frontières, October 2017. https://reliefweb.int/sites/reliefweb.int/files/resources/2017_10_mental_health_greece_report_final_low.pdf.

New York Times. 2020. "Afghan Migrants Charged with Arson in Fires That Destroyed Lesbos Camp." September 16, 2020. https://www.nytimes.com/2020/09/16/world/europe/afghan-migrants-charged-arson-lesbos.html.

Phillips, J. 2019. *Working with Detained Populations in Greece and Libya: A Comparative Study of the Ethical Challenges Facing the International Rescue Committee.* International Rescue Committee and Stichting Vluchteling, July 9, 2019. https://reliefweb.int/report/libya/working-detained-populations-greece-and-libya-comparative-study-ethical-challenges.

Slim, H. 2015. *Humanitarian Ethics: A Guide to the Morality of Aid in War and Disaster*. New York: Oxford University Press.

Stevis-Gridneff, M. 2020. "After Fire Razes Squalid Greek Camp, Homeless Migrants Fear What's Next." *New York Times,* September 13, 2020. https://www.nytimes.com/2020/09/13/world/europe/camp-fire-greece-migrants.html.

5

Are "Ethically Appropriate" Responses the Same for All of Us?

A SOCIAL WORK PRACTITIONER/RESEARCHER'S DILEMMA

Neil Bilotta

This chapter explores my experience of a specific interview with one participant for my doctoral research in Kakuma refugee camp, Kenya. As a new social work researcher who has "practised" social work for several years, I felt bewildered trying to navigate social work ethics that aligned with both social work practice and qualitative social work research. For instance, the social work profession mandates that as a social worker, I abide by a professional code of ethics. According to the *Code of Ethics* of the National Association of Social Workers (NASW),[1] the primary mission of the social work profession is to "enhance human well-being and help people meet the basic needs of all people, with particular attention to the needs and empowerment of people who are vulnerable, oppressed, and living in poverty" (NASW 2017, 1). The document goes on to state that social workers "promote social justice and social change with and on behalf of clients" (NASW 2017, 1).[2] In this code of ethics, a social worker's responsibilities are defined broadly, comprising direct clinical social work practice (counselling/therapy, case management), macro practice (e.g., community organizing, advocacy, social and political action, policy development, and implementation), education, and research and evaluation. Therefore, it is critical to note that as a social work researcher, similar to a social work practitioner, I am bound to the profession's formal code of ethics regardless of my exact "professional functions, the settings in which [I] work, or the populations [I] serve" (NASW 2017, 2).

The social work profession is guided by a set of values, principles, and standards to support decision making as ethical issues arise. These six core values – *service, social justice, dignity and worth of the person, importance of human relationships, integrity, and competence* (NASW 2017)[3] – are meant to support or guide us throughout our various roles. Broadly speaking, values undergird how *truth*[4] is understood, the existence of life, what morality requires, and what justice demands (Coghlan 2013). Values are critical to social work as they are key in contemplating ethical dilemmas that arise from conflicts in social workers' responsibilities. Thus, an ethical dilemma in social work arises when professional duties and obligations, rooted in core values, clash (Reamer 2018). As such, NASW accompanies each of the values of social work with an "ethical principle." However, concerns arise when determining how to pragmatically exercise these values in ethically complicated situations. For instance, the way a social work practitioner may engage in the value of social justice may not look the same for a social work researcher and a community organizer. While NASW maintains that a code of ethics cannot resolve all ethical clashes, it offers minimal guidance on what constitutes these six core values for social workers, specifically social work practitioners and social work researchers.

During my doctoral work in Kakuma refugee camp, I felt confused about how to implement or navigate the core social work value of *dignity and worth of persons* while envisioning that value as a social work doctoral student, specifically, a trained social work practitioner and an emerging social work qualitative researcher. To respect the participants' dignity and worth, I felt conflicted: Was there a significant difference in my engagement or interaction depending on whether I was donning my research or practitioner hat? For instance, the construct of "empathy" is critical to both social work practice and qualitative research. However, engaging in an empathetic interaction may look dissimilar from the respective perspectives of researcher and practitioner and is dependent upon one's culture. This results from the differing objectives of social work practitioners and social work researchers, despite both abiding by the value of the dignity and worth of the individual.

Furthermore, this chapter exposes the consequences of my decisions, how navigating this interview felt convoluted, how my training as a social work practitioner may have informed or influenced the research relationship, and how I may have handled this situation differently. Finally, this chapter encourages important conversations around ethics for researchers who are also involved in practice-based professions. It proposes that such professions would do well to consider exploring the complexity of ethical responsibilities for practitioners who also facilitate qualitative research. It does not advocate for a universal code of ethics to guide all professional practices; instead it encourages dialogue on the potential disconnect between ethics for those who practice professional work while concurrently engaging in research.

"IT'S MY FAULT"

The power and complexity of embodying my privileged positions has forced me to reflect on the ways that I navigate my existence. As a white, educated, able-bodied, cisgendered, heterosexual man from the Global North (US citizen/Canadian student), I am positioned in the elite realm of the asymmetrical power divide of this world. My daily life circumstances and experiences are inherently less challenging than for those situated in society's marginalized spheres. As a social work practitioner and an emerging researcher who works with those labelled "refugees," I have been concerned by the lack of urgency or desire by social workers to understand how our practice and research impacts those we intend to "support," particularly those who face heightened subjugation. Attempting to gain a deeper awareness of the inequities related to qualitative research that privilege and power impose upon marginalized populations drove my dissertation research. As such, in 2017, I undertook a five-month critical ethnographic study in Kakuma refugee camp, Kenya. The project explored research ethics, power, colonialism, and research participation from the perspectives of refugee young people living in Kakuma.

I am aware that simply acknowledging my identities does not equate to ethical practice or a depth in self-reflection. However, this chapter will not address this or the paradox or irony of me, a white, powerful researcher from the Global North, facilitating research about research ethics with refugee young people in an oppressive environment.[5] Instead, this chapter privileges one interview interaction between Afiya,[6] a twenty-something-year-old Ugandan woman who identities as a member of the LGBTQI[7] (lesbian, gay, bisexual, trans, queer, intersex) community, and me. In order to gain a richer awareness of the experience, a brief contextual landscape of Kakuma refugee camp is necessary.

Established in the early 1990s, Kakuma refugee camp is one of the world's oldest and most densely inhabited refugee camps. The camp is positioned in the semi-arid region of northwest Kenya, in Turkana County. It is situated about one hundred kilometres south of the South Sudan border and one thousand kilometres northwest of the capital, Nairobi. The protracted refugee camp encompasses four zones over ten kilometres and houses roughly 190,000 refugees, 90,00 above capacity (UNHCR 2017). The weather in Kakuma is especially harsh, with temperatures that regularly reach forty degrees Celsius, and the yearly rain accumulation is only between seven and fifteen inches (Ohta 2005). However, when the rain arrives, because of flat and barren terrain one can expect severe flooding, making homes and roads inaccessible throughout the camp. Dry riverbeds traverse the camp and infrequently rage with polluted water and random flash floods. Like many refugee camps, Kakuma is host to myriad non-governmental organizations and community-based organizations that provide a gamut of services. One of the most isolated regions in Kenya, the desperately impoverished Turkana County, which houses the refugee camp, is home to the Turkana people (Ohta 2005). The majority of Turkana have maintained a pastoral way of life – raising camel, sheep, donkeys, and goats. The abject poverty is undeniable, and scholars have theorized whether refugees or the Turkana face a greater deprivation of basic human needs (Grayson 2017).

Kakuma refugee camp also hosts a "protection area" for self-identified LGBTQI refugees from neighbouring countries. The oppression that members belonging to the LGBTQI community were subject to was exemplified in physical beatings and verbal and physical abuse by the police, local Turkana, and fellow refugees. Consequently, many members of the LGBTQI community chose not to depart from their makeshift living quarters (i.e., "protection area") because of safety concerns. After finishing my research, I was alerted that the United Nations High Commissioner for Refugees (UNHCR) transported many LGBTQI refugees from Kakuma to Nairobi. This was in response to several beatings of LGBTQI community members in the refugee camp, most specifically at the hands of Turkana community members. As it currently stands, UNHCR has shifted several refugees from Nairobi back to Kakuma, though many LGBTQI refugees currently remain in the capital.

It is important to note that my interview with Afiya intended to specifically focus on her previous research experiences while in the camp. It was not to ascertain information on the plight of LGBTQI refugees in Kakuma, though, as this vignette illustrates, the conversation quickly shifted to LGBTQI concerns, which caused a personal and professional dilemma for me, a social work practitioner and doctoral researcher. The interview was held in the home of Afiya, in the LGBTQI protection area of Kakuma refugee camp. Prior to "official" interviews for my study, I individually met with each potential participant to determine (a) their interest in the study, (b) general demographic criteria, (c) previous research experiences, and (d) expectations, motivations, and objectives for the participant and myself. The following interaction took place about four minutes into the official interview with Afiya. This was the second time we met. While this section will simply provide an excerpt from our exchange, the succeeding section of the chapter will problematize and unpack the situation.

NEIL: So, you mentioned that you were in two previous research studies. What were they about?

AFIYA: Well, one was not a research project but from a journalist from [name of publication]. And that was terrible for me. I think that guy exploited us. Sometimes they do that to us LGBTQI, these wazungu.[8]

NEIL: (*feeling remorse and frustration*) What do you mean these wazungu usually exploit you?

AFIYA: Yeah, this man came from [publication], do you know how many people read [publication]? He didn't even tell us that he was going to put our pictures on the Internet, and he did. And he never even provided us with anything after the interview. There still has been no word from him. He just published our stories and left us here in this place to be beaten.

NEIL: To be beaten?

AFIYA: Yes. You know most of us in our community cannot go out even to fetch water or pick up our rations [food rations] because we fear that we will be beaten or even killed. I know you have seen some of the ways we are treated here. Police, Turkana, even other refugees try to beat and kill us because we are LGBTQI. I'm so tired of it, and I am tired of these people coming to exploit our story and provide no help.

A barrage of emotions surface, and I am not exactly sure how to respond. I am acutely aware that my presence suggests I am one of "these people"!

NEIL: Gosh, Afiya, that sounds really terrible. I'm so sorry to hear all of this.

AFIYA: Yeah. That is our life here. But, you know, I guess I'm just mad at myself. It's my fault.

NEIL: What is your fault?

AFIYA: All of this ... If I wasn't a lesbian, I would be living in my country with my family and friends ... living a normal life. Instead, I'm here in this camp, constantly being harassed, beaten, assaulted, and scared for my life just because I love women and not men. So, yeah, it is my fault ... I'm a lesbian, and it's illegal to be a lesbian. I can only blame myself. (*stated with a flat affect and minimal emotion*)

At this point, I'm feeling worried, anxious, and unsettled. What should I do? What do I say? Is it even "ethical" for me to talk to Afiya about my interview topic anymore? How can I best support her? In this context, I'm a researcher and feel that if I respond the way I feel most comfortable, it will skew my research.[9] *Actually, this isn't even related to my research – she's talking about a journalist, but more importantly, she's discussing her safety and overall well-being.*

NEIL: So you feel that all of this is your fault?

AFIYA: How can it not be? Other people here are running from war – we are running from our sexuality. Yes, it's unjust, but it has to be my fault. No one is forcing me to love women, but I do. So it's just ... ya know ... confusing.

At this point, I consciously decide it may not be "ethical" to shift this interview back to my research topic. Based on her emotional state and affect, it would be wiser to abandon the interview and begin engaging in a way that I think most appropriately values the dignity and worth of Afiya.

NEIL: This is a really terrible situation that you are experiencing. This is sincere injustice, and it's wrong. And it sounds like blaming yourself could only make this situation worse for you.

AFIYA: I don't even know what to think anymore. I'm so tired of this life here in Kakuma.

NEIL: What do you mean, tired of this life?

AFIYA: I mean, I just want to get out of here and live normally again. I am determined that one day it will happen. At least we have each other, our community here. We really support each other.

NEIL: I'm happy you have a supportive community. That is very important.

AFIYA: Yeah.

NEIL: I can't even imagine the struggles of your community here in Kakuma. It's so painful to hear all of this, and you are absolutely being treated inhumanely. And it is definitely not your fault, Afiya. Have you sought help from the police here in Kakuma?

AFIYA: (*laughs*) Police?! It's even the police that are also beating us. It's like everyone in Kakuma is homophobic ... even UNHCR, they don't help as much as they could.

NEIL: That is so saddening and frustrating for me to hear. So I can't even imagine how it makes you feel.

AFIYA: It is too bad.

NEIL: Afiya, is there anything I can do to help try and be an ally or support to you and your community?

AFIYA: You know, you are a mzungu with a lot of power. People from here [Kenya] really listen to wazungu. Can you try to inform your people back there [Canada/US] about our problems here? We really need some help. Our people are suffering, and we are scared that some of us may be killed even.

At this point, I immediately think of a former acquaintance who works with the International Rescue Committee in New York City. Her dissertation focused on trans issues in Kampala, Uganda. I also consider contacting some global LGBTQI activist organizations and resettled refugees (in US and Canada) from the LGBTQI East African community. But I am also overtly aware of my colonial and privileged identities. Am I shifting my role from social work doctoral researcher to social work practitioner to "white saviour"?[10]

NEIL: Okay. I will try to reach out to some people who may have some ideas. I'm not sure what kind of response I will get, but I will definitely try to contact some people who may provide me with some information.

AFIYA: Thank you, Neil.

NEIL: Well, I'm not sure that I will get through to anybody, but I will surely try. This is a terrible situation, and I'm really sorry to hear about this. It pains my heart.

AFIYA: It's really terrible here.

We sit together for a few more moments and discuss our plans for the remainder of the day, who I would try to contact, and then arrange another time to meet to discuss this further.

QUALITATIVE RESEARCHER, SOCIAL WORK PRACTITIONER, WHITE SAVIOUR?

The interaction with Afiya was ethically concerning and unsettling for several reasons. These include power, privilege, position colonization, Othering, oppression, procedural and relational research ethics, and exercising the core social work value of dignity and worth of persons.[11] While it has been acknowledged that the identities and positionalities of the researcher are an essential and pervasive component of the research process (Dwyer and Buckle 2009), this felt explicit during our communication.

The following section will outline how my struggle to promote Afiya's dignity and worth was hindered by my being a white man from the Global North whose primary responsibility as a social work doctoral student was to facilitate research unrelated to LGBTQI constraints.

As noted, a fundamental value of social work is the dignity and worth of the person. This value indicates that "social workers treat each person in a caring and respectful fashion, mindful of individual differences and cultural and ethnic diversity ... Social workers are cognizant of their dual responsibility to clients and broader society. They seek to resolve conflicts between clients' interests and the broader society's interest in a socially responsible manner (NASW 2017, 5–6)."

The behaviours of a social work researcher and a practitioner may differ when attempting to affirm dignity and worth of the person. Considering that my primary role in Kakuma refugee camp was to facilitate my doctoral research, I was bound by institutional (i.e., my university, the Kenyan government) ethical codes, social work's ethics, and my personal ethics. As various sets of ethical codes diverge, how does a social worker, primarily a social work researcher, navigate the messiness of sorting through these principles? In this section, I explore the similarities and distinctions between the paths a social work researcher versus a social work practitioner could have led me. First, I provide some rudimentary distinctions between the roles of social work practitioners and researchers. Second, I will describe the "official" ethical clearance protocol I received before initiating my research. Moreover, I will illustrate how the concepts of "empathy" and "emotional labour" informed my conscious decision to abandon my researcher hat and embrace my social work professional practices while attempting to implement the value of dignity and worth to Afiya. Finally, I will discuss the consequences for this action and how shifting my role could constitute a white saviour ideology.

An important tool in qualitative research and social work practice is being self-reflexive and exploring one's positions and identities within the research or therapeutic process. Engaging in consistent self-reflexive exercises paved a path to, albeit minimally, assess how my positionalities and identities persistently impacted my daily surroundings in Kakuma. The ignorance that underlies my white, cis, heteronormative privilege was evident as I re-read the transcripts of our interview. At one point, I asked whether Afiya had sought help from the police in Kakuma. As a white man, my protected and naive upbringing engendered ignorance to assume that police protect all people equally. In my interaction with Afiya, this was apparent in her laughter when I asked whether the police were aware of the abuse she was facing. As a white man, my privilege inhibited my ability to recognize police as potential abusers.

Roles of Social Work Practictioner and Researcher

Before my interview with Afiya, it was clear that my roles as a social work researcher and practitioner would have reflected differing ideologies during my interviews. For instance, as a researcher, I initiated the relationship for my own research (i.e., dissertation) purposes. While my research objective was to identify power imbalances and inherent oppression between researchers and refugee research participants, this research project would surely provide me with more benefit than it would for any of my participants. This was contradictory to how I was trained in social work practice. For instance, in clinical social work, the client is commonly looking for support in processing mental health concerns, trauma, depression, or anxiety. Consequently, clients commonly seek direct support from social workers, and social workers attempt to "meet the client where they are at." In my research with Afiya, however, it was me, the researcher, who entered her home and pried into her life, primarily to serve myself. As such, we did not "meet" where she was at. Instead, we met at the discretion and direction of me, the social worker from North America.

Institutional Ethics

Prior to commencing my research in Kakuma refugee camp, it was mandatory that I receive ethics approval from five disparate bodies: (1) McGill University's (my home institution) Research Ethics Board; (2) the Kenyan National Government–National Commission for Science, Technology and Innovation; (3) the Refugee Affairs Secretariat of Kenya; (4) a National Commission for Science, Technology and Innovation-accredited Kenyan University; and (5) the local police chief of Kakuma town/camp. None of the five bodies posed questions specific to relational ethics, and only McGill's Research Ethics Board focused on procedural ethics. This suggested that it was not an ethics evaluation of my proposed research. Instead, the Kenyan entities were primarily concerned with (a) McGill University's accepted dissertation proposal, (b) an approval letter from McGill's Research Ethics Board, and (c) a monetary fee.

Obtaining approval from these five departments indicated that I was ethically authorized to conduct research in Kakuma refugee camp. These five institutions' approval, I understood, implied that so long as I maintained client confidentiality, provided informed consent documents, and abided by other procedural ethics, I, a social work doctoral researcher, would be illustrating a sense of dignity and worth to the research participants in Kakuma. The interaction with Afiya illustrates that regardless of official ethical approval to facilitate my research, an ethical conundrum surfaced. Such an ethical concern was not only unaddressed in the five ethical applications, but also any discourse even minimally associated with such experiences was excluded from my qualitative research training. This is not uncommon in doctoral research courses/pedagogy (Kumar and Cavallaro 2018).

Emotional Labour and Empathy

During the interaction with Afiya, I was palpably aware of my emotional labour. Concerning qualitative research, emotional labour consists of a process that may elicit particular feelings or emotions in oneself as a researcher (McQueeney and Lavelle 2017). Moreover, it refers to the effort a researcher invests in expressing or coping with their emotions to achieve "objectives" pertaining to their work (Nutov and Hazzan 2011). While emotional labour appears inherent in research interactions, I felt confused about how to manifest my emotional labour. My previous role as a refugee resettlement social work practitioner, coupled with my current novice researcher status, clouded my conceptions of "appropriate" emotion during interviews. How was I to illustrate empathy – the ability to share in and understand others' experiences vicariously (Decety and Cowell 2014) – in my interaction with Afiya? Indeed, displaying empathetic feelings is critical in social work practice (Gair 2012), though overly engaging in empathetic communication with a research participant may denote bias or an inability to remain critical in analysis[12] (McQueeney and Lavelle 2017).

Although a uniform definition of empathy is nonexistent, clinical social work has identified it as feeling *with* the client rather than feeling *for* the client; it moves beyond sympathy to enter imaginatively into the life of someone else (Gair 2012). Empathy is regarded as the establishment of caring rapport and support and may consist of "communicative attunement," which is a verbal response that includes reframing or paraphrasing the client's own words (Elliott et al. 2018). Empathy can also be conveyed non-verbally, including facial expressions and body posture (Gair 2012). In qualitative research, *cognitive empathy* focuses mainly on understanding the participant's frame of reference or attempting to understand their emotions (Elliott et al. 2018). In general, empathy is a part of the relational connection that would establish a less threatening environment and thus a worthwhile interview experience yielding quality participant responses (Mallozzi 2009). As culture, positionality, and identity impacted empathy, I struggled with how to display empathy in my time with Afiya. I was also concerned with how my research epistemology impacted my non-verbal empathy and the way that may have differed from my social work practice training.

If I had strictly abided by my institutional research ethical contracts, perhaps I would have exercised a cognitive empathetic approach by first actively listening to Afiya's concerns. This may constitute sharing an "empathetic" verbal response (i.e., "Wow, Afiya, it sounds like you are dealing with a lot here") or a non-verbal response (nodding my head while looking at Afiya) but, ultimately, shifting the interview back toward my primary research focus. Indeed, the social work value (not specific to research- or practice-based work) of dignity and worth suggests that I have a "dual" responsibility to both the individual/client/participant and the greater society. While my research did not focus on the plight of LGBTQI refugees in Kakuma, I wondered if navigating our conversation back to my research topic could be categorized as exemplifying dignity and worth, considering (a) my research study did directly focus on oppression in qualitative research and (b) I envisioned disseminating my research to the greater society. As such, if I chose to acknowledge yet minimize Afiya's urgent concerns related to her sexuality, I remain unsure that I would have been illustrating dignity and worth as a social worker, particularly a social work researcher. Moreover, my position was primarily a qualitative social work researcher and not a clinical social worker. Afiya had not come to me in my role as a social work practitioner, seeking support or advice for the appalling situation in which she found herself. Instead, I sought her out to assist me in my research endeavours, which were unrelated to LGBTQI affairs. While research suggests that qualitative researchers must be prepared for unexpected events in their research (Kumar and Cavallaro 2018), scholarship regarding empathy in qualitative research often appears convoluted, contradictory, or both and may be dependent on the research paradigm.[13]

While contemplating my responsibility in the interaction with Afiya, I briefly pondered how maintaining an alliance to my research obligations would affect the interaction. For instance, I signed documents for five independent ethical boards claiming that I would engage in "ethical research." Suppose I disregarded the information Afiya was conveying to me and instead focused on my topic. In that case, I am uncertain as to whether that would have constituted ethical research, considering her concerns were irrelevant to my research topic. While researchers who work with humans must "first and foremost" acknowledge "the well-being of the individual research subject" (Msoroka and Amundsen 2017, 5), I was unsure how to respect the well-being of Afiya in that particular moment. As I ruminated on her words and contemplated the convolution of the diverse ethical codes, it felt apparent that for Afiya's "well-being" and to acknowledge her ultimate dignity and worth, I should forgo my interview agenda and abide by conduct more closely associated with social work practice. This, however, was confounded by the notions that (a) I was not a social work practitioner in that context and (b) by taking on this role, I flirted with the danger of engaging in a white saviour, paternalistic relationship.

White Saviour Complex

Despite these concerns, I consciously decided to suspend my research objectives with Afiya. While this decision was made with minimal deliberation, I maintain that it felt more "ethical" in relation to dignity and worth. In this particular instance, Afiya's distress was palpable. She reported ongoing physical and emotional abuse. Although it was evident that the systemic oppression inflicted upon her was well beyond the scope of our interview, I could not detach my personal ethics from Afiya's experiences. I am not a member of the LGBTQI community, though I do attempt to root my work (research/scholarship, social work practice) in confronting oppressive forces that continuously encumber the lives of so many. As such, I viscerally observed personal feelings of anger and frustration at those identified as harming the LGBTQI community. Within moments of our engagement, I asked myself, "What is the most ethical path to follow as a social worker and as a white man from the Global North?" I determined that minimally addressing Afiya's concerns (with a brief empathetic response) and restricting the conversation to focus on my topic felt like the antithesis of acknowledging dignity and worth. In our engagement, it was explicit that Afiya was much less interested in sharing about her previous research encounters (my research topic) than in sharing about the overt and consistent harm she was facing.

Engaging as a clinical social worker consisted of my actively responding to Afiya, attempting to normalize her feelings of self-blame, and acting as an advocate. Immediately following my decision to abandon the interview, I thought about how my privileged and powerful identities and positionalities could, in fact, be useful. Indeed, a critical component of the social work discipline is advocacy. While disseminating research is a form of advocacy, Afiya's situation appeared more urgent and significant than my simply publishing a report on this situation. Moreover, the concerns that

Afiya shared were divorced from my research topic. Thus, I used my privileged and powerful identities and positions to expand beyond Kakuma in hopes of finding support, considering that the "supportive" resources in Kakuma refugee camp were overtly violating human rights. Therefore, I contacted several international organizations and activists working on LGBTQI issues. Throughout my time in Kakuma, I regularly met with Afiya and currently remain connected, despite her no longer living in Kakuma. Upon critical reflection, I continue to deliberate how my actions (a) instilled implications for my research and (b) could be considered to reflect a "white saviour" ideology.

With respect to research, I pondered how my interaction with Afiya would impact future interviews with other LGBTQI research participants. I considered the probability that other folks from the LGBTQI community in Kakuma were exposed to similar violence and whether it was "ethical" for me to bring that into our research-oriented relationship. Or would that "interfere" with my research topic? Conversely, I was confused about how future interview relationships with "ethnicities" that Afiya claimed to be discriminatory would be impacted by my aversion to the treatment of LGBTQI in Kakuma. On a more "formal" platform, I considered how research ethics boards would interpret my terminating my research objectives in order to "support" Afiya in a fashion that I deemed provided dignity and worth to her. Furthermore, would the academy[14] frown upon my decision, considering I was provided "permission" to facilitate "ethical research," not to terminate an interview without ascertaining how the participant may have provided beneficial information for my research study.

In my decisions to "advocate" for Afiya and other members of the LGBTQI community, I believe I was engaging in a "white saviour complex." Straubhaar (2015, 385) defines the white saviour complex as the privilege that Global Northerners exhibit while working in "developing" contexts in the Global South, by maintaining, albeit subconsciously, that they hold the "unique power to uplift, edify, and strengthen" those who face significant subjugation. Even though I recognized that Afiya sought my help, I still wondered how, as a white man with education and power attempting to provide "support" or to "advocate" for her and her community, I could ultimately save her from her unjust government and "immoral" society. Perhaps I was suggesting, albeit tacitly, that the Global North is more "advanced," considering LGBTQI persons are not publicly living in contexts of forced displacement. Furthermore, was my intuition to "help" rooted in an insecure desire for Afiya to recognize "I am not *that* mzungu," here to exploit you? This insecurity manifested in my concerted verbal and non-verbal empathetic responses to Afiya's concerns.

While these critical queries are invaluable, I was cautious not to have them inhibit or stymie my action or responses to Afiya's requests. Indeed, a person's ethical point of reference is influenced by the society that surrounds them (Amundsen and Msoroka 2021), possibly evidenced in Afiya's acknowledgment of both the micro-level and systemic oppression she faces, thanks to colonialism, power, Othering, and privilege. This may suggest why Afiya accurately acknowledged, "You know, you are a mzungu with a lot of power. People from here [Kenya?] really listen to wazungu." Whether paternalistic or not, actively responding to Afiya's requests for me to utilize my privilege in a manner that could conceivably assist her and her community felt closer to recognizing her dignity and worth than did (a) focusing on my research agenda and (b) not exploiting my privileged positions for fear of fully embodying the white saviour complex. Despite my justifications, could I be confident that my actions were "ethical" with Afiya? Although difficult to know, what appears more transparent is that neither research ethics guidelines nor social work's code of ethics address this nuance.

MOVING FORWARD: DIGNITY AND WORTH?

This chapter has illustrated that despite abiding by ethical codes of conduct, a dilemma arose when the prescribed ethical protocols lacked a clear framework for moving through a contradiction in my roles. Although my main focus was to provide dignity and worth to Afiya, I am still perplexed about how to truly engage with this core social work value as a researcher versus social work practitioner. In retrospect, I consciously decided to disregard my research agenda with Afiya and transitioned to a clinical social work role. While I feel confident that this assessment provided Afiya more substantial dignity and worth, I intermittently contemplate my decision, particularly one element of our interaction. It was not until after I decided to depart from the original interview that I asked Afiya about what she needed from *me*. I failed to inquire whether *she* deemed it important to forgo the interview or to shift our focus back to my original research agenda. I continue to ruminate on whether excluding this critical piece of engagement may have represented a failure to provide dignity and worth to Afiya. Instead, I ascertained what was "best" in the current context, without her consent or acknowledgment. This realization surfaced two months after the interview, during a critical self-reflexive journal writing session. I equate this lack of awareness to ask Afiya for her feedback with notions of privilege, power, colonialism, and Othering. As a white, educated, powerful social worker from the Global North, I employed my privilege and decided what was ultimately most appropriate for my research participant. For instance, the research was conceptualized, dictated, and implemented by me and my agenda. I came to Afiya's community and house and not only set the agenda but also decided to terminate the interview when I deemed it necessary. Clearly, asking Afiya, a woman who faces daily subjugation, oppression, and marginalization, for *her* thoughts would have showed a more equitable effort to support her *dignity and worth*? Despite my efforts to uphold dignity and worth, my inherent and unacknowledged white supremacy framework inhibited my ability to make that connection.

The ethical dilemma that surfaced in my interaction with Afiya indicates that ethical codes and values are often muddled and fail to account for the nuance in situational ethics. In order to redress such constraints, professionals who also facilitate research must continue to explore ways to implement ethical codes and values associated with their profession. More specifically, the profession of social work requires social workers to provide dignity and worth to our clients and participants. As this chapter explores, however, this value is convoluted and multifarious. In many instances, recognizing the dignity and worth of our clients and participants is uncomplicated. For instance, by maintaining procedural ethical codes in a research or interview interaction, the researcher is considered to uphold the dignity and worth of the participant. The challenges are nestled in the nuances of the research interaction, as this chapter has demonstrated. This is linked to the notion that procedural ethics are simply one variable of a complex research ethics agenda.

This chapter suggests that further ethical questions must be considered in the discipline of social work and other professions. For instance, future conversations should explore whether researchers and professional practitioners abide by identical codes. Indeed, NASW claims that the ethical code document "does not provide a set of rules that prescribe how social workers should act in all situations" (2017, 2). This statement appears to suggest the importance of assessing each ethical moment accordingly and considering core values and ethical codes on an independent basis. While I disagree with the universalization of ethical codes across contexts, by failing to deconstruct the underpinnings of each core value (e.g., dignity and worth), we lack evidence to suggest that we have engaged in a culturally responsive constitution of that core value. While NASW's *Code of Ethics* is not a panacea for all ethical dilemmas, the discipline of social work should do more to ascertain what constitutes dignity and worth of our participants/clients. By failing to do so, we may be replicating or perpetuating an inherent asymmetrical hierarchy in our social work relationships. Why are the participants and clients of our work absent from such discourse?

Moreover, this chapter is useful for those outside social work; human rights work is rife with ethical conundrums, as this book exemplifies. If "human rights advocates" anchor their work in similar core values, further consideration should be provided on *how* to engage with these values. Or perhaps some of the interactions are too complex to address in an ethical document and instead should be handled on an individual level. While this chapter poses far more questions than it answers, I argue that human rights work, social work, research, and other helping professions must make a concerted effort not only to conceptualize questions around ethics, but also to prioritize them. Moreover, in order to provide an equitable platform, all parties (practitioners, workers, clients, participants, students) must collaborate in advancing such ethical concerns. If academia, social work, and human rights work continue to promote skeletal constructions of core values and ethical codes, we can expect the exacerbation of ethically significant moments for helping professionals who also consider themselves researchers.

NOTES

1 As a US-trained social work practitioner, I reference the National Association for Social Workers (NASW) *Code of Ethics*. NASW claims that "among codes of ethics social workers should consider the *NASW Code of Ethics* as their primary source" (NASW 2017, 3), though it should also be noted that the Canadian Association of Social Work (CASW) abides by similar values and ethical constructs.

2 The term "client" has been debated in social work. This chapter will not engage in such debate but will loosely define "social work clients" as individuals, families, groups, organizations, and communities.

3 CASW identifies five core values: respect for the inherent dignity and worth of persons, service to humanity, integrity in professional practice, confidentiality in professional practice, and competence in professional practice.

4 Truth may be understood according to epistemology, cultural and social norms, and context.

5 Such an account is detailed in Bilotta (2021).

6 Afiya is a pseudonym.

7 LGBTQI is the acronym commonly used in Kakuma refugee camp.

8 Wazungu, plural of mzungu, is the Kiswahili term that literally translates to "aimless wanderer" (Che-Mponda 2013) and was initially coined to identify European colonists. Contemporarily, mzungu is commonly used to refer to white foreigners.

9 My research training did little to prepare me for ways to manoeuvre "data collection" methods that extended beyond "my" research topic. For instance, Afiya's concerns were not related to the research topic. In that moment, I was unsure if moving away from the research area would ultimately impact the "data." More importantly, I was reminded that my research training left me unprepared.

10 This question is with reference to "The White-Savior Industrial Complex" (Cole 2012).

11 Vervliet and colleagues (2015) distinguish between procedural ethics and relational ethics. Procedural ethics include informed consent, privacy and confidentiality, institutional ethical approval, the right to withdrawal, dissemination practices. Relational ethics consist of the recognition of value and respect (Lawrence, Kaplan, and Dodds 2015), reciprocity (Chilisa 2019), reflexivity (Guillemin and Gillam 2004), and privileging the agency of research participants while striving for dignity and connectedness between the researcher and participant (Vervliet et al. 2015).

12 It is important to note that I am relating specifically to my research training. Alternative theories would debate this methodological paradigm.

13 For further detail on research paradigms, see Chilisa (2019).

14 I have conceptualized "the academy" as a corporation that equates "knowledge production" (i.e., scholarship, funding) to "success."

REFERENCES

Amundsen, D., and M. Msoroka. 2021. "Responsive Ethics: Navigating the Fluid Research Space between HREC Ethics, Researcher Ethics and Participant Ethics." *Educational Review* 73, 5: 563–79.

Bilotta, N. 2021. "A Critical Self-Reflexive Account of a Privileged Researcher in a Complicated Setting: Kakuma Refugee Camp." *Research Ethics* 17, 4: 435–47.

Che-Mponda, C. 2013. "The Meaning of the Word Mzungu – Maana ya Mzungu." *Swahili Time* (blog), February 5, 2013. http://swahilitime.blogspot.com/2013/02/the-meaning-of-word-mzungu-maana-ya.html.

Chilisa, B. 2019. *Indigenous Research Methodologies*. Thousand Oaks, CA: Sage.

Coghlan, D. 2013. "What Will I Do? Toward an Existential Ethics for First Person Action Research Practice." *International Journal of Action Research* 9, 3: 333–52.

Cole, T. 2012. "The White-Savior Industrial Complex." *Atlantic*, March 21, 2012.

Decety, J., and J.M. Cowell. 2014. "Friends or Foes: Is Empathy Necessary for Moral Behavior?" *Perspectives on Psychological Science* 9, 5: 525–37.

Dwyer, S.C., and J.L. Buckle. 2009. "The Space Between: On Being an Insider-Outsider in Qualitative Research." *International Journal of Qualitative Methods* 8, 1: 54–63.

Elliott, R., A.C. Bohart, J.C. Watson, and D. Murphy. 2018. "Therapist Empathy and Client Outcome: An Updated Meta-analysis." *Psychotherapy* 55, 4: 399.

Gair, S. 2012. "Feeling Their Stories: Contemplating Empathy, Insider/Outsider Positionings, and Enriching Qualitative Research." *Qualitative Health Research* 22, 1: 134–43.

Grayson, C.-L. 2017. *Children of the Camp: The Lives of Somali Youth Raised in Kakuma Refugee Camp, Kenya*. New York: Berghahn Books.

Guillemin, M., and L. Gillam. 2004. "Ethics, Reflexivity, and 'Ethically Important Moments' in Research." *Qualitative Inquiry* 10, 2: 261–80.

Kumar, S., and L. Cavallaro. 2018. "Researcher Self-Care in Emotionally Demanding Research: A Proposed Conceptual Framework." *Qualitative Health Research* 28, 4: 648–58. doi:10.1177/1049732317746377.

Lawrence, J.A., I. Kaplan, and A.E. Dodds. 2015. "The Rights of Refugee Children to Self-Expression and to Contribute to Knowledge in Research: Respect and Methods." *Journal of Human Rights Practice* 7, 3: 411–29.

Mallozzi, C.A. 2009. "Voicing the Interview: A Researcher's Exploration on a Platform of Empathy." *Qualitative Inquiry* 15, 6: 1042–60.

McQueeney, K., and K.M. Lavelle. 2017. "Emotional Labor in Critical Ethnographic Work: In the Field and Behind the Desk." *Journal of Contemporary Ethnography* 46, 1: 81–107.

Msoroka, M.S., and D. Amundsen. 2017. "One Size Fits Not Quite All: Universal Research Ethics with Diversity." *Research Ethics* 14, 3: 1–17.

NASW (National Association of Social Workers). 2017. *Code of Ethics of the National Association of Social Workers*. Washington, DC: NASW.

Nutov, L., and O. Hazzan. 2011. "Feeling the Doctorate: Is Doctoral Research That Studies the Emotional Labor of Doctoral Students Possible." *International Journal of Doctoral Studies* 6: 19–32.

Ohta, I. 2005. "Coexisting with Cultural 'Others': Social Relationships between the Turkana and the Refugees at Kakuma, Northwest Kenya." *Senri Enthnological Studies* 69: 227–39.

Reamer, F. 2018. *Social Work Values and Ethics*. New York: Columbia University Press.

Straubhaar, R. 2015. "The Stark Reality of the 'White Saviour' Complex and the Need for Critical Consciousness: A Document Analysis of the Early Journals of a Freirean Educator." *Compare: A Journal of Comparative and International Education* 45, 3: 381–400.

UNHCR (United Nations High Commissioner for Refugees). 2017. "Kakuma Camp Population Statistics by Country of Origin, Sex, and Age Group." Refugees Operational Data Portal, November 12, 2017. https://data2.unhcr.org/en/documents/details/60695.

Vervliet, M., C. Rousseau, E. Broekaert, and I. Derluyn, 2015. "Multilayered Ethics in Research Involving Unaccompanied Refugee Minors." *Journal of Refugee Studies* 28, 4: 468–85.

6

Unequal Pay for Equal Work

ETHICAL REFLECTIONS ON EXPLOITATION AS A FUNDING REQUIREMENT

Maritza Felices-Luna

EXPANDING OUR ETHICAL GAZE

As practitioners, activists, artists, and researchers engaging in human rights work, our ethical gaze tends to be restricted or confined by regulating bodies, institutional guidelines, field conventions, codes of practices, procedures, protocols, and so on, and our own ethical principles. Although goals might be different (protection from liability, ensuring protection for those in vulnerable positions, guaranteeing standard practices, among others) these constraints provide us with a set of "valid" ethical questions to ask and "acceptable" answers to come up with. These constraints determine the focus of our ethical attention as well as help us prioritize when contending ethical principles arise.

Despite being necessary for multiple reasons, these constraints act as barriers delimiting what is within the purview of ethical consideration and what is exempt from it. Through this process of boundary making, unethical practices, relations, and situations go on unseen and unchallenged precisely because they are not thought of in ethical terms. Acting ethically, then, might demand that we reflect on the nature and logic of those constraints and the implications they entail.

As a case in point, countries such as Canada and the US regulate ethics in research through a national policy implemented by an external review body. In Canada, the public mandate of research ethics boards (REBs)[1] is to evaluate the ethical implications of a particular project on participants or potential participants. This means that the researcher's actions toward members of the research team, collaborators, local population, and the broader public as well as the impact the research might have on these groups lie outside the purview of the REB. While I am certainly not advocating for a larger role by REBs,[2] I do see as a problem the fact that ethical guidelines exclude from the realm of ethics the actions of the researcher in regards to all actors other than research participants. By reducing the researcher's universe of moral obligation, this narrow gaze opens the door to unethical practices, problematic attitudes, and exploitative relations in research that go on unimpeded.

As a researcher engaging in human rights work, I have come to the realization that I ought to expand my ethical gaze beyond the confines established by REBs, and to critically examine my practices, attitudes, relations, decisions, and considerations as they relate to everyone directly or indirectly involved in the research process or concerned by my research. However, doing such a thing is not easy or straightforward; it requires balancing sometimes opposing and even antagonistic considerations.

This chapter flows, akin to a stream of consciousness, through a series of questions that are not fully explored and for which I never attempt to provide an answer. In the text, I grapple with questions of scope and boundaries; questions of power and autonomy; questions of temporality and distance; as well as questions of angles of vision and prioritization when confronted with a common challenge for those engaging in human rights work: the difference in salaries, benefits, and working conditions between workers with the same previous experience and conducting the same tasks, whose only difference is the location of their permanent residency.

WHEN FILLING OUT BUDGETARY FORMS BECOMES AN ETHICAL DILEMMA

Many years ago, when I was a new hire in the criminology department at the University of Ottawa, I applied for a four-year research grant from the Social Sciences and Humanities Research Council of Canada (SSHRC).[3] The research project sought to analyze the continuum of human rights violations and other problematic practices by the police and the military in the Democratic Republic of Congo through changing political contexts (dictatorship, civil war, and emerging democracy). Having had the opportunity to visit the Democratic Republic of Congo on a few occasions, I had developed a connection with the Education Centre on Criminology and Human Rights (CEFOCRIM [Centre de Formation en criminologie et droits humains]) and wanted this project to be the starting point of a fruitful and mutually beneficial working relationship. In order to get the ball rolling in this partnership, I planned to hire a Canadian research assistant (RA) as well as a Congolese RA. Both RAs would conduct and analyze interviews in what I saw as not only a learning opportunity for both of them but also a way of sharing resources, knowledges, expertise, and so on, between researchers from the CEFOCRIM and the University of Ottawa. I wanted this project to produce knowledge regarding human rights violations by state institutions, but most importantly, I saw it as a way to funnel funding and begin a dialogue between academic institutions from the Global South and the Global North.[4] I was dreaming big!

While in the midst of my feel-good reverie where everything was possible, I reached the "budget section" of the application form. What I thought would be an uncomplicated mathematical exercise became an ethical conundrum regarding the salary of the Congolese RA. The salary of the Canadian RA was already set by the University of Ottawa, but I needed to determine how much I would be paying the Congolese RA. I considered three options:

1 Pay the Congolese RA the same amount as the Canadian RA;[5]
2 Pay the Congolese RA an equivalent amount to that of the Canadian RA, seeking to provide them with similar purchasing power;[6]
3 Pay the Congolese RA local rates.[7]

I was uncomfortable with the first and the third options; the two RAs would be doing the same type and amount of work, with probably similar previous experiences, but in each of the two scenarios I would be disproportionately compensating one RA over the other. At first glance, the second option appeared to me as fair given that it would ensure equity between the two RAs. However, I felt uncomfortable with the implications of paying a Congolese RA not only significantly more than what their colleagues get paid, but also more than people in higher hierarchical positions,[8] including the professors and researchers working in the CEFOCRIM, and I wondered about the potential negative implications of such a choice. Notwithstanding my unease, I decided to go ahead with option two, as it seemed at the time to be the least problematic of the three. When I submitted the application for internal review, the University of Ottawa's research facilitator indicated that SSHRC required researchers to pay local fees to local RAs, in other words, to pay the Congolese RA the same fees that Congolese RAs are paid in the Democratic Republic of Congo.

I was uncomfortable with this regulation because it concretely meant generating a serious discrepancy in terms of living conditions and compensation/acknowledgment for equal labour. I decided to attempt to make up for this discrepancy by including in the budget travel grants to international conferences for the Congolese RA. Once again, the university's research facilitator said SSHRC did not allow it; the grant was only to be used to finance the travel, accommodation, and conference fees for researchers and RAs from Canadian institutions.

Feeling troubled and at a loss but without having the insight to consult my Congolese colleagues, I decided to postpone dealing with the issue and simply fill out the application following the University of Ottawa's research facilitator guidelines. I told myself that if I got the research grant, I would figure out a way to solve the problem and redress the imbalance between the two RAs.

I see three potential ethical issues emerging from this vignette:

1 SSHRC's policy of paying local rates and excluding RAs not attached to a Canadian institution from travel grants for conferences, learning opportunities, and other benefits.
2 My decision to fill out the form following SSHRC's policy instead of challenging the policy; refusing to abide by their budgetary guidelines; or making the decision not to apply for the grant.
3 My original dilemma of how one should pay two people doing the same work in the same place with the same experience but attached to two institutions located in two different countries with starkly different living conditions.

Although each ethical question deserves serious thought and discussion, I will address only the last one. The core of my dilemma is that by paying the Congolese RA local fees – as set by common practice and prescribed by institutional guidelines – I would be establishing that their work was worth less than that of a Canadian RA, and I would be, for all intents and purposes, exploiting them by paying them less for equal work under similar conditions. However, by paying the Congolese RA the equivalent of what the Canadian RA was paid (by granting them equal purchasing power), I would be creating a rift between the RA and other Congolese researchers as well as with other members of their community, undermining local practices, and disrupting social hierarchies. My training on the *Tri-Council Policy Statement*[9] on ethics had certainly not prepared me for this.

In the end, I did not get the grant and, therefore, did not have to deal with the situation and the consequences of my choices. In the section that follows, I discuss the multiple questions that plagued me during the nine-month wait for the publication of the grant results. These questions continue to swirl in my mind as I have yet to figure out what is the "right" thing to do. How would it be possible to handle such a situation ethically?

THE IRRESOLVABILITY OF ETHICAL DILEMMAS

I am not privy to any ethical issues that might have been raised within Canada's research funding agency when it adopted the policy dictating that researchers ought to pay local fees to local researchers. I do not know on what grounds they based their decision, which arguments they put forth, what they took into consideration, and what they disregarded. I do know that on the application form required by my local REB to certify that my research was ethical, I did not have to answer any questions in relation to RAs, potential collaborators, other members of the population from where I was recruiting my participants, or the local community where I was conducting the research. The REB was concerned only with what *I* planned to do or not do with *participants*, how *I* would do it, what *the participants* would know about what *I* was doing, and whether *the participants* would be in a position to consent freely to their involvement in the project.

Neither the REB nor SSHRC helped me work through the ethical dilemma; the message I received from the two organizations I was depending on to conduct the research was that there was no ethical dilemma to solve. The impression I got was that doing the project ethically did not require me to consider the implications of remuneration given that the grant agency was the one making such determination. SSHRC, the REB, and the university's research facilitator framed the remuneration of the RAs as a technical or administrative issue that lay outside the realm of ethical conduct in research. I was confounded and disturbed by the fact that I could exploit someone, and that while doing research I could harm an individual, a community, or both, and the research would still be considered ethical simply because I was following what I had said I would be doing when it came to the research participants.

While awaiting the results of the grant application, I engaged in "watercooler" conversations with more experienced colleagues accustomed to managing grants. I was surprised to find that they also did not see this as an ethical issue but as a matter of policy and resource management. When I insisted that I would be exploiting the Congolese RA, they acknowledged the situation was problematic but did not deem it unethical because they shared the REB's and tri-council policy's scope of what ethics in research entails and to whom we are ethically responsible: the presumably less powerful participant.

What never crossed my mind was to talk to my Congolese colleagues from the CEFOCRIM about how they saw the situation, what insights they could offer, the potential impact of the different options I was thinking about, and possible solutions or ways to move forward. By trying to solve it on my own instead of reaching out, I was not involving those directly concerned in my dilemma, toward whom I was trying to act ethically. In hindsight, it seems absurd that I wanted to create a collaborative relationship with the CEFOCRIM, yet I did not think it might be relevant, let alone necessary, to talk to them about an ethical dilemma I was grappling with. This lapse might be a good indicator that I was not as ready as I thought to work in collaboration with them and to create a genuine partnership. Notwithstanding, if I had had the sense to reach out, whose perspectives should I have privileged: those of potential RAs? those of the researchers from the CEFOCRIM? those of the administrators of the CEFOCRIM? those of other local or international agencies conducting research in the city of Lubumbashi? Given how my decisions would impact them differently,[10] most probably they would have provided me with opposing views, and I would have had to decide whose perspective I would prioritize, whose angle of vision I would give precedence to, in other words, whose interests I would privilege and on what grounds.

Without a sounding board to bounce ideas off, I found myself attempting to navigate on my own the following myriad of questions assailing my mind.

Who should be the focus of my ethical action: the RAs? the research community? the local population? Should my actions be geared toward ensuring I treat both RAs in a fair, respectful, and equitable manner? Was I responsible toward the local community, making sure not to disturb local dynamics or practices, not to risk interfering in hierarchical relations? Or was my responsibility toward the local and international research community at large, meaning that I should not set a precedent that other researchers might not be able to follow? Whom should I prioritize? For whom was I responsible?

Whereas SSHRC frames the issue as a matter of what is best for the individual versus what is best for the community, REBs' mandates limit the ethical gaze to participants or potential participants and thus exclude the community from ethical consideration. Despite taking opposing sides, this dualistic framing of individual interests and rights as intrinsically in competition with community interests and rights is foreign to the Democratic Republic of Congo and implies values and logics from the Global North.[11] My ethical gaze, however, does not allow me to privilege one over the other. I know myself to be responsible to both at the same time, which renders acting ethically an impossibility in this situation. I would have to choose between privileging the negative impact on the RAs or the negative impact on the community. By acting ethically toward one, simultaneously and inescapably I would be acting unethically toward the other.

I considered defining my ethical duty based on the proximity of the relationship. If that were the case, I would be more responsible toward the RAs because they would be relationally closer to me, working daily side by side. I would be less responsible in regards to members of the CEFOCRIM and the École de criminologie de l'Université de Lubumbashi (ECOCRIM)[12], with whom I would be contributing occasionally, and even less responsible toward the local community, whose members I would only occasionally meet, if at all. This questioning helped me realize that, in fact, my universe of moral obligation extends only as far as I allow my ethical gaze to roam. If I narrow my gaze, then my responsibility is toward the two RAs. If I expand it and look beyond the individual, I would see the Congolese RA as part of a Congolese research community as well as a member of the local community. If I were to expand it even further, I would also see my ethical responsibility toward the CEFOCRIM and ECOCRIM, with whom I wanted to establish a long-term collaboration.

Yet, if I were to pay the Canadian RA considerably more than the Congolese RA for the same work under the same conditions and with the same work experience, the exploitation would be even more apparent and the humiliation direct and constant as they would be working in close collaboration on a daily basis. Every day would be a constant reminder that the Canadian's RA work was "worth" more than the Congolese RA's work. I saw this situation not only as exploitative and humiliating but also as reinforcing the privilege and superiority of whiteness.[13]

I was aware of the injustice felt by local workers, particularly those working in the area of international aid and human rights organizations who are paid local fees and have poor, even dangerous, working conditions while white people from outside Africa get better pay and better conditions and benefit from a "risk" bonus. By not worrying about the possibility of negative repercussions for the Congolese RA, I would be purposefully ignoring the impact of my choices, decisions, or actions and placing them outside any ethical consideration. By not finding ways to balance the inequity created by SSHRC, I would be acting unethically and endorsing the Congolese RA's exploitation. However, by fighting against the discrimination and exploitation of the Congolese RA, I would also be imposing foreign standards of equity and fairness on a society that does not have the same perceptions of it and values and practices it differently.

The question then becomes, Who am I to disturb local ways of working in the name of equality, fairness, justice when I do not permanently live in that locality? What right do I have to generate conflict or tension, to undermine local practices and then leave? On the other hand, should I let problematic practices go on because I am not part of the community that is concerned by them? When does "respect" for local practices become a reason to let suffering or problematic situations go on, and when does "helping" become a reason to impose values and ways of living that *I*, a Peruvian living and working in Canada, consider important or good?

The issue of how far my ethical responsibility as a researcher extends was compounded by questions about the temporal frame of my responsibility. Should I consider the possible or potential harms the Congolese RA might face in the short term, such as personal and property damage,[14] or in the medium and long term, such as loss of other job opportunities out of jealousy, vendetta, or bridges burnt if I were to pay them the equivalent of the Canadian RA's salary? Should I consider how it could potentially affect the dynamics within the CEFOCRIM and the ECOCRIM while the research was taking place as well as afterward?[15]

These concerns raised yet another issue for me: On what basis was I making assumptions about what could happen to the research assistants and what the potential negative consequences or impact might be? My thoughts on what might be at stake or how the community might react to the perceived benefits that the Congolese RA would enjoy came from multiple conversations with members of the local population and with professors, researchers, and students, as well as from interviews conducted previously for a different research endeavour. During those conversations, they had described the physical violence, destruction of property, loss of employment, social isolation, legal proceedings, and even criminal charges either they or people they knew had experienced when someone in the community felt they were more deserving of some perceived or real benefit. Notwithstanding the fact that this information came from those living within the community, I still worry that my interpretation and analysis of the information might be imbued with unconscious biases, privileges, and stereotypes I carry with me. More importantly, as I justify or provide grounds for my concerns in this paragraph, to what extent am I actively engaging in perpetuating stereotypes of the Global South?

I also ask myself whether I was adopting a paternalistic attitude by wanting to protect and defend the Congolese RA from potential jealousy, envy, resentment and to prevent a vendetta by the local researchers and community. Was I undermining the RA's agency and resourcefulness, their autonomy to decide whether they wanted the job or not? This issue also came up when I was attempting to find ways to make up for the exploitative salary of the Congolese RA. The problem, at the core, involved me deciding the best way for someone to spend their money. If it would be unacceptable for me to take part of the Canadian RA's salary and dispose of it by making them go to a conference, why would it suddenly be acceptable when it came to the Congolese RA? This was a matter of autonomy and self-determination; they each had the right to do what they wanted with the money they had earned. Furthermore, my choice of paying for international conferences in Europe or North America revealed what I implicitly deemed valuable for their professional development, and it was based on certain standards that (re)produce the Global North as a site of pre-eminence.

In experiencing the dilemma, in working through the dilemma, the driving force has been an incessant questioning: How do I act ethically – without damaging social relations? without reinforcing systems of discrimination and exploitation? without imposing my interpretation and actualization of equality and equity? And how do I do this without betraying who I am or harming those with whom I am working? Through this relentless questioning, am I giving myself way more power and way more importance than I actually have? In fact, how far do my actions actually reach? Could hiring one person for three or four years really or deeply affect the local community and the research community? To what extent would determining the salary of the Congolese RA or providing them with other benefits, such as attending international conferences or giving them their own computer, impact their personal and professional lives? Could any of my actions or a combination of them really "alter" or "disturb" local practices and social hierarchies?

More than ten years later, the answers to these questions remain the same:

I do not know.

BEYOND ACTING ETHICALLY

Taking time to think before doing is not only important but also necessary as we strive to act ethically. However, asking myself these questions has brought me almost to a standstill. It has stopped me from moving forward. I have withdrawn and held back from engaging in fieldwork while attempting to figure out how to do so ethically. I cannot fathom going into the field to research the dynamics and consequences of state violence, political violence, and human rights violations until I figure out how to do so in accordance with a broadened ethical gaze.

What follows is where I currently am in my journey of trying to find a way forward.

Throughout the past ten years I have read a lot, thought a lot, sought for answers in different ethical approaches. During these ethical explorations, I have been sometimes persuaded by ethics of duty, ethics of consequences, and ethics of care.[16] Although none of them helped me solve the question of how I should remunerate two individuals doing the same work under the same conditions, with similar previous experiences but whose permanent address is located in different parts of the world, I still believe each approach can be a useful point of reference in navigating some of the other ethical dilemmas I have encountered while engaging in human rights work. Yet, I have not been fully satisfied by any of the approaches for two main reasons.

First, they each necessitate the creation of artificial boundaries to circumscribe the temporality, scope, and geographical and social distance of our ethical responsibility. In other words, in order to avoid information overload, which would impair and render the approaches inoperable, we are required by each of these three ethics to selectively consider what is within the realm of ethics and to exclude components that, although integral to the situation, must be deemed ethically irrelevant. These approaches are, therefore, insufficient because I am looking for one that does not require me to wilfully limit my ethical gaze.

The second reason I have been dissuaded from embracing ethics of duty, ethics of consequences, or ethics of care is they appear to share the premise that we can discover or identify an ethical course of action in each and all situations when, as we have seen in this chapter, it is not the case. Any "solution" carries the potential for negative, unintended, or unethical consequences. Whereas it is possible to determine that an action is unethical, it is not feasible to claim that an action is ethical.[17] Acting ethically in absolute terms (without simplifying situations, without imposing boundaries that restrict our ethical gaze, without banishing certain factors out of the realm of ethical evaluation) is an impossibility.

I find myself facing a stark choice: either I narrow my scope and reduce my ethical gaze, or I give up entirely trying to act ethically because my ever-expanding universe of moral obligation and the ongoing need to solve the new ethical problems created by my solutions to previous ethical problems render it an impossible task.

Frustrated by either choice and unwilling to give up, I have come to realize that a way for me to move forward might be to abandon the goal of acting ethically as an absolute in any specific situation and strive instead toward engaging ethically with the world.

Virtue ethics have become a viable alternative as they are an approach geared toward being and not doing. They are an ethics that are centred on the agent and not in the act (van Zyl 2019), directing us to ask "What should I be?" not "What should I do?" (van Hooft 2006). By *being*, we are not disconnected from our actions; we can only *be* through commitment and action, by constantly and repeatedly doing (Hursthouse 2001). Being is not about making the correct choice at any given time but about constantly balancing and prioritizing our actions, aware of their limitations and consequences without constantly attempting to solve the unsolvable or prevent what cannot be prevented and, instead, shouldering our responsibility over our doing (van Hooft 2006).

Although virtue ethics have been criticized for their Eurocentric views on what constitutes virtue and which ones we should be striving for, virtue ethics do not impose a set of virtues. On the contrary, they invite us to explore, discover, and choose the virtues that resonate with us personally, culturally, and spiritually.[18] To this effect, I am currently attempting to work through the myriad of questions that assail me by exploring and reflecting on the virtues I value.

By focusing on the agent, virtue ethics might appear individualistic but are, in fact, centred on the Other and bound to the Other. Virtue ethics adopt Emmanuel Lévinas's ethical imperative that we can only be when we are with others and more specifically, when we are for others (van Hooft 2006). Our being is thus conditional on our being responsible for others, on being accountable to others (Barber 1998). The ethical gaze is, therefore, not directed inward, toward the agent, or outward, toward the action. Virtue ethics render the ethical gaze continuous and boundless by compelling us to constantly search for and look after the Other.

As a researcher engaging in human rights work, virtue ethics help me transcend the institutional restrictions placed on my ethical gaze. I am no longer only responsible for acting ethically toward participants; I am responsible for *being* ethical, period.

NOTES

1 The US and Canadian federal governments established ethics review boards as a means to prevent questionable practices in medical and military research as well as by social science researchers (Pimple 2008; Speiglman and Spear 2009). In 1998, the Canadian Federal government adopted the *Tri-Council Policy Statement: Ethical Conduct for Research Involving Human Subjects,* mandating all Canadian universities and hospitals adopt and implement the policy using in-house committees to review and approve all research involving human subjects (Gotlib Conn 2008). According to the University of Ottawa's research ethics board (REB), "The mandate of the REBs is to assess and sanction the ethical aspects of all research projects involving human participants conducted under their jurisdiction by their professors and students, prior to their inception and during their execution. The REBs also verify how researchers plan to take on their ethical responsibilities. The REBs must also approve all projects in which students, professors or support staff of the University of Ottawa serve as research participants" (https://research.uottawa.ca/ethics/reb, accessed September 16, 2020). There is an extensive literature criticizing the existence or the functioning of REBs (see Felices-Luna 2014 for an account of some of the criticisms).

2 Many researchers see as problematic the REBs' tendency to overextend their reach (Bosk and De Vries 2004; Guillemin and Gillam 2004; Haggerty 2004; Librett and Perrone 2010; Nelson 2004).

3 The SSHRC is "the federal research funding agency that promotes and supports postsecondary-based research and training in the humanities and social sciences" (https://www.sshrc-crsh.gc.ca/home-accueil-eng.aspx, accessed November 19, 2020).

4 Controversy exists regarding the use of global North/global South as being reductionist, homogenizing, without nuance, and as glossing over complex historical, economical, political, cultural, religious, social ... realities (Waisbich, Roychoudhury, and Haug 2021). Notwithstanding, I agree with Tobias Berger (2021), who sees an epistemological value to the use of Global North/Global South as a relational category. In this regard, the Global South is an epistemic South, post-national and deterritorialized (de Sousa Santos and Meneses 2020). It refers to subjugated peoples and spaces negatively impacted by capitalism and colonization, thus opening the possibility for Souths in the geographical north and Norths in the geographical South (Mahler 2017).

5 If I had to pay fifty-four hundred Canadian dollars to the Canadian RA, I would be paying that amount but in Congolese francs to the Congolese RA.

6 If the amount paid to the Canadian RA provided them with the purchasing power to lodge, clothe, and feed themselves for four months, then I would be paying the Congolese RA the amount that would allow them to lodge, clothe, and feed themselves to a similar standard.

7 Local fees would be determined by the amount that a Congolese RA was paid at the time by the CEFOCRIM.

8 I do not know how much professors or researchers earn, but from previous research in Lubumbashi, I knew that judges at the time were reportedly paid approximately thirty US dollars a month. At the time of the application (2010), 71 percent of the population lived with less than one US dollar a day (Weijs, Hilhorst, and Ferf 2012).

9 Tri-Council Policy Statement: Ethical Conduct for Research Involving Humans (2018). Accessed May 31, 2022. https://ethics.gc.ca/eng/education_tutorial-didacticiel.html.

10 I presume that potential RAs would advocate for equivalent pay with the Canadian RA whereas the researchers of the CEFOCRIM, administrators, and other research agencies would advocate for local RAs to be paid local rates.

11 For further discussion on how the Global North's contrasting of individual versus collective rights is irrelevant to many in the Global South, see Nagar (2014), Smith (2005), and Wilson (2008).

12 École de criminologie de l'Université de Lubumbashi (School of Criminology, University of Lubumbashi). The ECOCRIM is closely tied to CEFOCRIM. Even though they are two distinct institutions, they share office and classroom space. Furthermore, the researchers at the CEFOCRIM are professors for the ECOCRIM and the students at ECOCRIM are research assistants for the CEFOCRIM.

13 Even if the Canadian RA were racialized, their Canadian nationality would still be seen as a carrier of whiteness. This assumption comes from my own experience: as a Peruvian working in a Canadian institution, I was commonly referred to as Belgian by members of the CEFOCRIM, ECOCRIM, and other people I met. Whiteness is "a form of subjectivity that is socially constructed, historically contextual, and inherently unstable ... particularly problematic for its furthering of colonial and imperialist projects" (Razack, Smith, and Thobani 2010, 10–11). Whiteness is intrinsically tied to the perceived entitlement to manage all racial Others (Thobani 2007).

14 In my previous trips to Lubumbashi, individuals told me about personal experiences with their homes being vandalized, even destroyed, out of jealousy over perceived material advantages or economic benefits.

15 Although a relationship had been built with members of both institutions through various trips, it had not always been smooth or easy. I had seen the negative impact of being in a position to hire someone when I briefly and informally paid a student to collect empirical material necessary to start a small research project. On the one hand, I witnessed how he was mistreated by his colleagues and professors for the presumed "privilege"; on the other hand, he never delivered on the material he promised to collect, and others took this opportunity to challenge my decision to give him the "job." I experienced students, professors, and researchers vying for my attention when they thought I had power or money, only to be ignored once I demonstrated that I did not have either. There was tension when students and researchers, jockeying for better positions within the CEFOCRIM and the ECOCRIM, attempted to use me to gain some sort of perceived advantage. I had to manage situations when, on multiple occasions, those in positions of power displayed their authority and dominance over those with less power as a means to prove a point and get my attention, admiration, or recognition. Some students and researchers made disparaging comments and undermined their colleagues to me when they thought it could somehow benefit them.

16 Ethics of duty: ethical action is determined, defined, and justified universally by an abstract principle. Ethics of consequences: ethical action is determined, defined, and

justified contextually by the consequences of the action. Ethics of care: ethical action is determined, defined, and justified situationally by engaging in receptivity, relatedness, and responsiveness.

17 According to Bauman (1993, 11), "Few actions (and only those which are relatively trivial and of minor existential importance) are unambiguously good."

18 For some, those virtues might be represented in the four Rs of Indigenous research and education: reciprocity, respect, responsibility, relevance (Kirkness and Barhnardt 1991), and the fifth R, "relationships," added by Amy Parent (2009). For others, it might be the African concept of *ubuntu* (community). See van Hooft's (2014) *The Handbook of Virtue Ethics* for a starting point on important virtues within different communities and spiritualities.

REFERENCES

Barber, M. 1998. "Lévinas and Virtue Ethics." *International Philosophical Quarterly* 38, 2: 119–26.

Bauman, Z. 1993. "Introduction: Morality in Modern and Postmodern Perspective." In *Postmodern Ethics,* 1–15. Cambridge: Blackwell.

Berger, T. 2021. "The 'Global South' as a Relational Category – Global Hierarchies in the Production of Law and Legal Pluralism." *Third World Quarterly* 42, 9: 2001–17.

Bosk, C., and R. De Vries. 2004. "Bureaucracies of Mass Deception: Institutional Review Boards and the Ethics of Ethnographic Research." *Annals of the American Academy of Political and Social Science* 595: 249–63.

de Sousa Santos, B., and M.P. Meneses. 2020. *Knowledges Born in the Struggle: Constructing the Epistemologies of the Global South*. New York: Routledge.

Felices-Luna, M. 2014. "Fighting the 'Big Bad Wolf': Why All the Fuss around Ethic Review Boards?" In *Demarginalizing Voices: Commitment, Emotion and Action in Qualitative Research,* edited by J. Kilty, M. Felices-Luna, and S. Fabian, 195–215. Vancouver: UBC Press.

Gotlib Conn, L.G. 2008. "Ethics Policy as Audit in Canadian Clinical Settings: Exiling the Ethnographic Method." *Qualitative Research* 8, 4: 499–514.

Guillemin, M., and L. Gillam. 2004. "Ethics, Reflexivity, and 'Ethically Important Moments' in Research." *Qualitative Inquiry* 10, 2: 261–80.

Haggerty, K. 2004. "Ethics Creep: Governing Social Science Research in the Name of Ethics." *Qualitative Sociology* 27, 4: 391–414.

Hursthouse, R. 2001. *On Virtue Ethics*. Oxford: Oxford University Press.

Kirkness, V.J., and R. Barhnardt. 1991. "First Nations and Higher Education: The Four R's – Respect, Relevance, Reciprocity, Responsibility." *Journal of American Indian Education* 30, 3: 1–15.

Librett, M., and D. Perrone. 2010. "Apples and Oranges: Ethnography and the IRB." *Qualitative Research* 10, 6: 729–47.

Mahler, A.G. 2018. *From the Tricontinental to the Global South: Race, Radicalism, and Transcontinental Solidarity.* Durham, NC: Duke University Press.

Nagar, R. 2014. *Muddying the Waters: Coauthoring Feminisms across Scholarship and Activism*. Chicago: University of Illinois Press.

Nelson, C. 2004. "The Brave New World of Research Surveillance." *Qualitative Inquiry* 10, 2: 207–18.

Parent, A. 2009. "Keep Them Coming Back for More: Urban Aboriginal Youth's Perceptions and Experiences of Wholistic Education in Vancouver." Master's thesis, University of British Columbia.

Pimple, K. 2008. "Introduction." In *Research Ethics*, edited by K. Pimple, xv–xxxi. Burlington, VT: Ashgate.

Razack, S., M. Smith, and S. Thobani. 2010. "Introduction: States of Race; Critical Race Feminism for the 21st Century." In *States of Race: Critical Race Feminism for the 21st Century*, edited by S. Razack, M. Smith, and S. Thobani, 1–19. Toronto: Between the Lines.

Smith, L. 2005. "On Tricky Ground: Researching the Native in the Age of Uncertainty." In *The SAGE Handbook of Qualitative Research*, edited by N.K. Denzin and Y.S. Lincoln, 85–107. Los Angeles: Sage.

Speiglman, R., and P. Spear. 2009. "The Role of Institutional Review Boards: Ethics – Now You See Them, Now You Don't." In *The Handbook of Social Research Ethics*, edited by D. Mertens and P. Ginsberg, 121–34. London: Sage.

SSHRC. 2020. https://www.sshrc-crsh.gc.ca/home-accueil-eng.aspx. Accessed November 19, 2020.

Thobani, S. 2007. *Exalted Subjects: Studies in the Making of Race and Nation in Canada*. Toronto: University of Toronto Press.

van Hooft, S. 2006. *Understanding Virtue Ethics*. New York: Routledge.

–. 2014. *The Handbook of Virtue Ethics*. New York: Routledge.

van Zyl, L. 2019. *Virtue Ethics*. New York: Routledge.

Waisbich, L.T., S. Roychoudhury, and S. Haug. 2021. "Beyond the Single Story: 'Global South' Polyphonies." *Third World Quarterly* 42: 9: 2086–95.

Weijs, B., D. Hilhorst, and A. Ferg. 2012. *Researching Livelihoods and Services Affected by Conflict: Livelihoods, Basic Services and Social Protection in Democratic Republic of the Congo*. Working Paper, Wageningen University.

Wilson, S. 2008. *Research Is Ceremony: Indigenous Research Methods*. Halifax, NS: Fernwood Publishing.

Interlude

BACK AT YOU, JOSEPH CONRAD

Juliane Okot Bitek

Joseph Conrad's *Heart of Darkness,* a canonical text in English literature, has haunted me ever since I studied it at school. This novella, much celebrated and much critiqued for its articulation and seeming critique of colonial Africa, fully retained its racist trope of African people and was most famously debunked by Chinua Achebe, who did not say much about the misogyny of this text. In this poem, I perform an erasure of an excerpt from the novella, by deleting most of the words but retaining the presence of Conrad's words by maintaining his punctuation and select words. The exposed words are words spoken at the end of a narration about the only African woman in that novella. She is beautiful but voiceless and can only perform anger. I write back, as an African woman, a poet, and a literary scholar, to respond to Conrad with his own words and peel back the limitations, racism, and misogyny that can no longer hide behind the craft of this immensely harmful work of canonical British literature.

. A formidable silence

.

“ ,

, , ,

, .

.

“ , ,

, . ;

; ,

, , ;

, , , ,

. . . ,

; .

, ,

, ,

.

“ , , . ,

.

.

. ,

, . ,

. , ,

, . .

.

.

, ,

, ,

. .

“ , , .

.

“‘ ,’

, .‘

.

. . ,

, . I don’t understand

, , .

.... — ’ . Ah, well, it’s all over now.’

PART 2

Ethical Dilemmas When Challenging Business as Usual or When Taking the Unbeaten Path

7

"I Want My Name"

AUTONOMY, PROTECTION, AND ATTRIBUTION IN RESEARCH INTERVIEWS WITH "VULNERABLE" POPULATIONS

Kristi Heather Kenyon

How do we balance principles and practices of autonomy and protection in research with human participants? As a qualitative human rights researcher who uses interviews extensively this is a question I face often – particularly when it comes to identifying or masking the identity of interviewees. Often the powerful, articulate, and passionate people I speak to are what ethics boards classify as "vulnerable" populations because of the stigma they face for their work, their identities, their activism, and their health status. Sometimes, as a result, I am advised not to allow participants the option of choosing to have their names used in my research. The aim is protection and, yet, for some participants it can feel like an oppressive muzzling, limiting their ability to tell their own stories, to defy stigma, and to claim their own narratives. Why do we assume that research participants are not the people best able to assess their own risk? Who is best placed to decide whether to tip the scales toward autonomy or protection? And who gets to define protection – as anonymity or a space to tell their story on their own terms?

The question of attribution may appear small and technical, but it is a critical question of human rights related to personal autonomy, participation, dignity, privacy, confidentiality, and safety and security of the person. Naming participants – particularly where they belong to groups that are criminalized or stigmatized – can result in real world consequences including job loss, arrest, violence, and even death. These risks lead many ethics boards to caution against, and sometimes explicitly prohibit, the identification of people they consider "vulnerable" (see also Krystalli 2021, 134). But anonymity is not benign. It, too, has human rights consequences, including diminished autonomy, restricted participation, and impugned dignity. If we view those who participate in our research as active, autonomous, and capable it is essential that we engage with them as participants and honour their voices through their preferred attribution. Doing so, however, can challenge our own comfort level with risk, and given the immutability of our research outputs can ask researchers to make fixed commitments in perpetuity, even though the contexts of research participants and the risks they face often change over time.[1] Deeply personal and unexpectedly complex, the question of attribution is, in fact, applied human rights work in the practice of human rights research.

This chapter is inspired by a dilemma I encountered while conducting my doctoral fieldwork and centres on grappling with the consequences of an ethics board decision. I trace this dilemma through a series of encounters as I conducted my research. In so doing, I reflect on the practical implications of critical concepts such as protection, harm, and vulnerability. This chapter is an active and iterative struggle with an unresolved ethical dilemma. It contains paradoxes, exceptions, and contradictions as I continue to wrestle with these questions through time.

VIGNETTE

This will not sound like a story of interview-based research with activists in Southern Africa. There is no building of rapport, no nuanced tones, no dramatic facial expressions, no ambiance from background noise, no posters on the walls, no co-workers walking by, no protest slogans, no shared laughter.

I sat at a big oak desk in my bedroom in a graduate college at the University of British Columbia and composed a Human Subjects Research Ethics Application. A long way from the context in which I would conduct my research, alone, and in silence, I tried to imagine the ethical risks and benefits of my research and determine how I might mediate them.

Inspired by the HIV activists I had worked with during an earlier career in Botswana, I hoped my PhD would explore why organizations conducting advocacy on HIV in sub-Saharan Africa chose the language of human rights. Activists are often strategic in the language they use in their slogans, chants, protests, and campaigns, and I was curious about why, unlike many health activists, HIV activists often referred to human rights, even though using the language of public health or development, for example, might be more familiar and less confrontational. In my research I chose to focus on organizations in four countries: Uganda, South Africa, Botswana, and Ghana, along with a small number of interviews with United Nations (UN) agencies. I was eager to learn from this vibrant, dedicated, and creative group of activists and advocates and committed to bringing their insights into academic conversations.

I entered my ideas in precise, technical black and white, taking care to leave no box unticked. I had been told it was important to be specific, to avoid ambiguity, to address all conceivable risks, and to be consistent.

In composing my ethics application, I was influenced by my experience as an activist, and working alongside activists. I intended to interview people in high-profile organizations about their work. Some of these organizations were very well-known. Their objective was to be loud, visibly drawing attention to the plight of their constituency through radio campaigns, dramatic protests, marches, political advocacy, protest songs, and community mobilization. Some of the people within these groups were very vocal. They were regularly cited in newspapers and interviewed on the news. They made submissions to Parliament and took cases to court.

I decided to give each participant several choices about how (or whether) they wanted to be identified in publications resulting from my research. I offered these choices: identify me by my name and the name of my organization; identify me by organization only; do not include my name or the name of my organization.

A four-country study necessitated multiple ethics approvals.[2] One of these, the South African Human Sciences Research Council responded to my application with an unexpected request. They asked that, for reasons of protection,[3] "when publishing ... the investigator preferably makes no link to the organizations and individuals interviewed" (South African Human Sciences Research Council, personal communication, February 5, 2010).

I was puzzled. The primary organization I intended to work with in South Africa was the Treatment Action Campaign (TAC). They were, for lack of a better word, famous. They sought attention (and action) for their cause. That is why they existed. It would be difficult to anonymize them and difficult to explain why I would try to do so. Ultimately, the South African Human Sciences Research Council ethics board accepted my argument and allowed participants the option of identifying organizations.

The ethics board did not, however, allow me to include in my consent form the option of individuals identifying themselves by name. I was permitted only to identify individuals if "a particular respondent specifically asks to be named" (South African Human Sciences Research Council, personal communication, February 22, 2010). This did not feel right to me, but identifying people was not important to my research and I agreed to this condition.

I did not fully realize at the time that although individual identification was not particularly important to me, it *was* particularly important to many of those who would participate in my research, particularly those living openly with HIV.

A month later, in the thick of fieldwork, I would write in my field notes:

> A lot of people, when I go over the different ways they can choose to be identified (or not) in my study, look almost offended at the idea of not having their names used. [They ask] "But I am open, why should I hide?" We assume we're protecting people by not naming them, but that's also a way of silencing people, of denying them a voice. And a lot of the people I am working with have worked very hard to reclaim that voice, and they want to be named. (author's field notes, March 21, 2010)

FRAMING THE DILEMMA: INTERVIEWS ARE RELATIONAL, RISK IS PERSONAL

Applying for ethics review is in many ways the diametric opposite of the experience of doing qualitative research. The ethics review is important and essential; it forces researchers to think through the nitty gritty of a variety of ethical conundrums: Will we endanger our participants by speaking with them; who will benefit from our research; where will we store the data; who will have access to it? But in contrast with interview-based research, which can be highly personal and nuanced, ethics applications tend to be a process that values certainty and that treats people as though they have universal desires and risks. It rightfully places responsibility on the researcher to protect participants, but in doing so does not always provide ample space for participant agency and voice and can implicitly make paternalistic assumptions.

Protection is and should be a central component of research ethics (CIHR, NSERC, and SSHRC 2018, 10.4; Kaiser 2009). Much of the intellectual history of research ethics builds itself in contravention of studies that placed participants at significant harm, often without their knowledge or consent (see Resnick n.d.; Rhodes 2010). In many of these early studies, research subjects were clearly seen as less important than research outputs – they were, to put it frankly, seen as means to an end. When reflecting on the history of research ethics it is important to note, also, that these egregious historical examples relate primarily to medical research, where harm and benefit have often been quite concrete – the experimental treatment cures you or makes you ill, for example (see Rhodes 2010).

Social science and humanities research draws on the same framework in much muddier terrain and is far more open to diverse interpretations (McCormack et al. 2012). As a social science researcher working on questions related to health, I am often required to submit my application for ethics review to a medical- or health-related ethics review board.[4] This means I am asked whether I will take blood or tissue samples and whether there is a risk of death, the loss of limbs, or blindness as a result of participation in my study. I could answer these, with reference to my interview-based research on HIV activism, with some confidence. No, I would not take any biological samples, and, no, there should be no physical risk from the interview itself.

But an interview is not exactly a procedure that one is subject to. It is an interaction that two (or more) people participate in. It may be situational and time limited, but on a micro scale it has many of the elements of a relationship – there is the process of introductions, getting to know each other, and often the discovery of common interests. An interview with rich, honest data depends on rapport between the interviewer and interviewee – trust built or assumed through factors as various as personality, tone of voice, and assumed intentions, as well as the ability of interviewee to place the interviewer into an existing web of connections.

In the semi-structured style of interviews I used in my thesis research (see Longhurst 2003), I had the leeway to allow each interview to flow into its own unique shape. To reveal this shape I probed for detail, pulled on intriguing threads, sought examples, followed breadcrumbs, skipped redundancies, and altered the order of questions to fit the flow of each conversation. As I noted in my thesis:

> People's views may shift from day to day and their expression of them often varies by context, including who is doing the interviewing. Interview content and depth may be affected by mood, time of day, work schedule, previous interaction, gender, or perceptions about the other person (for both the interviewee and interviewer). Interviews are nuanced communication interactions where individuals respond to subtle cues both verbal and non-verbal as well as setting, clothing, vocabulary and intonation. As an example, in one instance I unexpectedly gained

> respect for having walked to an interview from a village 3 kilometres away. This may have had an impact on the lengthy and fruitful interview that followed, along with a meal. On another occasion, when I unconsciously cracked my neck, in the process jerking my head slightly to one side, the person I was interviewing mirrored the action. He then responded as though I had expressed doubt or surprise in relation to what he had just said, elaborating on his last comments as a result. (Kenyon 2013, 101)

Interviews are intricate, fluid, and intimate dances of interpersonal communication. Nothing about them is static. They are rarely replicable. As complex acts of relational co-creation, in many ways interviews are themselves living things.

The beauty and irreplicable relationality of interviews does not mean that they are without risks. As I often say to potential participants (and in my consent forms), there is a risk that you may find some questions upsetting, or they may remind you of unpleasant experiences. You may worry about upsetting colleagues if you are identified, or you may have concerns about how donors or partners may react. I have begun adding, as I introduce the consent form, that risk is personal. A question that may be neutral or positive to one person can be upsetting to another. I started adding this comment after a woman I was speaking to burst into tears partway through an interview. I had not asked an invasive question or prompted her to recall something difficult or painful. It was not anything that I, or the ethics board, anticipated being particularly triggering or upsetting. I was asking a conceptual question about how she understood human rights and was using a series of photos to help spark the conversation. I showed her an image of an older man using a wheelchair. Unbeknownst to me, she was caring for her ailing father and had recently learned he was dying. The photo reminded her of her father. We stopped the interview, found some Kleenex, and talked about her dad.

Some harm is predictable and generic. But in an interview, harm is often personal and specific. I could not have known that particular image would upset that interviewee. I did not know her life story and her family history. I now often say, "You know yourself and your situation best. You are the best judge of your own safety and well-being," while reminding participants they can skip any questions they choose or stop the interview at any time. This is not to abdicate responsibility, but to highlight agency and self-knowledge. Meaningful protection requires knowledge.

UNPACKING VULNERABILITY

> I had to prove to the ethics board that I would not be asking invasive questions (and I am not), and yet, people have been very open about sharing personal stories and heartache with me. I do not know if it is because they think that is what I expect, or because that is the starting point, the endpoint, the everything point for them when it comes to this issue. A lot of stories of death, lost husbands and wives, and children. Also, very honest, unpretentious, and unprotected (and unsolicited) sharing of personal experiences of self-stigma, internal struggles, and support structures. I have been ... I guess the word is impressed by the way people are open in saying "This is what I need." It is an admission of both strength and vulnerability in ways that I do not encounter often, especially from people I have only just met. When meeting a participant for the first time at her home, for example, she pointed out her brother and said, "He's an important part of my support network." (author's field notes, March 21, 2010)

Two years spent working in HIV advocacy in Botswana taught me some of the complexities of publicly identifying as HIV-positive. Some people were very open, proud, and in some cases even known for their HIV status and related activism. Many others kept it a guarded secret. Confidentiality was a right. There were still people who faced horrible consequences from their status being disclosed – including abuse, isolation from family, losing their housing and jobs, and, in a few horrific instances, losing their lives. As I put together my ethics application, I wanted to be very clear – under no circumstances would I ask anyone their HIV status. I was interviewing people working in HIV advocacy about their work.

And yet, the reason people undertake this work is often very personal; in places with some of the world's highest prevalence rates it is almost impossible for it not to be. The often quoted slogan "If you're not infected you're affected" is true. Every family, every workplace, every community is directly affected. Even though my research was organization-focused and institutional, I gradually realized it was also necessarily personal.

> **INTERVIEWER:** I think I just have one last question. Why do you think that people join TAC?
>
> **INTERVIEWEE:** Right. Let me talk about myself first. I didn't know that I'm living with HIV at first. But my sister was living with HIV. (TAC employee in Ekurhuleni, interview, August 12, 2010)

Even though it had not been my intention, for many people I was effectively interviewing them on their own lives – because the professional and the personal were so closely intertwined.

Many people became involved in HIV advocacy because they had been personally affected. My work included groups with strong grassroots components where, in many cases, women living with HIV, living in poverty, with relatively low levels of formal education (but a wealth of life experience) became involved after learning their status. I also conducted some more global policy–level interviews with United Nations agencies, where the people I talked to were typically highly educated career bureaucrats, some with personal connections to HIV, and some without. I also interviewed many people whose life experience and education fell somewhere in the middle of these two groups, including highly educated people living with HIV.

These first two groups would often be classified quite differently in terms of vulnerability. The former would be considered a population with a particular need for protection due to their HIV status, their gender, their poverty, and their "lack" of education. This vulnerability could be increased in some cases if that woman was also a sex worker, identified as gay or lesbian, or had sex with women. All of these features and facets of identity and life entail real tangible risks to health, safety, and well-being within and beyond participation in research. And yet, it is a UN employee in Geneva who insists that her interview be used only as "deep background," with no attribution or quotation because of worries about job security, and an HIV-positive woman in Ekurhuleni who insists that her name be used because it is her story. Each woman had the strength and wherewithal to challenge the options provided on the consent form and make requests that better suited her needs. One of these women, however, had the option she desired removed from the list of choices on the consent form at the request of her country's ethics board in order to protect her.

In the interview with Nontyatyambo, the woman who wanted her name to be known, I found myself saying, "It really strikes me when you're speaking that you sound so strong" (K. Kenyon, interview with N. Makapela, August 10, 2010). She explained, for example, when I asked about the meaning of human rights in HIV activism:

> As a woman who is living with HIV, who knows a little bit about our constitution, for me it mustn't be something which is written there. It must be something that reflects on a daily basis. For me, rights are all about human rights for a woman who is living with HIV, for a woman

> who is negative, for a woman who is sleeping with another woman. All these things that our constitution addresses – non-discrimination to race, sexual orientation and so forth – it mustn't be something that we just read. It must be practicsed. (N. Makapela, interview, August 10, 2010)

She goes on to talk about how the government is sometimes intimidated by Treatment Action Campaign's (TAC) "HIV POSITIVE" T-shirts, and that TAC works on building relationships toward positive change with health services, all the while conducting education on human rights and treatment literacy in informal settlements. She is informed, convincing, experienced, capable, independent, a leader. These are not traits that are typically associated with the word "vulnerable."

What does it mean to be vulnerable? The emphasis on vulnerability comes again from a history of egregious research practices. Its inclusion as a critical consideration in research "signals mindfulness for researchers and research ethics boards to the possibility that some participants may be at higher risk of harm or wrong" (Bracken-Roche et al. 2017). Rather than being precisely defined, however, it seems to be a word that falls into "I know it when I see it" territory. A detailed analysis of national and international research ethics policies and guidelines "exploring their discussions of the definition, application, normative justification and implications of vulnerability" found that "[f]ew policies and guidelines explicitly defined vulnerability, instead relying on implicit assumptions and the delineation of vulnerable groups and sources of vulnerability" (Bracken-Roche et al. 2017). The Canadian *Tri-Council Policy Statement on Ethics* (CIHR, NSERC, and SSHRC 2018) follows this trend. The document pays great attention to vulnerability, including consideration of risk, gender, decision-making ability, age, appropriate and inappropriate exclusion, and a wealth of contextual and circumstantial factors. The document does not, however, define the term. This is reasonable as vulnerability is necessarily contextual. In social science research, we are talking primarily of personal, emotional, and social risks, and each of these is difficult, even inappropriate, to generalize. Without definition, however, vulnerability can easily be couched in "implicit assumptions." These assumptions can be damaging and can impede the agency and impugn the dignity of research participants deemed vulnerable.

In common parlance, vulnerability is often referred to in two ways. First, it is used as a way of describing precarity or weakness (being "vulnerable to infection" often suggests that the body's defences are weakened and less able to handle a threat). Second, it is used to speak of the emotional openness needed to forge meaningful, close personal relationships. The latter is typically described as an example of strength and maturity, though it can sometimes fall into the gendered binary wherein showing emotion is seen as female and weak, and reliance on rationality is seen as strong, professional, and male.

How does this apply to interviewing HIV activists, some of whom were living with HIV? The *Tri-Council Policy Statement on Ethics* speaks of "individuals, groups and communities whose situation or circumstances make them vulnerable in the context of a specific research project" (CIHR, NSERC, and SSHRC 2018, Chapter 4, Introduction). This describes many participants in my research, and yet their situations and circumstances do more than make them vulnerable. Some of these factors are also what made the people I spoke to authoritative, knowledgeable, and powerful. One of the things that struck me was the ways in which vulnerability and strength were intertwined. In many interviews, the (mostly women) interviewees that I spoke to were frank about their journeys, their pain and loss, and the web of support they had built and continued to reinforce. This frankness, this openness, this "vulnerability" enabled them to establish meaningful connections, to find new purpose in their lives, and to embody a bruised but resilient strength. I was in awe of the bare honesty of these accounts and the matter-of-fact way people spoke about support as a necessity to give and receive, a part of being human and affirming humanity. I am often asked if my research is depressing. I struggle to explain the energy, vitality, and commitment of the activists I speak to. The work they do is devastatingly hard, as are many dimensions of their lives. But there is also real, palpable, fierce, proud, and hard-fought joy alongside a furious desire for change.

To speak of the activists I interviewed as vulnerable is not inaccurate, but it is insufficient and misleading. Many of the people I interview face very real risks. But words like vulnerable can obscure strength, capacity, and agency. They can reduce and simplify people who, like each of us, are multifaceted and complex. To say that Nontyatyambo faces risks because of her gender, health status, socio-economic status is true. To say that she is not capable of understanding her risks and making decisions for herself is not. Like many women with HIV, she has profound lived experience of negotiating and navigating risk and making difficult decisions. This is where the problem lies – that vulnerability was used to constrict her agency. She wanted her name used and she knew very well that there were risks involved in being identified (see also Krystalli 2021, 134, for a related discussion). She made this choice anyway. In Geneva, another woman evaluated her own risks and made a different choice.

WHAT IS PROTECTION AND WHO GETS TO DEFINE IT?

> I attended the Treatment Action Campaign's Gauteng Provincial Congress in the old Johannesburg city hall. An old ornate room with high ceilings and a balcony, full to the brim with (mostly women) in light blue shirts saying "HIV POSITIVE" in the largest possible letters. I've never been to a meeting with so much singing – at five minute intervals, after every presentation, one person would start and then the entire room was on its feet, singing, in harmony, in call and answer, until singing was no longer enough, and the room began to dance, first toyi-toying (a step side to side, and forward and back, traditional protest dance), then groups moving to the front to stomp, until the floor, the chairs, the tables and everything on them was vibrating, jiggling, dancing along. (author's field notes, August 29, 2010)

In interview-based research, "protection" is often understood as obscuring the identity of participants. This structure of protection is built on particular ways of thinking about harm. The assumption here is that if you are not named, and identifying details are not revealed, you will be kept safe. Harm is assumed to be social and due to identification, connection, and openness (see Kaiser 2009). Are these assumptions about harm meaningful to participants in my research? Can structures of protection be sources of harm?

Ubuntu is a sociocentric concept in much of Africa, known by various names in different languages (Kagame 1976; Kamwangamalu 1999, 24–25), that is often explained through the aphorism "I am because we are and since we are, therefore I am" (Mbiti 1990, 16; see also Gade 2011). It is the idea that we create, reflect, and recognize our own and each other's humanity through our interactions (see Mmolai 2007, xi; Mmualefhe 2007, 1). Although there is no universal story of HIV, for many people living with the virus, especially for many women, being diagnosed results in the severing of social and familial ties. One woman in Ghana, now a vocal activist, stated simply, "Because of this I don't have a family." She recalls thinking to herself, "I am no longer a human being" (Women United against AIDS Ghana employee, February 10, 2010; see also Kenyon 2017). For her and many others, involvement in support and advocacy groups filled crucial human needs for connection and recognition. She is now active in a group called Women United against AIDS Ghana (WUAAG), where every meeting begins with a call and response chant of "UNITED – We Stand!" She says "WUAAG is my family" and through this connection describes herself as "bec[oming] bold" (WUAAG employee, February 10, 2010; see also Kenyon 2017). This story was echoed through organizations in other places I studied, with heartfelt descriptions of finding and building a family to replace the one they had lost. Alongside this reconstruction there was often a story of moving from shame and silence about their HIV status to a place of strength and pride as they learned about their condition, helped educate and support others, and advocated for change. Connection and openness were often part of the "cure" to the social isolation, shame, and stigma, which many described as worse than the virus itself. In Botswana there even became a "Miss HIV Stigma Free" (Curtiss 2016) beauty and advocacy pageant, with extensive media coverage, where all participants were HIV-positive. For some, but certainly not all, the ability to be open, to tell their own stories in their own words and with their own names became an important act of reclaiming identity, voice, self-worth, and power.

What if it is silence and isolation rather than identification that is harmful? What if not being able to tell your story and claim it in your own name reminds you of the shame you felt while hiding your HIV status? What if not being able to make choices reminds you of the loss of control you felt when you were diagnosed and the lonely clinical experience of the medical system? In these cases protection can feel like oppression, another instance of being told it is "not a good idea" to tell other people about your life, or for people to know what you have lived through. It can be a way of once again being silenced, once again being stigmatized, and once again being separated from family, this time a found family of shared experience.

This is not a type of harm that is akin to a side effect in a drug trial. It is highly dependent on the details of an individual's life: their relationships, their personality, the stability of their employment and housing, their sense of safety, and even these factors in relation to those close to them who might be identified by proxy. The more I spent time with women living their activism, the more I realized the danger in assuming that anonymity always means protection. People need to be respected as experts on their own lives. The idea that I, a foreign researcher, or even an ethics board in Pretoria, is better equipped to assess risk in someone else's daily life is problematic. I have not walked in others' shoes, and I do not have to live the consequences with the same depth as those whose lives I write about. They are honouring me with their trust; I need to honour them and respect their agency.

COMPLICATIONS AND COMPLEXITIES

> It's March 2010 and I'm headed to conduct interviews with an LGBTI group that does HIV advocacy in Kampala. When I arrive there's someone no one recognizes fiddling with the lock on the gate. I go in and start an interview. A piece of legislation known as the "Kill the Gays Bill"[5] is before [P]arliament, which proposes the death penalty for same-sex sexual activity. I spend extra time on consent and make a point of recording our conversation about attribution. The person I speak to tells me about holding a conference on LGBTI issues and the police starting to arrest people before the first speech is done. He says he wants his name used in my research; "Let them come and arrest me," he says laughing.
>
> In October 2010 *Rolling Stone,* a newspaper in Uganda, published gay activist David Kato's photo on the front page alongside others with the headline, "Hang Them." He is brutally murdered in January 2011. In October 2019 gay activist and HIV educator Brian Wasswa is killed. The news is devastating and unsettling.
>
> I did not interview either of them. I know the man I spoke to faces the same risks. I am not naming him. (author's field notes summary)

I believe strongly in the autonomy and capacity of the people that I interview. I consider limiting or overriding their choices to be patronizing and disrespectful. I am a human rights researcher, and respecting the dignity and autonomy of research participants, particularly those who have already experienced such disrespect and marginalization, is of paramount importance. But what if those who participate in my research are willing to take risks with their lives that I am not? And what if risk changes with time?

These are terrifying questions, so terrifying, in fact, that I did not include this in the mass email I sent to friends and family while conducting fieldwork in Uganda. The interviews I did with LGBTI activists[6] in Uganda did not appear in my thesis or subsequent book. While their exclusion from my book can be explained by a situation of too many case studies, I could have written an article from the data I collected. If I had, I have no doubt that I would not have included any individual's name.

How do I navigate this glaring contradiction? Is this not precisely an example of the paternalism I have been arguing against? Is it a situation of "autonomy to a point, until I think that I know better than you"? The activists I spoke to were utterly cognizant of the risks they faced, so much so that they mentioned them in interviews. Their activism was an act of defiance, solidarity, and celebration in the midst of ongoing risk. Like the women I spoke to in South Africa, the LGBTI activists in Uganda that I met with built a vibrant, welcoming community in their organization. Some of them revelled in being out and open. But while some of them were willing to take on serious risks to their freedom, safety, and lives, ultimately, I was not willing to risk their safety[7] even if they were willing to risk their own. It was not a level of risk that *I* could live with. This reveals another level of complexity. While an interview is largely the story of the interviewee, it is, as stated earlier, a dynamic co-creation. I, too, am a participant and creator. As a co-creator I, too, have a voice and a say in how this creation is represented. In this instance, I choose to exercise a veto on identification. I am simultaneously at peace with and unsettled by this decision. It feels like a contradiction, but it is the only decision that feels safe. This in itself is troubling. Ultimately, in these precarious circumstances, it comes down to my comfort, my moral compass, and my level of risk tolerance or aversion. I would have chosen not to reveal the names of people for whom I feared identification could lead to serious harm, even death, even if those same people, knowing those risks, would have made a different choice. This raises a number of critical questions that I cannot quite answer. Does it matter if that person has already identified themselves (or been identified) in local media? What is the threshold of risk that justifies overriding the preference of research participants? What biases shape the way I think about risk? How does access to information shape perceptions of risk? Am I more likely, for example, to perceive risk where violence is sanctioned by the state and receives media coverage than, for example, where it is within families or relationships? And is this risk assessment specific to risks from participation in my research, which may be difficult to separate from other forms of communication and advocacy?

If interviews are dynamic, living co-creations, another serious complication is that we represent this dynamic creation in a static, immutable form. Academic outputs consist almost entirely of written publications, which are essentially unalterable once published. Once something has been on the Internet, even if corrected or removed, it leaves a trail that is nearly impossible to erase. In comparison with this permanent record, risk is contextual and ever changing. Changes in the political climate (elections, new laws, rising populism, new social movements) affect risk, as do individual circumstances like a new job, relationship, or a move to a new town or country. How can I anticipate, not what is dangerous now, but what might be dangerous is one year, or five, or ten? Should I invoke anonymity in research as a safeguard against not yet known future harm? This, too, is a struggle. To me, as a researcher, this seems the safest way forward. But safe for whom? As measured and defined by whom? In expressing dynamic lives in static outputs, all I can do is be informed by current and past events and trust in the self-knowledge of interview participants. I cannot muzzle the present in fear of the future.

CONCLUSION

It has been ten years, and this dilemma is still one I return to regularly. It remains a complex navigation of autonomy, agency, dignity, overlaid with often external perceptions of vulnerability, limited mechanisms of protection, and very real risk. It is an uneasy triad between research participants, ethics boards, and researchers. I have to believe that those who participate in my research are the best placed to assess their risk and understand what protection and harm mean in their circumstances. Particularly when studying activists who make a point of vocal and often controversial public expression, it is reasonable to accept that they have a nuanced understanding of their own political and social context. In a small number of cases I will be unwilling to tolerate that specific level of potential harm.

The aspects of this journey that I continue to carry with me are fourfold. First, there are human rights and values in the fine print and the technical details. In these small black and white spaces we show what we believe; we proclaim the rights of research participants; we express our ideological approaches; and we announce who we are.

Second, human rights research inevitably involves risk, now and in the future, for everyone involved. Some risks are small and some are horrific. Risk cannot be eliminated and that is unsettling, frightening, and uncomfortable. Risk should never be taken lightly, and we must do everything we can to understand and address it, but we cannot use the possibility of generic risk as a blanket trump card. I need to accept that to do human rights work means being uncomfortable and scared at times but also striving for the real rewards it brings.

Third, human connection is at the centre of human rights work. Gradually I have learned that long chats with tea and biscuits are not distractions from the work – they are the process of building a critical foundation. We need time to get to know and trust each other. Relationships are what makes work possible and meaningful. Interviews can be powerful spaces of recognition and expression. It is important to take the time, sip the tea, walk the three kilometres, eat the biscuits, come back the next day, eat a third lunch, and do the things that help build a relationship. These casual interactions help us relate as people and enable the deeper conversations about risk, harm, and benefit that will enable me to better understand and meet the needs of the generous people who participate in my research. To protect each other we need to know each other.

And, finally, there is no generic harm or benefit in human rights research, because there are no generic humans. Each of us is particular, and a meaningful assessment of risks, benefits, vulnerabilities, and protections needs to engage with these particularities.

NOTES

1 Once a piece is published, it is technically possible to submit retractions or corrections, typically in the case of inaccuracies or misrepresentations. However, even in these limited windows of permitted change, given that most academic publications will be online, it is virtually impossible to "erase" original versions. For all intents and purposes, publications are static and permanent. By contrast, personal risk assessments are inherently contextual and fluid. Risk may intensify or subside with shifts in political currents, family circumstances, and employment, for example.

2 Every process was different, but despite some logistical challenges (i.e., applications sent by mail being returned unopened months later and applications sent by email being "lost") or unexpected adventures (needing to travel to a hairstyling products distributor to meet an honorary consul general, or by boda boda [motorbike taxi] to an outlying office), most approval applications were constructive, interesting, and useful dialogues. The Uganda Virus Research Institute particularly stands out in this regard – it was a pleasure to have detailed in-person discussions about my research plans with such interested and interesting people. The main structural challenge to ethics review for social science research on health continues to be decisions about which ministry or agency is best suited to review such applications. In some instances, interview-based work with health activists by a graduate student is placed in the same category as multiyear pharmaceutical trials by multinational corporations.

3 In this instance the board referenced the "possible negative reaction from donors" that I had listed as a possible risk in my ethics application (alongside possible favourable reactions from donors that I had also listed as a potential benefit). There are, of course, other risks, particularly to identifiable individuals.

4 This was the case for this research in Uganda and Botswana.

5 The Uganda Anti-Homosexuality Act was introduced as a private members bill by MP David Bahati in 2009. Same-sex sexual activity was already criminalized in Uganda,

as in many former British colonies, with a penalty of up to fourteen years in prison. The original draft of the act included provisions for the death penalty for same-sex relations, but this was amended to life in prison. It was signed into law in February 2014. In August 2014 the act was ruled invalid by the Ugandan Constitutional Court. There have been periodic reintroductions of similar acts, most recently the 2023 Anti-Homosexuality Bill which passed third reading in March 2023 but was not signed into law by President Museveni, who instead returned it to parliament for further consideration in April 2023 (see Okiror 2023).

6 Here, I am using the dominant terminology of the groups I worked with in Uganda, South Africa, and Botswana. I was not able to meet with LGBTI activists in Ghana.

7 I am acknowledging here that the risk of inclusion in a thesis or academic text is not comparable to the risk of being local front page news.

REFERENCES

Bracken-Roche, D., E. Bell, M.E. Macdonald, and E. Racine. 2017. "The Concept of 'Vulnerability' in Research Ethics: An In-depth Analysis of Policies and Guidelines." *Health Research Policy and Systems* 15, 1: 8. doi:10.1186/s12961-016-0164-6.

CIHR, NSERC, and SSHRC (Canadian Institutes of Health Research, Natural Sciences and Engineering Research Council of Canada, and Social Sciences and Humanities Research Council). 2018. *Tri-Council Policy Statement: Ethical Conduct for Research Involving Humans*. December 2018. http://www.pre.ethics.gc.ca/eng/documents/tcps2-2018-en-interactive-final.pdf.

Curtiss, K. 2016. "Miss Stigma Free HIV Pageant Helps Empower HIV Positive Women." *Global Citizen*, April 24, 2016. https://www.globalcitizen.org/de/content/these-women-are-beautiful-brave-and-hiv-positive/.

Gade, C.B.N. 2011. "The Historical Development of the Written Discourses on *Ubuntu*." *South African Journal of Philosophy* 30, 3: 303–29. doi.10.4314/sajpem.v30i3.69578.

Kagame, A. 1976. *La Philosophie Bantu Comparée*. Paris: Presence Africaine.

Kaiser K. 2009. "Protecting Respondent Confidentiality in Qualitative Research." *Qualitative Health Research* 19, 11: 1632–41. doi.org/10.1177/1049732309350879.

Kamwangamalu, N.M. 1999. "Ubuntu in South Africa: A Sociolinguistic Perspective to a Pan-African Concept." *Critical Arts* 13, 2: 24–41. doi.org/10.1080/02560049985310111.

Kenyon, K.H. 2013. "Choosing Rights: The Puzzle of the Rights Frame in HIV Activism." PhD diss., University of British Columbia.

–. 2017. *Resilience and Contagion: Human Rights in African HIV Advocacy*. Montreal and Kingston: McGill-Queens University Press.

Krystalli, R. 2021. "Narrating Victimhood: Dilemmas and (In)Dignities." *International Feminist Journal of Politics* 23, 1: 125–46. doi:10.1080/14616742.2020.1861961.

Longhurst, R. 2003. "Semi-Structured Interviews and Focus Groups." In *Key Methods in Geography*, edited by N. Clifford and G. Valentine, 117–32. London: Sage Publications.

Mbiti, J.S. 1990. *African Religions and Philosophy*. 2nd ed. London: Heineman Publishers.

McCormack, D., T. Carr, R. McCloskey, L. Keeping-Burke, K. Furlong, and S. Doucet. 2012. "Getting Through Ethics: The Fit between Research Ethics Board Assessments and Qualitative Research." *Journal of Empirical Research on Human Research Ethics* 7, 5: 30–36. doi:10.1525/jer.2012.7.5.30.

Mmolai, S.K. 2007. "Introduction." In *The Concept of Botho and HIV and AIDS in Botswana*, edited by J.B.R. Gaie and S.K. Mmolai, xi–xiv. Eldoret, Kenya: Zapf Chancery.

Mmualefhe, D.O. 2007. "Botho and HIV and AIDS: A Theological Reflection." In *The Concept of Botho and HIV and AIDS in Botswana*, edited by J.B.R. Gaie and S.K. Mmolai, 1–28. Eldoret, Kenya: Zapf Chancery.

Okiror, S. 2023. "Uganda's President Refuses to Sign New Hardline Anti-LGBTQ+ Bill." *Guardian*, April 21, 2023. https://www.theguardian.com/global-development/2023/apr/20/ugandas-president-refuses-to-sign-new-hardline-anti-gay-bill.

Resnick, D.B. n.d. "Research Ethics Timeline." National Institute of Environment Health Sciences. Last reviewed June 27, 2022. https://www.niehs.nih.gov/research/resources/bioethics/timeline/index.cfm.

Rhodes, R. 2010. "Rethinking Research Ethics." *American Journal of Bioethics* 10, 10: 19–36. doi:10.1080/15265161.2010.519233.

8

Your Mandates Aren't Ours

Katsi'tsí:io Splicer, Cougar Kirby, and Sarah Fraser

SOCIAL POSITIONING

Cougar Shakaien'kwarahton (He Clears the Smoke) Kirby – I am a Coast Salish and Nuu Chah Nulth Native from Tsawout, BC, on my mother's side. My father is Kanien'kehá:ka from Kahnawà:ke, and I represent both sides of my family proudly. The Creator's game, lacrosse, has been a significant aspect of Haudenosaunee culture for centuries – I value the game and its traditions. The skills have been instilled in me from birth, and at fifteen years old, I was chosen to play at IMG Academy in Florida for my final years of high school, then selected for the NCAA Division 1 Lacrosse Program at the University at Albany, which finished in the top four in 2018. Lacrosse has let me grow into the passionate, hard-working man I am today. I am honoured and grateful to say I am a full-time student at McGill University and obtaining my bachelor of arts in sociology and Indigenous studies. I am a member of the men's varsity lacrosse team in Montreal and a research assistant for Indigenous Youth Empowerment. I am deeply interested in my cultural background and love to explore Turtle Island and the many cultures people have to share. I hope to continue studying, along with my wife, in the Kanien'kéha Ratiwennahní:rats Language Immersion Program, to revitalize our language and create a first language–speaking household for our two-year-old daughter SEMSEMÍYE (Bumblebee). I am a caring man and passionate about every person and their individual stories. I am a young father, and I am deeply honoured to say I would not have all of these opportunities if it were not for my grandparents, Douglass Lafortune and Kathleen Horne.

Katsi'tsí:io Splicer – I am a Kanien'kehá:ka (Mohawk) woman from Kahnawà:ke; however, I grew up in Brooklyn, New York, and moved back to Kahnawà:ke after finishing my Western education. There is a long tradition of Kanien'kehá:ka men ironworking in New York City, and my father was one of them. Most Kanien'kehá:ka ironworkers, such as my grandpa, would work during the week and drive back to Kahnawà:ke on the weekends. My parents decided they didn't want this type of lifestyle, so we stayed in Brooklyn full-time and visited Kahnawà:ke during school breaks. I grew up in an Italian American neighbourhood, and all my friends were white. Since I don't look like the traditional "Indian" you see in movies, I grew up with a lot of white privilege. When people would ask about my heritage they would say I looked "exotic." I grew up learning white, Brooklyn, Western culture. I knew a few words in my own language, Kanien'kéha, and barely anything about my own culture besides what I learned about the "pilgrims and Indians" when we covered Iroquois in third grade. I never felt like I belonged in Brooklyn, and I always felt like I was so different when I would visit Kahnawà:ke. Once I got older, I realized I had "identity issues." I did not have a full understanding of my own culture and therefore of myself as a person. It wasn't until I was working at the American Indian Community House[1] that I learned about colonization and all of the horrors that my ancestors experienced. This experience made me realize the importance of my culture and history, and so I began my journey to rediscover my identity as an Onkwehón:we woman. Since one of the only measures of success I knew at this age was to achieve higher education, I went on to achieve two master's degrees with the intent of moving back to Kahnawà:ke to help in whatever capacity I could. Shortly after I moved back, I was gifted with the greatest role I will ever hold, being a mother. As I write this, my daughter just turned four. Because of her, I am even more motivated to learn about my identity, namely language, culture, and tradition, so that she will grow up not having to wonder who she is. Since then, I have been on a journey of decolonizing and re-indigenizing my being.

Sarah Fraser – I am a colonial settler born in Montreal, Quebec. My ancestors travelled from France and Scotland and settled in the regions of Dundee and the Eastern Townships, in Quebec. The log cabin built by the first settlers of my family tree on my father's side is still standing as a reminder of their journey to what I now know is called Tsi:karistisere. For the first twenty years or so of my life I hadn't grasped what this story of resettlement meant other than for myself. During my childhood, my grandfather would take my family to Akwesasne for lunch and treats. Akwesasne is one of three sister Kanien'kehá:ka territories in the region of Quebec. It felt special and important. I knew I was an outsider but did not know why. My education about First Nations and colonization was severely limited as our history classes are, to this day, devoid of such knowledge and facts. Years later, when I passed an internship interview in Kahnawà:ke, the director of the institution explained to me sternly, "Never forget, you leave to go back to your home every evening, but this is our home, we don't leave." The words mark me to this day. They are a reminder that my words and actions impact humans and the land both when I am present and when I am absent. Ultimately, as a colonial settler working with First Nations, the everyday realities of people of Kahnawà:ke will never impact me the way they impact the community. Fifteen years have passed since that interview. I am now a researcher in the field of Indigenous health, well-being, and self-determination. With all the reading, the discussions, the relationships that I may have accumulated in my heart and memory, I still feel that the space between myself and the people I work with is always "unresolved" in the sense that it constantly needs to be watched, heard, worked on, respected, and transformed. The ways in which we choose to work together is an ethical terrain of possibilities. Our roles and relationships transform over time based on context. These roles and relationships can have positive repercussions and negative ones simultaneously. And for this reason, ethics (the space of questioning what may be appropriate and respectful ways of being and doing) is the core of who I am and how I interact with others. My interactions are forging who I am as a person, a soul, a partner, a mother, a friend, and a researcher.

BACKGROUND

The project described in this chapter takes place in Kahnawà:ke (By the Rapids). Kahnawà:ke is Kanien'kehá:ka territory on the south shore of what is known as Montreal. The Kanien'kehá:ka are Rotinonshon:ni (People of the Longhouse) and their original territories were in what is now known as upstate New York. Due to colonization, Kanien'kehá:ka were pushed to a Jesuit mission, Kahnawà:ke.

The history of research in Onkwehón:we (Kahniekaha word meaning original people) communities is a dark one. Research has been a contested space and activity throughout the history of Onkwehón:we since contact with colonial institutions. As will be discussed in this chapter, while the reasoning for ensuring that outside researchers conduct research ethically is important, it may be inconvenient and potentially harmful to have community members conducting research and applying the same stringent ethics guidelines that were initially developed and imposed by Western institutions. In the following pages we discuss the ways that we experienced ethics and how our research practices evolved over the course of our project to honour and protect the dignity and well-being of the individuals we worked with in this youth-led and youth-developed project we have come to call Teiethihsnitie Ahonata'kariteke Tsi Ronatehiarontie (Nurturing Health Growth). We begin by describing the project, and then we discuss the ethical questions and dilemmas we encountered that ultimately underlined the points of tension between Kanien'kehá:ka ways of knowing and doing and more academic ways of conducting research.

(COUGAR) The objective of sharing our story is to support and encourage ongoing reflection and practices related to ethics in Onkwehón:we research, as well as to support the self-governance of Onkwehón:we research by highlighting the practices that would best fit our conduct of research with our own community members while respectfully representing the opinions of youth we would work with. To avoid misrepresentation or fears of a Western researcher coming into our community and sending false information to the public, we felt it was right to conduct research by community members, for community members, so that their voices were properly heard and translated to the contemporary settler colonial vocabulary to better understand our current situation in terms of youth engagement and their needs to survive today. It is through this process that we have come to reclaim Kanien'kehá:ka ways of doing research.

THE PROJECT

(SARAH) The project started in 2018 with a government call for proposals for a research network on youth, with a subsection on Onkwehón:we youth. Our small academic research team composed of five settler women not only felt uncomfortable proposing to lead the project as settlers, but also felt that Onkwehón:we youth would have much to teach us about ways of viewing the entire project. We wanted to hear from Onkwehón:we youth. We were interested in knowing how youth conceptualize well-being, how they might imagine research governance, and what would be ways of meaningfully supporting youth. In collaboration with Kahnawà:ke Schools Diabetes Prevention Program, a long-term partner specialized in community mobilization research and Onkwehón:we governance of research, we posted two part-time job applications for youth of Kahnawà:ke. Interviews were co-led by myself and our amazing colleagues Alex McComber and Elder Amelie McGregor. The hope was to encounter youth who were curious about, and interested in hearing from, fellow youth from the community and to then collectively build a way of working together that would feel right to youth. Two beautiful people were invited to take on this role: Katsi'tsí:io Splicer and Lily Deer.

(KATSI'TSÍ:IO) Once Lily and I were hired as youth representatives, we began our work thinking about how we could engage youth. We had numerous discussions and turned to the literature to figure out how to begin. We came up with different ideas about how we could start engaging youth, and one idea became the turning point of our thought process. An initial thought was to create a youth council, a forum where youth could be heard. We asked ourselves, How would we get youth to join the youth council? and realized that many youth may not want to participate in such a group. It may be too formal of a process and might not allow us to hear a diversity of voices from the community. Through more critical thought processes, we realized that we needed to take many steps backwards before contacting youth and having them all come together. We felt that before asking them to come to a one-off meeting they needed to know who we were, and we needed to hear who they were.

Holding discussions and breaking down our thoughts led us to realize that we needed to ask youth what they wanted and how they wanted to be engaged. We then began to rethink the term "engagement," and we realized we didn't know what this meant for ourselves. I eventually began to define it for myself as "an activity that you are interested in and participate in, in some way." From here we decided that we needed to have discussions with youth in our community about what they spend their time doing, what they want to be doing, and what they want to see in the community to better support youth like themselves. We recognized that youth aren't asked what programs and activities they want to participate in. On the contrary, programs are most often developed using a top-down approach. Adults are deciding and creating what projects they think would benefit youth, without consulting youth. Our objective was to give a space and platform for youth to express what they want and need. The population that we wanted to reach was youth from Kahnawà:ke who are between the ages of fourteen and thirty-five.

(ALL) Once we realized that we wanted to explore youths' interests with them, we needed to develop the research methods we would use. We wanted to have casual conversations with other youth in Kahnawà:ke. Although the scope of what we wanted to do was simple, the process to decide on our methods was more complicated. As with any research project that is supported by a university, the project needed to be approved by the university ethics review board. Kahnawà:ke also has their own research review board, Onkwata'karitáhtshera Health and Social Services Research Council, which oversees health and social science research in the community. The project was also supported by the Kahnawà:ke Schools Diabetes Prevention Program, which has their own ethics protocol. Thus, to begin the project we applied to three different ethics review boards. The process was time consuming; however, as described below, it gave us space to understand that the university ethics committees had different ways of assessing the project and different concerns with regard to what is ethical and what may not be. Through our research process, and our discussions with youth, we experienced multiple points where the protocol "didn't feel right" or situations where we realized we needed to question the initial ethical paradigms that guided decision making related to the research protocol and then modify our approach to ways of doing that were more congruent with what *felt* ethical. The following presents the various ethical dilemmas that we encountered while enforcing Western-developed ethics mandates and carrying out an Onkwehón:we youth–developed and –led research project. This process allowed us to refine and reclaim our own ethical guidelines and paradigms.

RELATIONSHIPS AND RESPONSIBILITY AS A FOUNDATION: ETHICS OF RECRUITMENT

(ALL) The first ethical dilemma we encountered was around our recruitment strategy. Our initial strategy was to use snowball sampling: inviting the youth in our own environments and soliciting community youth organizations to invite us to their events and meet with youth in groups. Through these exchanges with youth, we hoped to foster a certain connection and then to invite them to research group events and to offer youth participants the option of being members of the research team by participating in a short research training that would allow them to conduct interviews.

The ethics committee of the university had some initial concerns with the proposed methods of recruitment. First, they were concerned about direct solicitation of youth. They were worried that the youth might feel obligated to participate in a project if they were being solicited by young adults they knew from the community (the research team). In order to ensure that the youth participated of their own free will, the Institutional Research Ethics Board wanted the potential participants to receive the informative pamphlets and consent forms and have approximately one week to think over their interest in participating. The youth would then contact the research team to confirm their interest. Additionally, the ethics committee requested that flyers be placed on the walls of public spaces to invite a greater audience to participate in the project and to ensure that the solicitation be passive.

The ethics committee's concerns were well-intentioned. How do we ensure that people can freely choose to participate? How do we ensure that youth do not participate only to please an older youth or another person they know? On the other hand, we felt that youth would not proactively inquire about a research project if they were not directly invited to do so. This would make it difficult to recruit youth. We felt that not hearing from youth at all would also be an ethical issue, considering the importance of hearing directly from them and making decisions based on their experiences and knowledge.

(KATSI'TSÍ:IO) Being youth ourselves (Katsi'tsí:io, Lily, and Cougar) and from speaking with other youth, we knew that the best method of engaging youth and asking them to contribute to the project would be to meet with them and talk about the project in person. A great deal of self-reflection contributed to determining the best way to approach youth. We reflected on our own experiences of speaking with others in various scenarios and unpacking situations when we felt comfortable versus when we didn't. We asked each other what conditions would make us feel comfortable and motivated to have a personal discussion, such as having a conversation versus an interview, having food and coffee available, and being in a physically comfortable environment. We also considered the countless different personalities and experiences that each youth carries with them, and how these factors could affect how they would want to be approached and in what way they would feel comfortable contributing.

When trying to connect with youth and ask them to participate in the project, we found it easiest for us to reach out to people that we knew and had existing relationships with. We did this for a while and had continuous discussions about how we could reach other youth that we didn't already know. Initially, we thought that reaching out to youth we knew was unethical or biased. After much dialogue and rumination, I had the realization that our situation was normal, and that I was problematizing our recruitment methods because I was thinking from my Western, colonized, academic mind frame. Academic research ethics and the caring professions tell us that we shouldn't hold relationships with research participants. This is difficult to achieve when conducting research in one's community because we have a relationship of some type with so many people. I came to the conclusion that it is natural to reach out to people you know to have discussions.

In fact, for most it is probably more natural and comfortable to have a deep conversation with someone you know and are comfortable talking to. On the contrary, it's unnatural and uncomfortable to sit down with someone you've never spoken with before and ask them a list of questions about their personal feelings and beliefs. We did create a list of interview questions, but we knew we wanted to avoid asking a list of questions one by one. Our goal was to have casual conversations with other youth about their hobbies and interests and what they wanted to see in the community. Thus, we continued to connect with youth we knew, while also deliberating on how we could reach youth that were outside of our circles. We decided to teach other youth how to have these discussions with youth they know. This method would help build trust among youth and in research. We would teach them about conducting research, specifically community-based participatory research, provide support with interviewing skills, provide a job opportunity, and develop relationships.

(COUGAR) Another method of reaching youth was to be present in environments that they frequented. At the beginning stages of the project, a new café opened in a central location of town. We started having team meetings at Tóta Ma's Café and noticed the flow of youth coming in after school. Since it was in a central location of the community, we decided it was a good place to try and create connections with youth. The café was new, had no history or stigmatization as to "who hangs out there," and was a friendly, modish environment with great roots trying to incorporate aspects of Kanien'kéha (Mohawk language) in their facility. This, along with the free rental space for community projects, made it a great space to hold our discussions as it was a relaxed and comfortable environment for youth.

Ultimately, as we discussed these different questions and emotions around recruitment and ethics, we realized that it boiled down to trust and engagement. What is the mechanism that encourages youth to engage in research (or in any activity, for that matter)? We believe it is trust – feeling comfortable and confident enough that the discussion is respectful of one's own story and knowledge. What are the elements that will foster a feeling of trust in the activity they are invited to participate in? We believe it is through relationships: prior experiences of respect and reciprocity between two people that allow the individual to feel a certain degree of confidence in the other.

BUILDING ON AGENCY: ETHICS OF INFORMED CONSENT

(SARAH) All research projects that pass through a university ethics committee will have consent forms. In a Western context, the written contract is a mechanism to protect the participant from the researcher and from the institutions behind the research. It is a way of ensuring that the participant knows what they are getting into and of defining the obligations of the researcher. Certain committees will allow or encourage the possibility of verbal consent rather than written. Committees might also accept or encourage that forms be simplified and rendered visually easy and interesting to read. In our case the committee felt comfortable with both of these adaptations of the more traditional formal consent forms. However, they asked that a few sentences be removed from the consent form. We had initially written "if you agree to help us" but were invited to write "if you agree to participate." By writing "if you agree to help us," the ethics committee felt that we were subtly encouraging youth to participate in the project, ultimately creating a bias in the "informed" component of consent. The logic here is that if youth are told that by doing research they are helping, they may feel as if they need to participate in order to be helpful.

(KATSI'TSÍ:IO) This situation is an example of the differences between Onkwehón:we and colonized ways of knowing and doing. For us, the word "help" simply acknowledges the fact that participants would be helping us in the process. It is an acknowledgment of the existence of a helping relationship and reciprocity. Contrarily, the Institutional Research Ethics Board understood this word to persuade or influence youth to participate. We felt it was important for youth to know that they were helping, as it would empower them in the process. In a context where research has historically, and to this day, been experienced as a practice that is done *on* people rather than *with* them and that has taken rather than given, the notion of using research to *give* to community is an ethical standard. Indeed, youth we spoke with wanted to know that they were helping their community. They wanted to ensure that the research was not "just" for research but was going to offer something concrete to the community. Moreover, for many Onkwehón:we youth, contributing to community may be the only reason for participating in a project. In order to honour this promise that youth are helping their community through research we needed to speak honestly about our intentions and limitations, and to involve youth in the project beyond the initial discussion. Indeed, being a youth-led project, it was constantly evolving based on what youth would share in the discussions. Therefore, questions about what would be done with the research data or what it was for were relatively unknown. We explained to youth that they didn't have to talk about anything they didn't want to, and they could end the conversations at any point. We explained what we foresaw happening with the data from the conversations but also explained that we wanted youth to guide the project and help decide what would be done with the information. This was discussed and understood by the ethics boards.

On another note, from our experience with research in community and with consent forms, we understand that most people don't want to read a lengthy document, and some might not feel comfortable signing a document. We finalized a five-page consent document that we initially were proud of, as we felt it was simple and as clear as possible. However, when we actually started the research process and began handing the consent form to youth, it felt uncomfortable. The formality of the document and the process went against the values we wished to put forth. We explained that because the discussion we would have is part of a research project, we had to receive consent to have the discussion. We then offered to read it to them or for them to read it themselves. This process felt awkward for numerous reasons. First, the term "research" can be intimidating to non-academics because they may not understand what research is, or that it seems too "smart" or "boring." The procedure was tedious and felt overly formal.

(COUGAR) "Ethical" forms of research felt very robotic and unnatural. Our intent in the project was to make the process as natural and comfortable as possible, and handing over a consent form in order to start a conversation did not feel natural. Indeed, pulling out large documents that needed to be reviewed before the interview automatically created a rift. The large volume of documentation and the signing felt like overkill for ninth graders. Conversations meant to create fluidity and honesty and to derive from a passion to create thoughtful interest for the community had to begin with a very onerous process. When sitting with a group of youth in the early days of our research, we started with the recitation of the main points of our ethics document, followed by a solemn silence while they signed the document in order for the process to begin. Within months, we decided it would be much more comfortable to begin the process with traditional approaches, like providing a meal to thank the youth for their support and to reassure them about their participation and how the research would be used. So with the latter process, our ethical problem would be solved by beginning with meals and proposing activities or prizes that would incentivize the youth to begin conversations and speak about what they enjoy and would like to see in the community in order to better their future. They could then later determine whether or not they wanted this information to be used, and how they wanted it to be shared (in scientific journals, only in the community, anonymized or not). This approach focuses on notions of agency and autonomy by giving options to youth only once they have a clear idea of what they have shared and who they are sharing it with. We discussed this with the university ethics board, and they understood the challenges and felt comfortable with the proposed approach.

(SARAH) Passive recruitment strategies and formal processes for consent make sense when the meeting between a researcher and a participant is punctual, when the relationship that exists between the researcher and the participant is hierarchical. The consent form allows the participant a form of protection. But youth-led community-based research is far from being punctual; it is far from being just a researcher-participant relationship. People will maintain relationships over decades. The responsibility of the researcher does not rest on the formal consent form; it is practised through relationships and by honouring what was said and shared. Does this mean that consent forms are not useful? That they should be eliminated? I don't presume to know. The fundamental values behind the passive recruitment strategies and consent forms are fundamental: protecting individuals from participating in something that they did not wish to participate in, and reducing the potential negative impacts of research and dissemination of research on participants. The mere development of the research protocol and the consent form is a way to ensure that these notions are reflected upon and that measures are taken to protect youth and their dignity.

ACKNOWLEDGING RECIPROCITY AS A FUNDAMENTAL VALUE: ETHICS OF COMMUNICATION

(KATSI'TSÍ:IO) Self-disclosure was one aspect that we were challenged with throughout the project. Having come from a clinical and Western research background, I was under the impression that self-disclosure might be considered unethical. I was used to seeing protocols where researchers ask questions and participants answer. I didn't feel comfortable just asking questions (retrieving answers from people) without giving some of myself. I often felt the desire to reciprocate and share my experiences and feelings when it seemed right; however I was often hypervigilant about doing so. I was nervous that individuals wouldn't want me to share or would be bored by my story, or that I was imposing some type of bias. After sitting with this for a while, I concluded that healthy communication and conversation consists of reciprocity. Being that we were actively trying to have conversations, as opposed to interviews, I embraced this concept and allowed myself to share when I felt it was relevant. I felt that in order to foster a sense of connection and trust, I needed to share my story and experiences. I wanted the individuals I was connecting with to know that I could relate to them and that I understood them.

We tried to gear away from "research" terminology as much as we could. We did this because we didn't want to sound intimidating and because, in reality, what we were having were conversations, not structured interviews. Also, when working in community, it is important to use language that people will understand and can relate to. It is important to remember, as academics we are taught a different language. It can seem pretentious and intimidating to use this language with those who don't speak it. It creates and maintains power dynamics between people based on their education and career orientations. Our responsibility as researchers is to consistently check our ego and remember that first and foremost, we are community members. Instead of using the term "interview," we used "conversations" or "discussions."

(COUGAR) These tweaks helped resolve some of the tensions of using a formal process to hold one-on-one conversations, but also made the process feel more comfortable. "Interviews" made us feel like we were in charge and created this feeling of hierarchy between the interviewee and the interviewer. In reality we, as community members and youth, felt like equals. Many of the youth were family or friends. Transforming the vocabulary had a profound change on the way we felt about our project, specifically about presenting it and interacting with youth through it. The vocabulary was more congruent with our understanding of research as a process of learning through reciprocity and dialogue. These conversations are not for us to benefit individually from research, but to better the overall understanding of youth engagement in the community and to address the needs of the youth through our findings.

ETHICS OF CONDUCTING COMMUNITY-LED RESEARCH FOR SOCIAL CHANGE

(SARAH) Youth conducting research with youth in their own community brings layers of considerations. As described above, youth participate in research in order to see social changes for their community. Therefore, the ultimate "contract" that binds us, as researchers, and youth, as participants, is using the data for social change. This is also the foundation of

Participatory Action Research. Our work highlights two major considerations that directly impact the process toward social change.

The first consideration for us was finding a balance between conducting the work efficiently in order to produce impactful results that could be shared, and also going at a slow enough rhythm to be able to truly integrate youth within the research process, but fast enough that our own well-being was being nurtured and respected. We felt that if we wanted to see social change within organizations and in the community, we had to also participate in our own change. We felt we needed to be learning from youth and from the Onkwehón:we literature we were reading. We were compelled by questions surrounding decolonization and Indigenization, and we needed time to contemplate. If we wanted to be making recommendations to youth and organizations about engagement and wellness, we needed to be sure we were engaged in activities we love and that help us to maintain wellness. Part of the research process included interviewing ourselves, taking time for ourselves, and participating in activities that would help our growth and passions. On the one hand, we took the time we needed to flourish in our own identities as parents, athletes, artists, and language learners. Engaging in activities such as basket making or gardening, and having our kids present in our activities and meetings allowed us the space to ensure we were honouring all roles we have as well as nourishing our identities and well-being. On the other hand, we wished to give back concrete, finished products to organizations, to ensure that the messages youth were offering through words were being heard and integrated by adults within the community.

The research process takes time. Meaningfully listening to the discussions and truly learning from youth takes time; honouring our responsibilities as parents, family members, partners, community members takes time. Each step evokes thoughts and emotions. Doing research "in a good way" means constantly rethinking our actions and words, asking ourselves if we are doing things a certain way because of what we have been taught through formal institutions and dominant norms. Are there other ways of doing that might *be* and feel more ethical? This constant questioning was a process of decolonizing our own minds, and it is time consuming.

(COUGAR) Not only did we take time to decolonize our minds, we also took time to learn to work with youth differently and to decolonize research activities. Youth asked to learn certain things, such as creating their own medicine bags, taking a cold winter walk to find the available medicines of the season, or ice fishing, for example. Developing activities for youth and leading gatherings was a new experience for us. Once again, taking time, working as a team, recognizing our interdependence and our strengths and those of others helped us gain confidence.

CONCLUSION

(COUGAR) Some of the ethical dilemmas with conducting youth research within our local community was also related to the diaspora of our origins. Katsi'tsí:io and I would reference our heritage and connect our stories about living off of the reserve and back to the community throughout the conversations we had. Striving for trust through interdependence was no easy feat. Maintaining a relationship with youth would have been frowned upon by Western research ideology and connecting with the "subjects" noted as an unethical form of research. But when it came to the youth in our community, seeing as we had our own connection to their needs, we felt untied from such boundaries, as we are all bound together in some relation or another. As a youth myself, it was not just a point of extracting information for self-determination, but also simultaneously collaborating and recording for the betterment of what we could fabricate together. This is, in a sense, our form of community building through research: combining traditional ideologies of community nexus with contemporary research practices.

Throughout the process we did make changes to our original ethics applications and communicated this to the Institutional Research Ethics Board, which was very understanding and open to our changes. The process that we experienced through this project provided us the time and space to think critically about the ethics process. Being aware of our intuition, questioning our feelings and thoughts, and challenging the process that we had in place led us to relearn and reconnect with our own Kanien'kehá:ka ways of conducting research. Moving forward we will be able to develop an ethics application with the concepts and design that we know to be true to our own ways of doing, being, and understanding.

Onkwehón:we communities should be supported and empowered to learn and do research in ways that align with their values and belief systems. The research process should be guided by relationship and connection with the self, participants, and the knowledge itself. While we appreciate the application of ethics in its intention of protecting research participants, we as community members have experienced at first hand the consequences of imposing a Western framework of research ethics in community. We advocate for the notion of research ethics to be an adaptable process, where the level of rigour is based on context. For example, there may be different requirements necessary for community-based researchers versus outside researchers going into community. These requirements should be thoroughly explored with the intent of, first and foremost, preserving and promoting the knowledge and ways of Onkwehón:we.

NOTE

1 The American Indian Community House is a not-for-profit organization serving the needs of Native Americans residing in New York City.

9

When Life Isn't a Moment

PARTICIPATORY PHOTOGRAPHY, PHOTOJOURNALISM, AND DOCUMENTARY PHOTOGRAPHY

Myrto Papadopoulos and Shayna Plaut

Myrto Papadopoulos is a documentary photographer and filmmaker specializing in intimate long-form projects that often involve human rights and social justice, particularly as it relates to people who are too often rendered marginal or invisible.[1] *Originally from Athens, Greece, she worked and studied abroad for many years and returned to Greece in 2009, where she began to work intensely for international media.*

It was a dark time. The financial crisis was escalating, as was an increase in migration – including refugees and those seeking asylum – from Syria, Afghanistan, and sub-Saharan Africa. There was also a dramatic increase in HIV rates.[2] *These ingredients created a toxic cocktail of nationalism, xenophobia, and a search for blame among those on the margins. At the same time, the sex industry that had always existed and was previously fairly low-key, was growing, and becoming more and more multilayered and transnational.*

Although sex work has been legal in Greece since 1999, within this increasingly hostile and suspicious environment, political leaders publicly blamed and shamed sex workers on more than one occasion, for everything from increased HIV rates (although there was no correlation), to being foreign (although many, if not all, were Greek themselves), to being evidence of – and contributing to – general societal decline.[3]

It is within this context that Myrto began working on a photographic project documenting the booming sex industry in Greece.[4]

A few years later, in the summer of 2013, while working on an assignment to cover the financial crisis in [the Greek part of] Cyprus, Myrto was walking around and unexpectedly came across a "sex workers hub" (a small red-light district).

She was looking around, with her camera around her neck, when she was called over by a man who was "in charge" of the women working in this small, confined courtyard (piazza). While talking briefly with the self-confessed trafficker, Myrto became increasingly interested in speaking with the women themselves. It was in this tension-filled space that Myrto's ethical dilemma emerged: How does a photographer ethically create, and sustain, a shared and evolving narrative between camera, photographer, and "subjects" in politically, culturally, and socially complex environments?

Although the National Press Photographers Association calls for photographers to "treat all subjects with respect and dignity,"[5] *how this manifests differs for each photographer. It is fairly rare for a photojournalist to seek permission to take a picture. The photojournalist's first instinct is to shoot the picture and maybe ask later, because once a moment is gone it cannot be recaptured. Myrto is different. Before taking a picture, Myrto almost always asks for permission from the person, "the subject." Usually, the people appreciate being asked and they agree.*

This time, Myrto was told "No" by one of the sex workers with whom she had developed a good rapport. The fact that she was told no, and the subsequent conversation, forced Myrto to rethink her entire approach to photojournalism: her methods, her reasons, and her voice. It has been a powerful and, at times, lonely shift – professionally and personally.

True to her commitment to shared narrative, Myrto chose to reflect on her journey from "capturing" a good portrait to participatory photography in conversation with Shayna Plaut, one of the editors of this book who works at the intersections of journalism, academia, and activism. In the spirit of full – dare we say, ethical – disclosure, it is worth noting that Myrto and Shayna worked together previously.

SETTING THE SCENE: A SUMMER'S NIGHT IN CYPRUS

MYRTO (INTERVIEWEE): In the summer of 2013 I was in Cyprus. I was there [on a different assignment] to record the financial crisis. I had already been working on a project exploring the sex industry in Greece for a couple of years, but I did not seek out their work this time, I just kind of bumped into a situation that caught my attention.

SHAYNA (INTERVIEWER): And if I understood you correctly, in Cyprus sex work is not as open, but this was like a red-light district.

MYRTO: Right. The model in Cyprus is different than the one in Greece. The sex industry in Cyprus was and is currently unregulated.[6] The actual pay at the time was much better, and usually sex work took place indoors rather than on the street. Sex workers would work either in apartments or the so-called "studios," which are basically modern brothels.

SHAYNA: Okay. So, take me to that night in Cyprus.

MYRTO: I was wandering about photographing and I found myself in this small square. It was late afternoon. I was quite tired. It was a nice summer weather. And I immediately saw all these neon lights and these girls – you didn't see many men around there. The bars were quite empty. It was a quiet situation. And I think the fact that it was a quiet situation kind of helped me focus, and it brought out a curiosity in others – to take that slow pace and understand what was happening around me.

And so I saw this man looking at me, middle-aged man around fifty-something, a bit chubby. I remember he didn't have lots of hair.

And he called out to me and he said, and he asked – because he saw my camera hanging off my neck – "What are you doing here?"

I was very honest. "I'm here in Cyprus. I'm a photographer. And I'm covering the financial crisis ... But I'm also very interested in what is happening here." And he invited me for a drink.

He started talking and I asked him very politely, "What's happening here? What are you doing?" One thing my work has taught me is to listen. So I think I kind of have the face of someone that can be trusted, someone you can talk to.

He basically told me that he was the one responsible for all these girls that I was looking at in the bars. He also told me he had been doing this for a long time and that he had spent time in prison for trafficking.

Throughout this entire conversation, it is important to know that the girls were [physically] very close to us – we could almost touch them.

The girls were looking at me in quite an aggressive way, which was understandable. There was a lot of tension and suspicion. "Who is she? Why is she here? What does she want? What are they doing?" I let him talk but I didn't spend much time with him. I wanted to approach and to talk to these women.

I was trying to balance those two worlds: this trafficker and the women.

I was particularly struck by this [one] girl – she was Bulgarian, as she later told me. She was very young, early twenties. I thought she was just so pretty. I could not stop looking at her. She looked extremely fragile to my eyes, and somehow she kind of shared her vulnerability with me. I, too, can choose to be vulnerable. I think it's important to be open; being vulnerable helps us to connect, to share experiences, and a way to create relationships and start a dialogue. It felt as if she wanted to connect.

THE ETHICAL DILEMMA

MYRTO: We started talking. She told me about her life in Bulgaria, that her family had moved to Athens, that she had a son, a baby boy.

While we were talking, it felt as if something was not right; I needed a bit of time and space to understand the energies around me and of the other girls.

I recognized their hostility was not *me,* but by the fact that right behind me was, again, their pimp – the trafficker. So the situation didn't feel clean. It felt controlled. I wasn't in *their* space. I was in his space.

However, we kept talking, and at some point I asked her if I could take a picture of her. I said, "Could I please take a portrait [photograph] of you?"

SHAYNA: And why did you ask her that?

MYRTO: I just felt we had connected and that she was beautiful. I just thought ... I just wanted a portrait of this woman. She had something ... that vulnerability ... that fragility spoke to me. I felt she had something that I was personally connected to. And I wanted to capture that feeling, that narrative, that moment. Remember: I am a photographer.

To be clear, I would never intend to exploit her or anyone. It's just, there are those moments when you look and connect with some people. She was one of them.

So this is why I requested permission to take a portrait. And she stopped, and she looked at me, and I froze. And she looked at me, and she said, "If I let you take a picture of me, this is how you will portray me. You will create an identity of me, which I don't want to be a part of." And she told me afterwards, in a very exasperated and frustrated way that, "I really don't want to do this. Fuck. I really don't want to do this shit. I have a young boy. I'm here alone, but I just have to do this."

And that was it. Her words felt like a knife through my heart as I would never exploit the identity and reality of a person. I never want to portray someone in a way that they do not identify with. She didn't want to be identified like that – like a one-dimensional sex-worker. Like a victim.

Over the years in documenting sex workers, I met and spoke with a number of women, and often they didn't want to describe or identify themselves as victims, even if they were victimized in certain situations. It is important to me to never portray people in a way they don't want to be portrayed.

I wanted to show them as women, as individuals, with their dreams and aspirations and, of course, to report on their very difficult realities. They are not only their struggles or circumstances.

I have been taking photographs for over sixteen years, and when I am part of a story that represents someone else's life I would never carelessly photograph someone to increase their pain. I never want to take away their voice. Never.

But in this situation, she thought that by taking her portrait that is exactly what would happen.

And from there on, my approach around the project and photography as a whole changed completely. By being told "No," my own role as a photographer became much clearer.

At the beginning of this project, I was very focused on the women. And while I was getting more involved, I felt as if I was being very one-sided and not being an actual researcher. I cannot talk about the women if I don't know of the role of the client nor the role of the pimp. They, too, are part of the story.[7] This is an industry. It moves. It's dynamic.

SHAYNA: What brought about that shift to you?

MYRTO: I had the chance to meet with clients who viewed themselves as victims of their own circumstances. So I thought that if I wanted to understand the sex industry, then as uncomfortable as it might be I really needed to understand those voices, too.

THE RADICAL POWER OF EMPATHY – OR – WHAT DOORS OPENED WHEN I WAS TOLD "NO"

MYRTO: I went quite deep into this project.

And I understood I wasn't only in this project as a photographer. I was part of it. I was part of this narrative. After working on it for years, this project also became personal. I was trying to explore a part of my own understanding of sexual morality, the role of women and sexuality. Women and sex. Women and violence. Women and sexual assault ...

SHAYNA: I'm just wondering, when she said, "No, you cannot take my photo," what did you learn about yourself? You said you were stopped in your tracks. Why? Why did you react that way? What did you learn about yourself?

MYRTO: One thing I learned and realized about myself was that I *want* to go deep. To go deeper with my narratives and with those whom I meet. To go beyond the one-dimensional layer of a story. To search for more than one truth. To push myself and to be more of a thinker and, in turn, to be more accepting of different, sometimes conflicting, truths – even or especially – within one person.

Also my interaction – both with the trafficker and with the Bulgarian woman – definitely helped me to be more empathetic.

There's much more to learn and to see and to accept, even – or maybe especially – if you don't like it. You can work to accept it. Acceptance is a powerful thing. Empathy is a powerful thing.

I also realized that when this woman said "No" that she was reacting to our power to represent and to misrepresent. We – photographers – can have a massive impact in our society, and it takes a significant level of responsibility from our part to represent someone else's life, culture, and country. Photographs bring attention: "Photographs of an atrocity may give rise to opposing responses. A call for peace," as Susan Sontag [2003] described it in *Regarding the Pain of Others,* but they can also cause great harm.

How can the benefit or harm be measured? I don't know. But visual journalists should continuously study and reflect on their craft and the ethics that guide it. This is what I am always trying to do; however it is a process and not an easy one.

SHAYNA: Now, I'm assuming ... I'm assuming that you already thought of yourself as an accepting and empathetic person. So what is new here? What changed for you? Did this situation make you *more* accepting and empathetic or ... ?

MYRTO: I can see the pain in people. However, as I mentioned earlier, I would never carelessly take a picture that would increase someone else's pain. I saw this woman's pain – she shared it with me but she didn't want to share it with anyone else. And I could only respect that, respect the situation she was in.

Previously, I thought asking permission before taking a picture was enough. To get permission to tell someone's story was enough. But this interaction – being told "No" and being told *why* this was not something she wanted – caused me to realize that, one, asking permission is not enough and, two, I want my photography to do more

Myself in front of a window | *Photo: Myrto Papadopoulos*

than that. I want it to change the power imbalance. To raise questions. To bring about more justice.

So if I did learn something about myself, [it] was that I want to approach my storytelling in a very specific way.

SHAYNA: So one of the things you learned was your own professional method?

MYRTO: Yes, but it wasn't *just* about my professional method. It was also about recognizing my voice, my values. The fact that this woman told me, "Please, no, I do not want you to take my picture; I do not want myself pictured like this," made me understand the importance of my role as a storyteller and the importance of my voice as a woman. We both played a vital role within the same narrative.

And it is here where my approach to the project and narrative changed. I let it guide me. I became more free both with myself and storytelling.

WHAT PARTICIPATORY PHOTOGRAPHY MEANS IN PRACTICE: FINDING AND WORKING WITH AND PLAYING WITH PARTNERS/COLLABORATORS/PARTICIPANTS

MYRTO: I also recognized that these women did not have only one specific angle to their realities. For example, some of these women who would describe themselves as victims of trafficking would also reflect on their situation as if they somehow accepted it. But there was also a sadness within that acceptance. Was it a way of protecting oneself? A survival mechanism? I don't know – it was nuanced but it was there: the sadness and the acceptance.

Some of these women said, "Compared to where I come from, I may be a bit better now. So, therefore, I'm okay."

These moments and stories reminded me once again [of] the complexity of humans and that my personal interest in storytelling is to take a broad approach to understanding the many different aspects of the human experience.

Method + Practice + Myrto

MYRTO: To be able to better understand the stories, the larger narratives, I first put myself to experience various situations in the sex industry. The reason for this was to understand how the systems and methods worked on the ground – on the streets, in the brothels, in the strip clubs, in the studios [modern brothels]. I had to talk with the madams all over Greece who were running the houses and so on ...

At first I began to capture these various truths in quite of an organic way, as I met women and men that didn't want to be visually portrayed – mainly for their safety – but wanted to share their stories with me. So I started collecting handwritten stories, quotes, sounds, and images of the environments, to structure the multilayered reality that I was living.

As I moved forward I decided to become more specific with my methods – my participatory methods[8] – and to interact even more with my subjects using Literacy through Photography techniques.[9] This type of interaction is always presented in the narrative, and it allows more than one voice to coexist in the same narrative.

SHAYNA: Well, it's a joint narrative then, right? I mean, in academic spheres we would call it co-constructed. You're both constructing the story.

MYRTO: Exactly. You basically ask for the subject to participate, right? The interaction itself creates a very different dynamic between photographer – participant. Photography provides an accessible way to describe realities, communicate perspectives, and raise awareness of social and global issues to different audiences. It encourages sharing, facilitating dialogue and discussion. Jim Goldberg's photography in *Rich and Poor* [1985] and *Raised by Wolves* [1995] and Michael Moore's

A story that some people hide | *Photo: Myrto Papadopoulos*

films such as *Fahrenheit 9/11* [2004] are great examples of the *participatory* methodology in documentary photography and filmmaking.

SHAYNA: But it's also risky, right? Because it may not go the way you want it.

MYRTO: That's the idea. We could maybe say that the participant becomes a co-director when engaging in this process. You don't want the process to be performative. You want it to be participatory. To add that other truth – that other voice, that other identity – that cannot be seen nor heard otherwise.

After having structured my ideas and methodology for this project, I had the need to search for collaborators and to focus on the social impact of this project. Not to give answers but, rather, raise questions.

Finding and Working with Partners in the Project

SHAYNA: And by collaborators, do you mean collaborators who were in some way or another involved in the sex trade?

MYRTO: No. I was looking to collaborate with social workers, NGOs [non-governmental organizations] that were working hands-on, on the ground *with* sex workers.[10] Not "rescuing them" or trying to convert them but working *with* them. It took me a really long time to discover those that I was actually able to work with, without them trying to reshape my identity – or the identities of the women.

From my experience, most NGOs follow their own rules and ways of working, which I respect and understand. However, for this project this couldn't be the case. There was no prescription – no *one* way. The NGOs could not set the stage. The women were the focus and the narratives themselves had many layers; it was very complex. The stories, the realities were all different. Therefore, I was very selective with whom I worked with.

One of the first organizations that I reached and finally collaborated with, which I highly admire, is Positive Voice, an NGO that "defends the rights of people living with HIV in Greece and to respond to the spread of the virus."[11] Their work focuses on populations who are vulnerable toward HIV, and at the time they were at their first steps in creating a program especially for sex workers.

Another NGO that could partner and did partner with me on the project was the Salvation Army. But although they were founded as a religious institution, they were not trying to convert anyone. And finally, as I was also in search for funds for the creation of a participatory photography workshop, I collaborated with the NGO Amaka that specializes in art therapy workshops with people who are often marginalized.[12]

We finally got a grant – in collaboration with Amaka – and we began to work in one of the most difficult areas in the city of Athens, near Omonoia Square. It was a hub of prostitution, drug dealing, homeless refugees, and police – a surreal microcosm in the heart of the city. It often felt like I was part of a Fellini movie.

THE PROGRAM IN THE LARGER PROJECT

The program that was designed especially for women [cisgender and trans] sex workers lasted for six months. It was operating once or twice week in an old building that was mainly used by the Salvation Army.

So every week I would meet with Maria, Alexia, Christina, Foteini, as well as with other women. I would pick them up from the nearby hotels and bars where they worked, to go to this "safe space" that we had all created. At the beginning it wasn't easy. There were times we were bullied by men in the area. I don't know who these men were, but we assumed they were those who controlled the streets, these women.

So after a few months, our idea had begun to take form, and for all it became some kind of a collaboration. For example, while we were operating our workshops in the building, in another space Positive Voice was distributing condoms and raising awareness of HIV and other sexual transmitted diseases, particularly how these affect women.

We all tried to create a safe space for these women where they could be themselves outside their harsh realities. We didn't always succeed, but that was part of the process – it was a reality.

Often there were days where we were there only to listen, to discuss, and sit with a cup of tea while painting our nails. Moving forward, when we gained the trust of the women we began to think on joint initiatives. An example is when Positive Voice invited a makeup artist to the space – to do the makeup of the women – and we on our part created a photo booth for whoever wished to participate – for a self-portrait session.

This project lasted for six months, and by the end I was no longer simply the photographer. It became something bigger than me and my photography. It became more about the women, their voice, and, concurrently, my own self-awareness process.

SHARING THE CAMERA AND MAKING IT PUBLIC

In one of our final lessons after months of being together, the women involved became the directors, the photographers. Using Polaroid cameras, they walked around the streets where they worked to capture moments that reflected their realities. The next step was to write their thoughts and feelings on their images.

And in 2016 we created a public exhibition of their work.

At the beginning, I believe it seemed unreal, not for us but for the public that was invited to an area that it would never visit.

The night was moving; it was a rare moment where people from all sorts of social backgrounds and realities coexisted, spoke, and respected each other. These women saw themselves under a different context in this exhibition and saw their creations – their portraits, their writings, their Polaroids, their poems, their drawings – being admired and loved. They were touched, themselves. This space gave them more attention and respect than they were used to.

Their pictures together with their narratives were very powerful. It became a multidisciplinary project that had my voice and their voices intertwined.

SHAYNA: What did the project turn into?

MYRTO: I really wanted to question, and also humanize, the idea of "the victim." She is a human. She is a mother. Just like you. She goes to the supermarket, just like you. She cooks, just like you. It's not that they

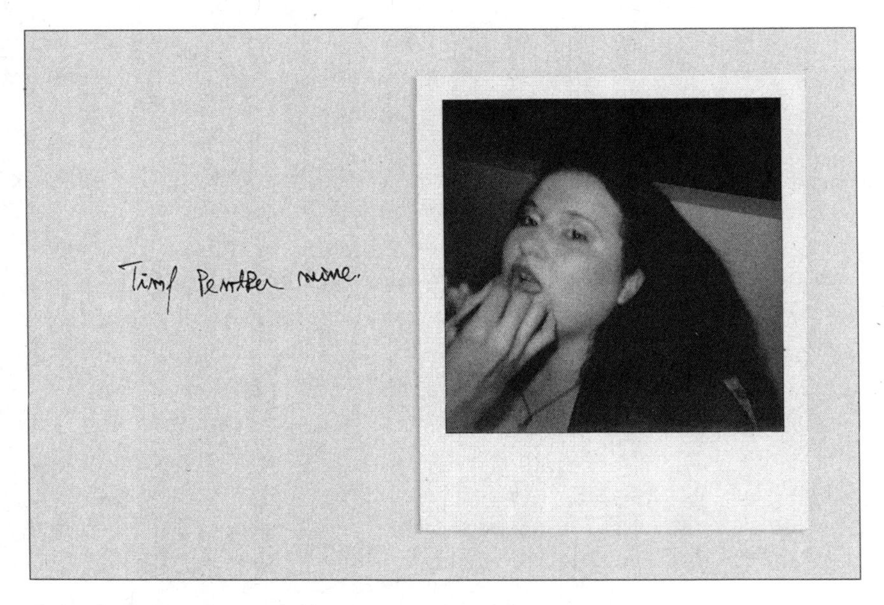

A perfect time for me | *Photo: Myrto Papadopoulos*

are only identified with the world of sex. That is not the only place they exist! But *she* will show you all the ways that she is a human, not *me*. These are her stories and she will choose if, and how, and when to tell them.

MAKING SPACE FOR MANY VOICES

MYRTO: The difference is that at the beginning, maybe, I was not as focused on the larger agenda of making sure it was *their* voice telling the story. This is the extra layer in my narrative, the layer of someone telling me, "No. If *you* photograph me, that's how *I* will be identified. I will choose how and when to show the parts of myself that I want to share, and the story, the stories, will change!"

I changed my focus ... yes, and methods. Those participatory tools helped me to capture those stories. I began to really recognize that the way a narrative is constructed is itself very powerful in regards to the actual context and subject matter.

SHAYNA: Whose stories?

MYRTO: Their stories.

SHAYNA: Who is doing the capturing?

MYRTO: They are doing the capturing.

It's their voice; they control the narrative.

In one of the Polaroid images, it shows a pack of condoms that has been thrown on the street. The caption writes, "My whole life." This image, for example, together with this woman's words became more important to me and the narrative. That is why I included the photographs and captions here, with our interview. It is *their* telling of their stories.

Their captions were really amazing. Some of the ones really stand out to me, such as "The cafes with the trans and Moroccan pimps"; "I am looking for a true love. Does it exist?"; "A happy time for myself," are all images and words that have been created by the protagonists of this project. These images were more important than any picture I took of them.

CONCLUSION OR NEW BEGINNINGS?

SHAYNA: I want to go back to something you said. The Cyprus situation in 2013 re-shifted your project. The project originally began because you wanted to stop the ongoing exploitation of the victim or the one-dimensional portrayal of these women as victims only, but what ended up happening in Cyprus was that it seemed that you recognized that to do this, actually, you needed to change your methods. The goal was the same, but to actually achieve that goal you had to radically change your methods.

MYRTO: Yes, exactly. It's like you're reinforcing, again, you're recycling a narrative that is simple and has been seen as we've seen it our whole lives. But this is my very personal perspective. I'm the person who dislikes the anti-domestic violence poster that shows the woman with the punched, bruised eye. It bothers me. I don't believe that the repeated, one-dimensional linear narrative that we all know – that we are all familiar with – is the only way to talk about victimization. To always portray the victim only as a victim. Why not show this woman under a different context? How can we create campaigns that matter, that can have an impact?[13]

I understand that we need these type of narratives in our societies. But in my personal work, I choose not to repeat the "classic" one, not the cliché one.

SHAYNA: So let me ask you two very clear questions on this. Knowing this now, if you were back in Cyprus in 2013, and you're back in that hub, what, if anything, would you have done differently?

I am looking for a true love. Does it exist? | *Photo: Myrto Papadopoulos*

MYRTO: I definitely wouldn't have asked for a portrait.

I would just go deeper in a more human way ... I would just listen more. I would focus on the process, not the end result. This is where I am at today.

In terms of the result of this project, I got more out of it as a person than as an actual photographer. I love it. It's a project that I'm going back to. It's a project that I feel now that I want to go back to and add more layers to it, somehow.

SHAYNA: Just going back to make sure that something is clear, what it sounds to me, like what you learned when the Bulgarian woman said "No" and how that really caused you to reflect and shift your methods, is that something that you've also taken now into all of your projects?

MYRTO: Absolutely.

Photography can be very psychoanalytical as a medium and especially documentary photography. And I think this is what I'm enjoying, and this is what I'm using. I understand more of my tools now to [be] able to ... I definitely have learned to use my tools better and my voice. But it is the *people* who have taught me – the actual stories of people, the actual narratives, the actual situations, not books or tradition.

SHAYNA: Right. It just, it makes me think back to what you said in terms of empathy. And it makes me think back in terms of what you said – it's not just *you* being empathetic as a photographer, or you being empathetic as somebody who's working with narratives. It seems like what you're saying is you're trying to use your photography and the process to *generate* empathy. That's what I heard you say.

MYRTO: Absolutely. The methods create the story told – the narrative – and the story is shaped by the methods, the "subjects," and the audience(s). Too often the narratives have become recycled, predictable. Overused. Tired.

I want my work to raise questions, not provide an answer. I want to expose the extra layers. For me, it is in the questions that one finds the most complete truth.

SHAYNA: I'm going to ask this last question: What was the ethical dilemma? What was that messy ethical dilemma where you made a decision or you chose not to make a decision? What was it?

MYRTO: If what I'm doing is actually the right way, my way, if it's actually ... if I'm actually portraying the people I photograph as they want to be portrayed.

SHAYNA: So then what are you wrestling with? Is this new approach working? Is this new approach actually accomplishing what you want? Is *that* the ethical dilemma?

MYRTO: Well, it's the approach that allows me to go to sleep at night.

NOTES

1 Myrto's current and past work can be found on her website (available in English) http://www.myrtopapadopoulos.com/.

2 Between 2011 and 2015, HIV infections increased 200 percent in Greece (Reid 2015). In April 2012, after the HIV rate had increased 60 percent in one year, the authorities in Athens arrested many drug addicts and prostitutes; and conducted compulsory testing for HIV on these individuals. The media were complicit in the crackdown and published names and photographs of those who were HIV positive (Reid 2015; Baboulias, 2013). This action made sex workers wary of getting tested in case their names were published if they tested positive.

3 For more information, please see Reid (2015) and Baboulias (2013).

4 Although there are men working in the sex industry in Greece, Myrto worked primarily with cisgendered women and trans women and thus she uses the term "women" throughout this interview.

5 In 2012, the National Press Photographers Association revised its code of ethics (one of the few that is specific to visual journalists), noting that photographers

should "treat all subjects with respect and dignity. Give special consideration to vulnerable subjects and compassion to victims of crime or tragedy. Intrude on private moments of grief only when the public has an overriding and justifiable need to see" (https://nppa.org/code-ethics).

6 Prostitution in Cyprus is not illegal, but operating brothels, organizing prostitution rings, living off the profits of prostitution, encouraging prostitution, or forcing a person to engage in prostitution are illegal activities.

7 Please see Plaut's piece in this volume regarding the need to speak with people you may not agree with, or where it may feel very uncomfortable, in order to get a more complete understanding of a dynamic/situation.

8 Documentary mode is a conceptual scheme developed by American documentary theorist Bill Nichols. In participatory mode, "the filmmaker does interact with his or her subjects rather than unobtrusively observe them" (Nichols [1991] 2001, 179). This interaction is present within the film; the film makes explicit that meaning is created by the collaboration or confrontation between filmmaker and contributor. Jean Rouch's (1960) *Chronicle of a Summer* is an early manifestation of participatory filmmaking. At its simplest this can mean that the voice of the filmmaker(s) is heard within the film. As Nichols explains, "What happens in front of the camera becomes an index of the nature of interaction between filmmaker and subject" (1991/2001, 179).

9 According to Duke University's Center for Documentary Studies website, "Literacy through Photography is a teaching philosophy and methodology that encourages children to explore their world as they photograph scenes from their own lives and to use their images as catalysts for verbal and written expression."

10 I had already been working closely from the beginning of this project with academics and the National Rapporteur on Trafficking, Heracles Moskoff, but at this point my main goal was to strive toward awareness-raising, and I recognized I no longer wanted to do it alone.

11 Translation by author. For more information on Positive Voice, view their website at https://positivevoice.gr/ (website in Greek).

12 For more information on Amaka's projects see their website (English): https://www.amaka.gr/en/.

13 A good and powerful example of the kinds of campaigns that question and shift social norms in an unconventional and provocative manner is Amplifier. See their website: https://amplifier.org/campaigns/.

REFERENCES

Baboulias, Y. 2013. "Remembering How Greece Used HIV to Terrorize Sex Workers." *Vice*, October 30, 2013. https://www.vice.com/da/article/znwv4y/remembering-greeces-hiv-witch-hunt.

Goldberg, J. 1985/2014. *Rich and Poor.* Steidl Publishers, Germany. https://www.magnumphotos.com/newsroom/society/jim-goldberg-rich-and-poor/.

–. 1995. *Raised by Wolves*. Art Pub Inc: New York.

Moore, M., dir. 2004. *Fahrenheit 9/11*. Dog Eat Dog Films. DVD.

Nichols, B. (1991) 2001. *Introduction to Documentary*. Bloomington: Indiana University Press.

Reid, R. 2015."Prostitution: The Hidden Cost of Greece's Economic Crisis." *Telegraph*, November 13, 2015. https://www.telegraph.co.uk/women/politics/prostitution-the-hidden-cost-of-greeces-economic-crisis/.

Rouch, J., and E. Morin. 1961. *Chronicle of a Summer*. France. Film. https://www.imdb.com/title/tt0054745/.

Sontag, S. 2003. "Regarding the Pain of Others." *New York Times*, March 23, 2003. https://www.nytimes.com/2003/03/23/books/chapters/regarding-the-pain-of-others.html.

10

"But Don't Believe Me, Believe Sex Workers"

AMPLIFYING VOICES, SPEAKING OUT OF TURN, AND KNOWING YOUR PLACE

Claudyne Chevrier

Popular portrayals of sex workers as well as large portions of the academic literature are plagued by simplistic narratives often ignoring and erasing the complex reality of people involved in the sex trade. They are shown as blameless victims or "victim-criminals" (Majic 2014), as mindless prey to systemic oppression or as perpetrators of exploitation, as inherently innocent or guilty. Only rarely are these portrayals informed by the experiences of sex workers, let alone presented by sex workers or experiential people.

For the past decade, much of my life has focused on doing my best to be an ally to sex workers in both my academic and activist worlds. Since 2010, I have done research with, for, and about sex work and sex workers on the topics of access to and experiences with health and social services, on sex work activism, community-based service provision, stigma, representation in media, self-representation, and sexual and reproductive health in Canada and India and for global organizations.

In all of my work, I am careful to "pass the mic" as often as possible, hoping to move beyond "giving a voice" to a community that is well equipped to speak for themselves – as long as people are willing to listen. As problematized by scholar Linda Martín Alcoff (2009, 118), while there is a strong current in feminism that holds that "speaking for others – even for other women – is arrogant, vain, unethical, and politically illegitimate," "moving over and getting out of the way" (119) does not always reconcile easily with the political responsibility to speak out against oppression. Without robust evaluation of the power relations and discursive effects at play in specific situations, is keeping silent to avoid speaking for others always the most politically effective strategy? As with many researchers committed to social justice and working with and for marginalized populations, the uncomfortable limits of reflexivity and musings on positionality are often made painfully evident to me. How do we both ensure the safety and confidentiality of our colleagues and, in some cases, participants, and also challenge the long history of researchers and other self-proclaimed experts speaking on behalf of sex workers, often reinforcing the very oppressions they claim to be fighting against? When is it appropriate to speak out of turn, if ever? How can we centre the experiences of groups historically silenced by stigma and violence when we *do* speak up?

Grounded in over five years of ethnographic fieldwork and activism in the medium-sized, conservative city of Winnipeg, on Treaty 1 territory in the Canadian Prairies, this chapter explores the intricate dilemmas emerging from not only witnessing and documenting but also actively participating in the complex socio-political processes surrounding sex work. Crowned in recent years as the "most racist" place in Canada (Macdonald 2015), Winnipeg is a place where the spectacular seasonal contrasts in temperature – even by Canadian standards – are rivalled only by the contrasts between the poverty line of its neighbourhoods (Silver 2016). Like the rest of Canada, Winnipeg is built on lands stolen from Indigenous groups, in this case the Anishinaabeg, Anishininewuk, Dakota Oyate, Denesuline, and Nehethowuk. It is also the heart of the birthplace of the Métis Nation.

My work as a founding member of the Sex Workers of Winnipeg Action Coalition (SWWAC)[1] – the first and only advocacy group in 2015 challenging the notion that sex work is inherently exploitative – has forced me to explore ethical questions without finding clear answers. This chapter presents some partial answers to when – if ever – it is appropriate to speak up for others as an ally and engaged researcher. I use as a starting point one ethically important moment where, after years of vocally committing to refrain from presenting myself as a "sex work expert," I ended up participating in a TEDx talk on sex work as the sole presenter.

> My knees are trembling and my hands are so sweaty that I am actually thankful that speakers are not allowed notes, and that presenters were given fancy clip mics. After months of debates, weeks of preparations, countless 2 a.m. mental battles between the activist and the researcher in my head, I am presenting today in the 2015 TEDxUniversityofWinnipeg on sex work, rights and stigma, on behalf of the Sex Workers of Winnipeg Action Coalition (SWWAC).

When the event organizer Hazim Ismail[2] originally approached me to speak, on the referral of a feminist community organizer I met while planning the annual International Women's Day march, I refused. I thought that it would be best to get a sex worker to speak about sex work. I suggested co-presenting with a SWWAC member or supporting one to present, should any of them be interested. I brought the invitation to SWWAC, and Anlina Sheng, founding SWWAC member and long-time activist, expressed their interest in presenting with me, and possibly sharing their experience as a sex worker. SWWAC was so new that Hazim and other organizers hadn't heard about it yet, and they were very supportive and met with us to discuss what we could talk about and what we would need to feel safe. It seemed obvious that, while the TEDx platform seeks to "uncover new ideas and to share the latest research in their local areas" (TEDx, n.d., line 3), the organizers were also interested in showcasing knowledges that come from community directly.

At the time, Anlina was involved in global advocacy for sex workers' rights with the prestigious Global Network for Sex Work Projects, and I felt confident that their personal experience, years of advocacy, and strong presentation skills would carry us through, no matter how the presentation went. In 2015 in Winnipeg, talking about sex work as work, in a perspective that was grounded in a labour perspective, was not at all common. Nor was it safe. Perspectives that viewed all sex work as inherently exploitative were the norm, and anyone challenging these ideas would see their reputation and credibility questioned, if not attacked. Just a few weeks before the TEDx talk, SWWAC (then known as the Winnipeg Working Group for Sex Workers' Rights) was banned from using space at the community health centre Klinic because we were, in their words, "pro-prostitution."

I feel the weight of these considerations as I listen to Hazim introduce me, and I walk to the centre of the stage. I scan the audience for familiar faces, trying to assess if there are known anti–sex work activists, if SWWAC members and other allies are there. I start my presentation, with the carefully scripted text I practised.

As I move through the slides, I point to the empty chair placed at the centre of the stage and explain to the audience that it represents the voices and people missing from this talk, that I am not doing it alone, despite being the sole presenter. When Anlina learned that they would not be able to join me on stage for the presentation because of scheduling conflicts, we asked all SWWAC members, and every sex workers' rights activist in the city if any of them would join me at Anlina's place. No one

> was able or willing to take the risk of outing themselves on such a public platform. At that point, I wanted to back out, and I tried to. SWWAC members made it clear to me that this opportunity was too important to pass up, and they worried about who else would talk about sex work, and what they would say, if we didn't do it. SWWAC member Craig Ross suggested that we use a chair to signify who was missing, and how, despite really wanting to have these things said publicly, no sex worker could speak about it.
>
> Later in the presentation, I play a recording where Anlina explains what whorephobia feels like to them: "The first time I spoke publicly about being a sex worker felt like stepping off a cliff," they say (Chevrier and SWWAC 2016, [00:05:43–00:05:47]). "Don't believe me, don't believe the research," I tell the audience in various ways throughout the talk. "Believe sex workers" (Chevrier and SWWAC 2016, [00:19:43–00:19:44].) Don't let my credentials and the research I present fool you into thinking I'm an expert, I tell them.
>
> My knees trembled throughout the presentation.
>
> Despite the discussions, the writing and re-writing with SWWAC members and other allies, I worry how it looks for SWWAC to have a non–sex worker speaking on their behalf. Am I just giving ammunition to our detractors who maintain that SWWAC is led by well-meaning but misguided white people who have no experience with the sex trade, pawns of the "pimp lobby" and of ongoing colonization? How am I contributing to the timeless tradition of self-proclaimed experts and researchers speaking in the place of sex workers? Because there is no doubt that I am.

Before the TEDx talk, SWWAC was unceremoniously forbidden to use space at Klinic, a progressive and feminist community health centre. As described elsewhere (Chevrier 2020; Sheng and Chevrier 2019), they disagreed with SWWAC's position that sex work is not inherently exploitative and with SWWAC's advocacy for decriminalization, and were furious that we had been using their space for meetings. They stated that they took "their leadership from Aboriginal women" when it came to the sex trade and refused to let SWWAC further meet there. In Winnipeg, where progressive community centres are not numerous, this was a very worrisome moment for sex workers, many of whom were clients/patients at Klinic who felt that they could no longer count on being safe there. While SWWAC advocated strongly in the years that followed and managed to get a formal apology and currently has a working relationship with Klinic, this event is representative of the constant fear that sex workers and sex workers' rights activists felt in 2015 – and to some degree today. If speaking of sex workers' rights in private, in a basement room of a feminist community centre, was risky, how could outing oneself on a public platform that would be filmed and available online in perpetuity be safe? Alternatively, what would it mean for SWWAC's message and reputation to have a non–sex working white researcher present on such a public platform? And if this opportunity was passed on, would it be taken up by someone painting the entirety of sex work as inherently and solely violent? Which option would be the least damaging to SWWAC's stated mission and reputation? What would it mean for my professional credibility as a student researcher to take a strong political stance publicly?

WHAT IS AT STAKE

My decision to participate in the TEDx talk, and the ways I chose to frame my talk, were informed by concerns around disputed expertise, considerations of the particular political situation in Winnipeg at the time around sex work, and the importance of representation.

Delivery of a public presentation on sex workers' rights and health is, of course, something that is aligned with my role and responsibilities as a critical researcher and something that I am trained and qualified to do. What complicates it is my relationship with both SWWAC and its particular social and political positioning on Treaty 1 territory and my commitment to SWWAC's mission and values. In other words, my dual roles as a researcher and activist are at odds in this moment, as they so often are for critical researchers engaging with communities they work with and advocate for. As a sex workers' rights activist, and as a member of SWWAC, speaking at the TEDx event was a crucial opportunity that allowed the perspective of our sex-working members to be heard and defended. As a researcher, taking a position publicly on this issue made me, to borrow from scholar and activist Chris Bruckert, a "suspect scholar whose commitment to research rigor is open to question" (Bruckert 2014, 310). As she discusses, the involvement of a researcher with activist goals is often used to discredit their work, as if commitment to a social justice goal was necessarily self-involved and self-serving.[3]

Language: A Field of Contestation

The language that surrounds the sex trade and everyone who participates in it is highly controversial, and it might not be possible to understand some of what was at stake in the situation described in the vignette above without some clarifications.

Generations of experts, academics, physicians, feminists, journalists, filmmakers, and other artists have dominated the portrayals of people in the sex trade and almost unanimously cast them in roles that fail to reflect the vast diversity of people and experiences. From "sinners" to "entrepreneurs," and from "bad girls" to "exploited/prostituted women" and even victims of "self-exploitation," the moralizing language used provides a glimpse of the surprisingly high-stakes nature of these conversations. Indeed, the exchange of sex for commodities or currency is a highly controversial issue in academic and policy arenas, reflected in highly dichotomized and reified sex workers' rights versus abolitionist positions.

Positions often defended by some are regrouped under the term "prohibitionist" or "abolitionist"[4] to refer to their belief that "prostitution is inherently exploitative, violent and akin to slavery" and thus "seek to eliminate prostitution through various regulations and prohibitions including a legislative model they call 'end demand'" (Bruckert et al. 2013, 1). The proponents of this position describe themselves as abolitionists with reference to the eighteenth- and nineteenth-century movements to abolish slavery. However, many sex workers, especially sex workers of colour, find the reference to the abolition of slavery offensive and inaccurate in its application to sex work both because many sex workers do not see their work as akin to slavery but also because many argue that using the term "slavery" trivializes the experiences of those who have and do endure slavery (Bruckert et al. 2013; Maynard 2010, 2012). Correspondingly, and following the leadership of sex workers' rights activists in SWWAC and elsewhere, I use the term prohibitionist to refer to a theoretical framework, a social movement, and organizations that seek to abolish all forms of prostitution.

Nahanni Fontaine, a member of the Legislative Assembly for the New Democratic Party and long-time advocate of Indigenous women's rights and justice for Missing and Murdered Indigenous Women and Girls (MMIWG), speaks publicly regularly on the topic of prostitution and describes its tie with colonization. In a public presentation at the University of Manitoba on the legalization of the sex trade in Canada in October 2014, Fontaine described her views this way:

> When discussing prostitution, we begin from the twisted and insulting premise of prostitution as the world's oldest profession, positioning

> prostitution as a legitimate and longstanding human – or male – right and experience, consequently justifying patriarchy's violence against, and claim over, the bodies, minds, and spirits of women, men, boys, and girls all over the world. Let me be unequivocally clear: in these lands, these Indigenous lands, prostitution did not exist within our territories prior to contact ... The narrative of "choice" circumvents women's and girls' lack of choice and the push-and-pull factors from which their exploitation derives itself. The only people who exercise choice are the predators, offenders, and pedophiles who make a conscious, methodical, and strategic choice to prey upon and sexually assault or rape the most marginalized, disadvantaged, and oppressed within our society, all the while justifying to himself with the ridiculous mythologies on why these women and girls are prostituting themselves. (Fontaine 2014)

MLA Fontaine's perspective echoes the perspective of many Indigenous community organizers and activists on Treaty 1 and all over so-called Canada.

The analysis of the sex trade in terms of labour and human rights is different from prohibitionist or abolitionist analysis in many ways. Perhaps most importantly, it does not consider the consensual selling of sex as a problem that needs policies, laws, or social programs dedicated to acting upon it. Rather, it views the selling of sex as a form of labour that should have the same safeguards against exploitation as other fields of work, such as the possibility to unionize and to report abuse or exploitative practices.

Terms like "sexual exploitation" and "human trafficking" are always looming in conversations around sex work, even though they refer to different realities. Their definitions are not directly relevant to the current discussion, and I will limit myself to highlighting that while there is ever growing attention and resources devoted to fighting these realities, the estimates regarding how many people are affected by it continue to be bitterly debated (Hunt 2015; Maynard 2015).[5]

SWWAC'S UNIQUE POSITION

Since its inception in 2014, SWWAC is the first and most vocal supporter of full decriminalization of sex work on Treaty 1 territory (UM Today 2019). In fact, SWWAC came together as a chapter of the Canadian Alliance for Sex Work Law Reform fighting against Bill C-36, the *Protection of Communities and Exploited Persons Act* that would eventually be passed into law in 2014.

As will be discussed later, the specific *local* context in 2015 made the high-stakes decisions about participating in the TEDx talk and who would present even higher. SWWAC members and I worried that if we did *not* take this opportunity to speak, it might be taken up by others who would reinforce dominant narratives equating sex work with exploitation and violence. This meant that SWWAC might miss out on an opportunity to fulfill its mission to confront this narrative. Additionally, SWWAC, as an organization, and myself, as an individual, also worried about how having a non–sex working person present for our group would play into harmful dynamics that place expertise on sex work solely outside of people with experience in it.

Whose Expertise?

The group of sex workers, researchers, healthcare people, and other allies that make up SWWAC came together in the spring of 2014 and quickly established our mission as challenging the notion that sex work is inherently exploitative.[6] I have been involved with SWWAC since it started, and although it became the "site" of my dissertation, my relationship with the organization goes far beyond that of an "ethnographic field site" and a "research project." In other words, my ethnographic research practice was deliberately a site of intense political engagement and participation, rather than the more classical and removed methodology known as "participant observation" (Robertson and Boyle 1984). In addition to my work with SWWAC, I also attended and closely followed public discussions regarding sex work, sexual exploitation, and human trafficking in the media. I spoke and wrote publicly many times on behalf of SWWAC as a researcher (Blaquiere 2015; Botelho-Urbanski 2018; Zoratti 2015), including on February 11, 2022, as a witness in the review by the House of Commons Standing Committee on Justice and Human Rights of the *Protection of Communities and Exploited Persons Act*. I supported SWWAC's tireless efforts to push back against the prevailing narrative in Winnipeg at the time, which stripped sex workers of all agency. In doing so, I was always careful to occupy only the necessary space and spotlight, and to position myself as someone trying to act as an ally to sex workers and who does research on sex work. In other words, I was careful to not be perceived as speaking out of turn and to not present myself as an expert on sex work.

The slogan "Nothing about us without us," coming from disability activism in the 1990s, resonates loud and clear in rallies and in the sex work "Twittersphere" (Grant 2014; van der Meulen 2012; van der Meulen,

Durisin, and Love 2013). The slogan's spirit is also reiterated in everyday life with vigorous demands for representation in public discussions. As a push back against centuries of experts speaking for and about sex workers, it is very important for the expertise and voices of sex workers' rights activists to be at the forefront of advocacy. This is part of the current in other feminist movements, mentioned in my introduction, where speaking for others is widely discouraged, if not deemed "politically illegitimate." The danger lies in the possibility that someone leveraging their privilege to speak for others, however close that someone may be, can reinforce the oppression of the group being spoken for or focus the attention on the speaker rather than on the issue (Alcoff 2009).

Of course, speaking openly about one's experience in sex work is also dangerous in general, and particularly in Winnipeg in 2015. As Anlina said in the TEDx talk, outing oneself as a current sex worker is akin to "stepping off a cliff" in terms of risks and unpredictable consequences. Stereotypes around sex work include assumptions of victimization, disease, drug addiction, and lack of agency (Ferris 2015; Jeffrey 2006). Indeed, the stigma that is attached to sex work, often referred to as whorephobia or whore stigma, and with it the constant threat of its manifestation as direct physical, psychological, verbal, and economic violence, can act as a powerful controlling mechanism for sex workers (for discussions of how it affects individuals, see, for example, Bahri 2019; Bruckert 2014). It is rooted in social beliefs about the impurity of mixing commerce with intimate acts in specific ways that challenge the heteronormative ideology and procreative norm of womanhood (Bahri 2017; Pheterson 1993). This stigma has permanence across space – affecting sex workers on a personal level as opposed to other occupational stigmas – and across time, where being an "ex–sex worker" is an ascribed identity that endures (Bruckert 2014). Of course, this complicates my positionality, as I have spoken publicly about sex work in an effort to give visibility to positions that cannot be represented by sex workers because they cannot say publicly that they are currently selling or trading sex.

Long-time sex workers' rights activist Amy Lebovitch reminds us in the preface of the 2015 publication *Street Sex Work and Canadian Cities: Resisting a Dangerous Order* (Ferris 2015) – and is quoted during the TEDx talk – of another layer of complications when it comes to who gets to speak for sex workers: despite what "those who speak for [sex workers] want you to believe, there are no 'representative' sex workers" (quoted in Ferris 2015, ix). Indeed, not all experiences in sex work are considered to be the same, equivalent, or "representative," especially in relation to the different fields of sex work (outdoors, in-call, massage parlours, cam workers, for example) but also to class, race, and gender identity. In Winnipeg, a large proportion of workers,[7] and the majority of experiential people who spoke publicly about their experiences in 2015, are Indigenous and share the position that all sex work is exploitative. This makes the question of who speaks a painful point of contention, with groups claiming that other groups cannot be representative if they do not have a person with certain experiences or characteristics speaking on their behalf. Alternatively, as will be addressed later, this requirement can be used to silence certain voices because of the immense difficulty in finding a diversity of people willing to publicly identify themselves as sex workers (Kaye 2017).

Specific Situation in Winnipeg

In Winnipeg, at the time of the creation of SWWAC and the event I started this chapter with, all programs catering to people in the sex trade adhered strictly to a narrative that reduces all involvement in the sex trade to exploitation, if not human trafficking. Through the work of people like then-member of Parliament Joy Smith, who is a vocal anti–sex work activist, the idea that all sex work is exploitation dominated the discourse in Manitoba and underpinned the approach taken to all sex trade workers and sex work. Underlying this approach is the fact that Indigenous women are over-represented in the poorest parts of the sex trade (Bruckert and Chabot 2010; Canadian Public Health Association 2014), a reality for which a variety of activist, political, and policy responses have emerged all over the country. Until quite recently, on Treaty 1 territory, those responses have not been focused on harm reduction – as they have in other places (see, for example, Muree Martin and Walia 2019; Sterling and van de Meulen 2018) – but on prohibitionist approaches to the sex trade, seeking to eliminate it entirely.

Critical anti-trafficking studies scholar Julie Kaye, in her research on the response to human trafficking in Canada (2017), reported that while the conflation of sex work and human trafficking happened in each of the three cities she focused on[8] – and, indeed, at the national level – it went a bit further in Winnipeg, where all experiences of children, youth, and adults were conflated under the banner of "human trafficking." The level of disciplining and silencing happening to those deviating from the dominant anti-trafficking narrative was unique to Winnipeg, where her participants reported feeling like they "can't speak openly." Furthermore, it was apparent that the strength of the dominant discourse and the single narrative it projected was such that "the actual voices of experiential workers and trafficked persons are silenced, whether directly or out of fear of such disciplining" (Kaye 2017, 152).

It is impossible to talk about sex work in Canada without addressing the ways in which the forces of white supremacy and ongoing colonization shape the distribution of violence and rights within the sex industry. The distribution of violence and vulnerability is undeniably impacted by race, class, gender, and legacies of violence such as colonialism. Indigenous women are over-policed and under-protected (Razack 2000), and the violence against them is dismissed, ignored, and minimized (Hugill 2010), as the abysmal treatment of MMIWG in the media and in political life attests. Critical race scholar Sherene Razack (2000), in her analysis of the 1996 murder of Pamela George, a Saulteaux woman, in Regina, Saskatchewan, by two middle-class white men, articulates the way interactions between certain raced, classed, and gendered bodies within these urban spaces, particularly in the context of prostitution, often shed light on historically violent and deeply racist, colonial, and patriarchal power structures. She highlights how George's ancestors were displaced from their land and confined in reserves. She writes,

> Pamela George's own geographies begin here. Colonization has continued apace. Forced to migrate in search of work and housing, urban Aboriginal peoples in cities like Regina quickly find themselves in places like the Stroll. Over-policed and incarcerated at one of the highest rates in the world, their encounters with white settlers have principally remained encounters in prostitution, policing and the criminal justice system. (Razack 2000, 127)

Razack argues that the over-representation of Indigenous women in outdoor sex work is a testament to the legacy and power of colonialism. She also argues that any universalized position on sex work privileges the voices of white women over racialized women, thus reinforcing the race privilege and, ultimately, patriarchy. Razack's position echoes Nahanni Fontaine, quoted above, and feminists and Indigenous activists and scholars who consider prostitution to be inevitably linked with violence and racial hierarchies.

CURRENTS OF DISSENSION

The last decade has seen a growing body of voices from experiential women stressing the ways in which sex work can and does resist and challenge hegemonic masculinity, and these voices do include Indigenous scholars and activists. For example, Naomi Sayers, Colleen Hele, and Jessica Wood have been active in discussing the harmful effects of mainstream Indigenous organizations and settler Canadian organizations conflating human trafficking, sexual exploitation, and sex work (Wood, Hele, and Sayers 2015). They describe the legacy of residential schools, the sixties scoop, and continued overrepresentation of Indigenous children in the child welfare system as a practice of human trafficking (Wood, Hele, and Sayers 2015). The continued reliance on those systems maintains the trafficking and violence against Indigenous women. The ongoing criminalization of sex work and ever broadening definitions of human trafficking and sexual exploitation can then contribute to the violence against sex workers and other people involved in the sex trade. These overly broad definitions also feed into the white-saviour complex, which legitimizes colonial institutions and their practices of "saving" Indigenous women and girls. Most dangerously, when the colonial state views all prostitution as human trafficking, these overly broad definitions contribute to the forced removal of Indigenous women and girls from their communities, all in the name of "saving" and "protecting" them. This is reminiscent of what scholar Gayatri Spivak (1988) phrased as "white men saving brown women from brown men" in processes that absolve them from any complicity in violence against those same women.

In 2015, a group of Indigenous sex workers and allies published a statement under the name Indigenous Sex Sovereignty Collective, calling for "centering the voices of people who trade or sell sex in Indigenous anti-violence organizing" (Indigenous Sex Sovereignty Collective 2015, homepage) and for recognizing the diversity of experiences and voices in the sex trade:

> The Indigenous Sex Sovereignty Collective represents a diversity of voices and we acknowledge that there is no one singular voice for Indigenous peoples, especially Indigenous two-spirits, trans* people, and women. We must begin to acknowledge the diversity in our experiences and acknowledge that organizations that unequivocally support colonial policies do not adequately represent the interests of all Indigenous peoples, especially those who trade or sell sex in sex industries or street economies. Turning away from colonial policies, we must instead value, respect and center the diverse voices of Indigenous people with experience trading or selling sex. Without these voices and perspectives, any efforts to reduce violence in our communities only contribute to the ongoing marginalization of sex workers – this, we say, is unacceptable.

The strong focus on experiences of exploitation in the sex trade was reflected in the services offered in Winnipeg in 2015 for people in the sex trade, where services focused almost entirely on people wishing to "exit the trade" and assumed that everyone's experience was one of exclusive exploitation (Chevrier 2020).

SPEAKING OUT OF TURN

My experience of conducting research on a topic which I am greatly invested in in other aspects of my life was guided by the reflections of generations of anthropologists and other researchers who have sought not only to produce knowledge but also to leverage that knowledge in order to participate in processes of social change. The thoughts of Alex McClelland (2017) on what he defines as the role of the "critical researcher" (building on the work of Andrew Sayer 2009) resonate particularly with my approach. McClelland, who works with people living with HIV who are criminalized, highlights that a critical researcher must "undertake work that can be in the service of challenging oppression and injustice of marginalized and criminalized peoples" by paying attention "to systems of oppression, and the resulting suffering of social actors, with the aim of making people contend with that suffering as an act supporting efforts toward forms of emancipation" (McClelland 2017).

In truth, the decision for me to speak for SWWAC at the TEDx conference was not my own, but that of SWWAC as a coalition of sex workers and allies. This opportunity was important for SWWAC in 2015; it was one of the first times that we were approached as a group with expertise on sex work, a group that deserved to have a public platform to talk about our work. My concerns about the space I was taking up, about speaking out of turn, were evidently superseded by the pragmatic need of SWWAC and its mission. SWWAC members asked me to act on my allyship, to be an accomplice in the broader goal of challenging the dominant narrative that sex workers are mindless victims and that sex work is inherently exploitative. They asked me to amplify their voices by speaking for them, and with them, to carve out space for their experiences, even though it was impossible for them to convey those experiences in person.

Alcoff (2009) offers a useful set of interrogatory practices to help guide the decision to speak for others, which include (a) analyze the need to speak (or fight against it, or both), (b) interrogate the bearing of our location and context, (c) fully accept responsibility and accountability for what is said, and (d) analyze the probable and actual effects of the words on the discursive and material context. I find this set of practices useful when thinking back to what guided the decision to participate in the TEDx event. Since the first practice was extensively discussed in the pages describing what led to the decision, I will focus on the three remaining practices in next section.

Interrogating Speaking Up and Knowing My Place

With the decision made, I settled into my discomfort, pushed back both the concerns this contributed to the legacy of "experts" speaking for sex workers and the accusations of SWWAC's detractors, and started planning the talk. In this moment, I considered my position and the context, my "specified, embodied location," to make clear that I was speaking "without pretense to a transcendental truth" (Alcoff 2009, 129), to borrow from Alcoff's second interrogatory strategy. I was wary of falling into the common trap of declaring one's autobiographical details "as a disclaimer against one's ignorance or errors" (Alcoff 2009, 129). Along with other SWWAC members, I looked for ways to reorient the talk, to focus less on issues regarding health, stigma, and rights, and to have at its heart the problematic issue of representation and the danger for sex workers to speak for themselves. We came up with several strategies to amplify the voices of sex workers while also marking their problematic absence from the presentation, such as the empty chair, which reminded us of those who should be speaking, and the audio statement from Anlina. I was careful to plan the presentation so I would repeatedly circle back to the words, the voice, the experiences of sex workers and remind the audience to believe workers before they believe me, at one point stating, "The most radical thing that you can do is probably to seek your information about sex work from sex workers, listen to what they have to say and believe them. If that happens, maybe disconnected academics like me won't have to take up their time and space" (Chevrier 2016, [00:19:34- 00:19:52]).

Alcoff, in her third strategy, suggests that in order for speaking for others to be justifiable, the speaker must commit to remain open to criticism and to accept responsibility for what is said. In the context of the TEDx talk, I considered the responsibility for the content, format, and delivery of the presentation to be entirely mine – following the guidance of my colleagues – and attempted to be accountable to SWWAC sex-working members who entrusted me with this task. Of course, I prepared to be challenged and to have potentially difficult conversations with other presenters or audience members, although I was relieved to be met only with curious and respectful comments and feedback.

Alcoff's fourth strategy is for the speaker to analyze the effects of the words on the discursive and material context. SWWAC's decision was made by carefully weighing the options and evaluating which option would be more damaging to SWWAC's mission: having yet another researcher speak for sex workers, or leaving a spot open that would surely be taken up by someone painting the entirety of sex work as inherently and solely violent. While it was a very clear possibility that my speaking could be seen exclusively as a non–sex working white researcher presenting a skewed, naive view of sex work, the strategies that we put in place were our attempt to mitigate this risk. I view the decision that was made by SWWAC as a pragmatic evaluation of what might be more beneficial to the group and to sex workers. Following the work of medical anthropologists Margaret Lock and Pat Kaufert (1998), I look at this decision through the lens of pragmatism based on a careful and continual analysis, balancing the need to protect SWWAC's sex-working members and the risk of reinforcing harmful narratives about the coalition and sex-working communities.

A Note on Pragmatism

Pragmatism has been used to break away from simplistic analyses of decision making by sex workers regarding their reproductive choices (du Plessis et al. 2020), and I find it a useful tool to highlight how SWWAC and I reached the decision to participate in the TEDx conference. Scholar Elsabé du Plessis and colleagues (2020) describe how Indian sex workers carefully weighed the possibilities offered to them by their context – the pressures made on them by their social networks and families – and enacted an "engaged form of resignation to the possibilities offered in the specific social situations in which they find themselves" (du Plessis et al. 2020, 1187). They were not passive victims of unfortunate life situations; they actively made the best decision for themselves. Similarly, SWWAC members assessed the possibilities offered to them in a context where sex workers who do not identify their experience as exploitative or violent (although they may face instances of exploitation and violence) are systematically silenced, and where opportunities to take up space were limited. Just like the Indian sex workers, SWWAC "both capitulates to and circumvents the wider power arrangements that surrounds" them (du Plessis et al. 2020, 1187) to carve out space for their reality to be represented, albeit imperfectly, by a non–sex working advocate. Far from simply giving up, this decision was deliberate and calculated. It aimed to reach an audience that would not otherwise hear SWWAC's perspective and to take up space that had, until then, been so difficult to claim. As an individual wrestling with my dual roles of researcher and activist seeking to work in allyship with sex workers, pragmatism is also what guides many of my decisions.

OPENING UP SPACE

In the recording that ended the presentation, Anlina said that sex workers need us "to create space for our voices so we can advocate for ourselves without risking everything." In this sense, my "out of place" participation in the TEDx talk contributed to carving out space and safety for sex workers to be able to speak publicly without fear. It also amplified voices and experiences that were (and still are) actively being silenced from denouncing a system that oppresses them.

Until I started to work on this piece, I had never watched the recording of the TEDx presentation, although I promoted it extensively along with SWWAC's social media page, and I hope I never have to watch it again. SWWAC received good feedback on it both locally and nationally. Since 2015, SWWAC has given dozens of presentations to students, service providers, activists, and the general public. It has grown to be a well-respected, published advocacy group (Mexico, Sheng, and Chevrier 2017; Sheng and Chevrier 2019; SWWAC 2022) that collaborates with many other grassroot organizations locally and nationally. In 2016, the Winnipeg Regional Health Authority published a position statement on harm reduction that endorses an approach of "full decriminalization of adult sex work" (Winnipeg Regional Health Authority 2016), which opened the door – given the nature of the public health care system in Canada – for SWWAC to have different conversations with service providers about their position on sex work. A plethora of factors and events have contributed to SWWAC's success and the changes in local conversations around sex work, including every opportunity where SWWAC's recognition of the diversity of experiences in the sex trade was showcased.

NOTES

1 The mission of Sex Workers of Winnipeg Action Coalition (SWWAC) at the time of the TEDx talk I participated in was to challenge the idea that sex work is inherently exploitative and represent the diversity of experiences in the sex trade (SWWAC, n.d.). SWWAC members worked to carve out space for their realities to be heard alongside those of people who have experienced exploitation and violence in the sex trade and who maintain that this is the only possible experience in it. This was done through public education, by holding discussions on the new laws once they were

passed, establishing a strong social media presence, engaging with media about issues relating to sex work, reaching out to journalists, organizations, and politicians to urge them to use exact language when discussing the sex trade, and encouraging service-providing organizations to clarify their commitment to the safety of sex workers, among other activities. SWWAC's sex-working members also led the development of workshops and presentations that are offered to students and organizations regarding health, human rights, decriminalization, and the history of the Canadian sex workers rights movement. Starting in 2015, SWWAC led an extensive community needs assessment for the updating of Winnipeg's Bad Date List system (Mexico, Sheng, and Chevrier 2017), which is now an online database supported by many local organizations. All of these activities were led by the desire to centre and honour sex workers' experiences, expertise, and rights.

2 Community organizer Hazim Ismail was a wonderful source of support, and we exchanged references on sex workers' rights, migrants' rights, and other topics in helping us develop the presentation.

3 Bruckert (2014) also describes how, in her 2010 decision, Supreme Court of Ontario Justice Himel gave higher credibility to academic expert witnesses who are not activists and who she seemed to assume were more objective.

4 Other terms used to describe the abolitionist position by people holding it include radical feminists, fundamentalist feminists, or second wave feminists. Sex workers often use the terms prohibitionist feminists, anti–sex work, or anti–sex worker's rights feminists to describe them.

5 Sexual exploitation in its legal definition occurs when the exchange of sex or sexualized intimacy is not based on mutually informed and transparent consent, or when one of the individuals involved in the transaction has not reached eighteen years of age (Canadian Public Health Association 2014). The term "human trafficking" comes from a distinct set of laws, laid out most clearly in the Palermo Protocol (United Nations General Assembly 2000), which Canada became a party to in 2002. Trafficking generally refers to situations when an individual is forcibly moved or coerced, sometimes –but not always – across borders for the purpose of forced labour, including that of sexual exploitation (Kaye 2017).

6 For a description of the beginning of SWWAC, please see the chapter "Changing the Conversation: The Sex Workers of Winnipeg Action Coalition" (Sheng and Chevrier 2019) in *Sex Work Activism in Canada: Speaking Out, Standing Up* (Lebovitch and Ferris 2019).

7 There are no definitive numbers available regarding the overall number of people involved in the sex trade, their demographic information, or in what field of sex work participants work. However, research consistently reports an over-representation of Indigenous women in outdoor sex work (Canadian Public Health Association 2014).

8 Kaye (2017) conducted fifty-six one-on-one interviews in Vancouver, Calgary, and Winnipeg in 2010–11 with representatives involved in various levels of anti-trafficking, including front-line workers, representatives of non-governmental organizations, sex workers and sex workers' rights advocates, policy-makers, politicians, immigration officials, judiciary, government officials, law enforcement, and some formerly trafficked persons.

REFERENCES

Alcoff, L.M. 2009. "The Problem of Speaking for Others." In *Voice in Qualitative Inquiry Challenging Conventional, Interpretive, and Critical Conceptions in Qualitative Research*, edited by A.Y. Jackson and L.A. Mazzei, 117–35. New York: Routledge.

Bahri, J. 2017. "Stigmatized in Stilettos: An Ethnographic Study of Stigma in Exotic Dancers' Lives." PhD diss., University of Manitoba. https://mspace.lib.umanitoba.ca/xmlui/handle/1993/32776.

–. 2019. "Boyfriends, Lovers, and 'Peeler Pounders': Experiences of Interpersonal Violence and Stigma in Exotic Dancers' Romantic Relationships." *Sexual and Relationship Therapy* 34, 3: 309–28. https://doi.org/10.1080/14681994.2019.1617415.

Blaquiere, S. 2015. "Winnipeg Is: Sex Work." *The Uniter*, March 25, 2015. http://uniter.ca/view/sex-work.

Botelho-Urbanski, J. 2018. "Closure of Free Advertising Website Spurs Fear, Anger in City's Sex Workers." *Winnipeg Free Press*, April 25, 2018. https://www.winnipegfreepress.com/local/closure-of-free-advertising-website-spurs-fear-anger-in-citys-sex-workers-480777443.html.

Bruckert, C. 2014. "Activist Academic Whore: Negotiating the Fractured Otherness Abyss." In *Demarginalizing Voices: Commitment, Emotion, and Action in Qualitative Research.*, edited by S.C. Fabian, M. Felices-Luna, and J.M. Kilty, 306–25. Vancouver: UBC Press.

Bruckert, C., A.-A. Caouette, J. Clamen, K. Gillies, S. Kiselback, É. Laliberté, T. Santini, K. Scott, and E. Symons. 2013. *Language Matters: Talking about Sex Work.* Infosheet No. 4, Stella. https://www.nswp.org/sites/nswp.org/files/StellaInfoSheetLanguageMatters.pdf.

Bruckert, C., and F. Chabot. 2010. *Challenges: Ottawa Area Sex Workers Speak Out.* POWER (Prostitutes of Ottawa/Gatineau Work, Educate and Resist). https://www.nswp.org/sites/nswp.org/files/POWER_Report_Challenges.pdf.

Canadian Public Health Association. 2014. *Sex Work in Canada: The Public Health Perspective*. Ottawa: Canadian Public Health Association.

Chevrier, C. 2020. "Deliberative Identities: An Ethnography of Sex Work and Health and Social Services in Winnipeg Manitoba, Treaty One Territory." PhD diss., University of Manitoba. https://mspace.lib.umanitoba.ca/xmlui/handle/1993/34801.

Chevrier, C., and SWWAC. 2016. "Sex Work, Rights and Stigma." Filmed January 27 at TEDxUniversityOfWinnipeg, Manitoba. https://www.youtube.com/watch?v=YPc4AVAUrXU&ab_channel=TEDxTalks.

du Plessis, E., C. Chevrier, L. Lazarus, S. Reza-Paul, S.H.U. Rahman, M. Ramaiah, L. Avery, and R. Lorway. 2020. "Pragmatic Women: Negotiating Sex Work, Pregnancy, and Parenting in Mysore, South India." *Culture, Health and Sexuality* 22, 10: 1177–90. https://doi.org/10.1080/13691058.2019.1662946.

Ferris, S. 2015. *Street Sex Work and Canadian Cities: Resisting a Dangerous Order.* Edmonton: University of Alberta Press.

Fontaine, N., presenter. 2014. "Visionary Conversations: Giving the Red Light the Green Light." Recorded October 16 at University of Manitoba, [00:19:21–00:25:46].

https://www.youtube.com/watch?v=f3OM6i0NAhE&list=FLo8_wkCLLtIAmCf0NBviCxw&index=1026.

Grant, M.G. 2014. *Playing the Whore: The Work of Sex Work*. New York: Verso Books.

Hugill, D. 2010. *Missing Women, Missing News: Covering Crisis in Vancouver's Downtown Eastside*. Halifax: Fernwood Publishing.

Hunt, S. 2015. "Representing Colonial Violence: Trafficking, Sex Work, and the Violence of Law." *Atlantis: Critical Studies in Gender, Culture and Social Justice* 37, 2: 25–39.

Indigenous Sex Sovereignty Collective. 2015. Indigenous Sex Sovereignty Collective, homepage. https://Indigenoussexsovereignty.tumblr.com.

Jeffrey, L.A. 2006. *Sex Workers in the Maritimes Talk Back*. Vancouver: UBC Press.

Kaye, J. 2017. *Responding to Human Trafficking: Dispossession, Colonial Violence, and Resistance among Indigenous and Racialized Women*. Toronto: University of Toronto Press.

Lebovitch, A., and S. Ferris, eds. 2019. *Sex Work Activism in Canada: Speaking Out, Standing Up*. Edmonton: ARP Books.

Lock, M., and P.A. Kaufert. 1998. *Pragmatic Women and Body Politics*. Cambridge: Cambridge University Press.

Macdonald, N. 2015. "Welcome to Winnipeg, Where Canada's Racism Problem Is at Its Worst." *Maclean's*, January 22, 2015. https://www.macleans.ca/news/canada/welcome-to-winnipeg-where-canadas-racism-problem-is-at-its-worst/.

Majic, S. 2014. "Beyond 'Victim-Criminals': Sex Workers, Nonprofit Organizations, and Gender Ideologies." *Gender and Society* 28, 3: 463–85. https://doi.org/10.1177/0891243214524623.

Maynard, R. 2010. "Sex Work, Migration and Anti-Trafficking." *Briarpatch*, July 1, 2010. https://briarpatchmagazine.com/articles/view/sex-work-migration-anti-trafficking.

–. 2012. "Carceral Feminism: The Failure of Sex Work Prohibition." *FUSE Magazine*, July 2012. https://robynmaynard.com/writing/carceral-feminism-the-failure-of-sex-work-prohibition/.

–. 2015. "Fighting Wrongs with Wrongs? How Canadian Anti-Trafficking Crusades Have Failed Sex Workers, Migrants, and Indigenous Communities." *Atlantis: Critical Studies in Gender, Culture and Social Justice* 37, 2: 40–56.

McClelland, A. 2017. "Epistemological Violence. Ethics and the Construction of People Labelled as Criminal into 'Cases' for Academic Inquiry." Public Scholars Blog, June 27, 2017. https://www.concordia.ca/content/shared/en/news/offices/vprgs/sgs/public-scholars/2017/06/28/epistemological-violence.html.

Mexico, J., A. Sheng, and C. Chevrier. 2017. *Needs Assessment regarding Winnipeg's Bad Date List among Sex Workers and Experiential Persons*. Sex Workers of Winnipeg Action Coalition, August. https://sexworkwinnipeg.com/wp-content/uploads/2016/09/Winnipeg-Bad-Date-List-Consultation.pdf.

Muree Martin, C., and H. Walia. 2019. *Red Women Rising: Indigenous Women Survivors in Vancouver's Downtown Eastside*. Downtown Eastside Women's Centre and Sex Workers United Against Violence. http://dewc.ca/wp-content/uploads/2019/03/MMIW-Report-Final-March-10-WEB.pdf.

Pheterson, G. 1993. "The Whore Stigma: Female Dishonor and Male Unworthiness." *Social Text* 37: 39–64.

Razack, S.H. 2000. "Gendered Racial Violence and Spatialized Justice: The Murder of Pamela George." *Canadian Journal of Law and Society* 15, 2: 91–130. https://doi.org/10.1017/S0829320100006384.

Robertson, M.H.B., and J.S. Boyle. 1984. "Ethnography: Contributions to Nursing Research." *Journal of Advanced Nursing* 9, 1: 43–49. https://doi.org/10.1111/j.1365-2648.1984.tb00342.x.

Sayer, A. 2009. "Who's Afraid of Critical Social Science?" *Current Sociology* 57, 6: 767–86. https://doi.org/10.1177/0011392109342205.

Sheng, A., and C. Chevrier. 2019. "Changing the Conversation: The Sex Workers of Winnipeg Action Coalition." In *Sex Work Activism in Canada: Speaking Out, Standing Up,* edited by Amy Lebovitch and Shawna Ferris, 168–80.Winnipeg: ARP Books.

Silver, J. 2016. *Solving Poverty: Innovative Strategies from Winnipeg's Inner City*. Halifax: Fernwood Publishing.

Spivak, G. 1988. *Can the Subaltern Speak?* Basingstoke, UK: Macmillan.

Sterling, A., and E. van der Meulen. 2018. "'We Are Not Criminals': Sex Work Clients in Canada and the Constitution of Risk Knowledge." *Canadian Journal of Law and Society* 33, 3: 291–308. https://doi.org/10.1017/cls.2018.13.

SWWAC (Sex Workers of Winnipeg Action Coalition). 2022. "DIY Defunding the Police: How Sex Workers Stopped the Police Services from Taking Drivers' Money." In *Disarm, Defund, Dismantle: Police Abolition in Canada,* edited by S. Pasternak, K. Walby, and A. Stadnyk, 113–17. Toronto: Between the Lines.

–. n.d. What Do We Believe? Accessed December 1, 2020. http://sexworkwinnipeg.com/about-us/what-do-we-believe/.

TEDx. n.d. Programs and Initiatives. TED. Accessed November 5, 2020. https://www.ted.com/about/programs-initiatives/tedx-program.

UM Today. 2019. "Showcasing Inter-Professional Collaboration." UM Today Network, May 9, 2019. https://news.umanitoba.ca/inter-professional-collaboration.

United Nations General Assembly. 2000. Resolution 55/25. *Protocol to Prevent, Suppress and Punish Trafficking in Persons, Especially Women and Children, supplementing the United Nations Convention against Transnational Organized Crime*. Adopted November 15. https://www.unodc.org/documents/treaties/Special/2000_Protocol_to_Prevent_2C_Suppress_and_Punish_Trafficking_in_Persons.pdf.

van der Meulen, E. 2012. "When Sex Is Work: Organizing for Labour Rights and Protections." *Labour* 69: 147–67.

van der Meulen, E., E.M. Durisin, and V. Love. 2013. *Selling Sex: Experience, Advocacy, and Research on Sex Work in Canada*. Vancouver: UBC Press.

Winnipeg Regional Health Authority. 2016. *Position Statement on Harm Reduction*. Winnipeg Regional Health Authority, December 2016. https://wrha.mb.ca/files/public-health-position-statement-harm-reduction.pdf.

Wood, J., C. Hele, and N. Sayers. 2015. "What's Missing from the Conversation on Missing and Murdered Indigenous Women and Girls." *The Toast* (blog), September 14, 2015. https://the-toast.net/2015/09/14/whats-missing-from-the-conversation-on-missing-and-murdered-Indigenous-women/

Zoratti, J. 2015. "Campaign's Goal Misses the Mark: Link between Sports Events, Sex Exploitation Unfounded." *Winnipeg Free Press*, October 30, 2015. https://www.winnipegfreepress.com/opinion/columnists/Campaigns-goal-misses-the-mark-338710462.html.

11

Breaching My Contract to Uphold My Responsibility

Nick Catalano

I am an educator at a national museum focusing specifically on human rights. As such I am bound by the same restrictions and obligations as other public servants – the most significant for the stories I explore in this chapter is a commitment to non-partisanship. In effect I am unable to criticize *or* support the politics or policies of the major political parties in Canada, whether federal, provincial, or municipal. Balancing non-partisanship and the moral obligation to advocate for and support the advancements of human rights is at the centre of the dilemmas I explore with you here.

Since starting this chapter in early 2020, several events occurred that exacerbated the challenges I initially wrote about in the earliest draft. The most prominent is the renewed movement for racial justice that swept the United States and the world in the summer of 2020, referred to by most as the Black Lives Matter movement, which has been ongoing since 2013. Contrary to popularly held opinions in Canada, police violence against Indigenous, Black, and People of Colour populations is a severe problem in Canada, alongside systemic racism, and highlights an ongoing system of oppression. The legacy and current reality of colonial violence is ultimately at the heart of many of the challenges and experiences I will outline below.

My workplace was rightfully called out during the summer of 2020 in light of the Black Lives Matter movement. Several former and current employees have spoken up publicly about experiences of racism, systemic discrimination, homophobia, as well as a policy of hiding 2SLGBTQIA++ stories. The museum's concrete actions and responses are still developing and ongoing at the time of writing. My response as an individual to these situations, as well as my professional response, are also ongoing, starting by asking myself, "Should I work here?" As someone living paycheque to paycheque, able to pay only the majority of my bills with student loans, the answer is clearly yes, however COVID-19 has made that decision increasingly complex. One factor I see shaping my response is how reform and change are undertaken in this institution as we move forward. My own identity and positionality, that is to say, being a white, queer, disabled person, also plays a significant role in that decision and will be unpacked in this chapter in more detail.

This chapter explores the implications of federal human rights work and some of the challenges therein. First, I present a dilemma that illustrates many of the challenges and, second, I explore my identity and the additional layer of complexity that identity brings to human rights work. Third, I analyze the strictures of being a public servant in the human rights sector in Canada, including the artificial delineation of human rights and social justice. Finally, I focus on the four largest groups of people I interact with regularly (public, donors, students, Indigenous groups) and the particular manifestations of the ethical issues outlined in the initial story within the context of those four groups' divergent wants and needs.

HUDBAY AND THE Q'EQCHI' MAYA

Being a public servant brings with it numerous contractual stipulations, including non-partisanship. While that can be read as simply not endorsing or condemning any political party over another, in practice it means not making comments on anything considered "political," with no clear definition of where those boundaries lie. Within my institution are further stipulations beyond what an ordinary public servant is bound by, notably that I am not able to present my workplace in any kind of negative light. Last, my workplace has determined that anything construed as "social justice" is political and thus outside the scope of what I can easily discuss. Keep in mind that in light of all this, and maybe paradoxically, I work as a human rights educator.

As a museum interpreter, and one who has been in this role for several years, I often deliver content to donors and stakeholders. It is my job not only to explore the subject of human rights with them, but also to engage and educate them. Ideally, while they may not leave their visit happy, they should not be upset with me or the museum but, rather, with the content we explored.

One donor I delivered content to in 2016, which was about a year into my position as an interpreter, was HudBay, the international Canadian mining company that operates primarily in South America. I was told about this tour three hours before delivering it, and very little context was provided as to whom I would be speaking with. Had I been given more notice, I might have been able to research who and what I would be talking about and come better prepared to handle the challenge in a way I felt appropriate, rather than needing to assess the situation on the fly. It was policy to provide far more notice to the interpreter, but it was inconsistently applied, so short-notice tours like this have been fairly common, though rarely with such high stakes. In the next section I will also detail some of the crucial context I would have appreciated having at the outset of the tour.

In 2011, eleven women from the Q'eqchi' Mayan community that had been forcibly evicted at the request of Skye Resources Inc. (which later merged with HudBay Minerals) filed a lawsuit in Ontario alleging that security personnel contracted by Skye Resources Inc. raped the eleven women. They further allege that "Skye Resources was negligent in requesting and authorizing the forced eviction of Lote Ocho without taking adequate and reasonable steps to guard against the use of violence by company security personnel during this eviction."[1]

Those same women submitted materials referencing this claim to the museum when a call for submissions went out to the public for a temporary exhibit. The submission was explicitly related to environmental rights but also made reference to the lawsuit and the allegations. The submission was successful, with the text making reference to the alleged sexual assault, the ongoing lawsuit, and the forced displacement.

HudBay was less than pleased with this inclusion in our gallery and sent a representative, whom I referred to previously as "the donor," to evaluate the situation. This was someone relatively high up in the company, and I learned only a few minutes before the start of the tour that I was meant to somehow defuse the situation with my tour. One of my executives explained to me that the representative was quite upset about some of our content and that they were being offered the tour in part so that they would not pull funding support from the museum. While I was unaware of this at the time, my task was to smooth over the relationship and highlight the value of the museum. I thus spent quite some time with the representative one-on-one. We spoke at length about many aspects of human rights, including Indigenous rights, land rights, migrant labour rights, and the right to cultural autonomy.

We discussed the responsibility of resource extraction companies in the face of increased public scrutiny and the demand to respect human rights, both in a Canadian context and with a broader international lens, alongside a discussion regarding the urgency of climate change. The representative felt that resource extraction companies were unfairly maligned by outdated characterizations and policies being used as the measure by which public opinion was formed, and I responded by talking about the impossibility of ahistoricism and the lingering impact of those same policies, despite their discontinuation in many cases.

This discussion, or what was officially designated a tour, was an ethical minefield and highlighted the main dilemma in federally mandated human rights work: *balancing public service neutrality and the inability to be neutral on the subject of human rights.* This can be best viewed as the balance I must hold between my contractual neutrality and my mandate as a human rights educator. I was caught between my responsibility to advocate for and support the rights of the Q'eqchi' women who, regardless of the results of the allegations in the lawsuit, certainly had their rights violated by the forced relocation, and the need directed by my employer to maintain a positive relationship with these stakeholders. Advocating too strongly or directly would also probably result in a violation of my contract. As a public servant, I have been sternly warned that failure to uphold this obligation could result in a visitor taking my words as representing the view of the government, my employer emphasizing that I cannot choose which Canadians to serve in this role – meaning I should not determine which opinions are valid and which are not, regardless of the content of those opinions.

Ultimately, after this exchange I felt relieved because I managed to navigate the interaction without seriously violating my contract and thus jeopardizing my job. I also had a generative conversation with the representative, who told me that I had managed to change their mind on some things and had given them a great deal to think about. I was troubled because I had had to face the choice of potentially risking my job to uphold my values. Further, I had had to navigate between what I feel is the responsibility of a human rights educator (with my level of perceived privilege) to deliver a message I believe in and prioritizing my safety and stability at the expense of an opportunity to have a meaningful conversation with someone in the resource extraction industry. Given my skill level at the time, I did the best I think I could have, but I will always wonder if I did enough, or if I should have pushed more.

I found out afterward that one of the vice-presidents of the museum, as well as members of the fundraising arm, had been aware of the controversy surrounding the situation, and while no one informed me about it, they all monitored the situation intently. I was never spoken to by the vice-president, but I became trusted by most others to handle the most challenging tours at my workplace, at least until I developed a reputation of being more "outspoken" some years later.

IDENTITY

No conversation about ethics can take place without assessing one's own position and the power it affords. In my case I have two separate positions, which are informed by the ethical challenges detailed above. Professionally, I am known to be a straight, cisgendered, white male and am able-bodied. Of that list the only identities that are uncomplicatedly true are that I am white and male. I am otherwise queer and living with several mostly "invisible" disabilities. Thus, the next section must be an unpacking of both my professional and my personal identities and the reasons why they are distinct.

The archetypal straight cis white male is highlighted as a locus of power, possessing incredible levels of privilege, often unexamined but jealously guarded. Assumptions of authority, knowledgeability, and expertise all follow. It is little wonder that I would cling to those privileges at the cost of my identity. It makes my job significantly easier; I do not have to spend the first portion of a talk convincing my audience that I have the expertise to be speaking. I can rage against institutional racism and discrimination without being dismissed as angry, emotional, or other demeaning and harmful phrases applied to my colleagues possessing various intersections of identities. I can denounce patriarchy and visibly declare myself a feminist without being labelled irrational, a "man-hater," or any number of other insults and slurs. I am also as insulated as possible from reprimand for violating my contract because of this positionality, making the delicate balance of violating my contract to fulfill my mandate a little easier.

The assumed authority does bring in a different complicated ethical dilemma, one that is encountered often by postmodern ethnographers: What *should* I say or do? I can speak on almost any topic, but there are many that I am patently unsuited to based on my identity, where my approach needs to be specifically conscious of my position as an outsider. Much of the issue rests on whether I should occupy the space I do as an interpreter, whether I am amplifying marginalized voices or speaking over them. This often comes down to an ideal versus a practical approach to the subject. For example, I am one of the more knowledgeable people in my workplace about the Inuit, as I am from an Inuit community and spent my childhood in that community. While I am not Indigenous, I hold a lived experience that, while incredibly privileged and complicated, is not often understood in southern Canada. I am often relied upon for answers regarding questions about the Inuit due to the lack of Inuit staff in the museum. This is far from ideal; a white person should never be the go-to person. Ideally, we would have someone on staff with both knowledge and lived experience who is Inuk and is hired to provide that kind of knowledge to staff rather than being tokenized. Lacking that institutional shift to value such an investment, however, my choice becomes using my privileged access to education, French language education, and a job in the south that gives me this platform to advocate for Inuit rights or keep silent so as to not self-aggrandize or profit professionally from the generosity that my community showed me in my youth.

I believe the ethical decision is to mobilize my privilege. I also recognize that I am walking a dangerous line that requires constant reassessment. I get dangerously close to "speaking for" the Inuit, rather than about, alongside, or with them. This also evokes another problematic aspect in museums: Inuit are not exhibits; they are people. The danger of speaking about them in the third person, as some vague monolith, runs the risk of dehumanizing them, similar to the way they are dehumanized to remove their rights. I must question a number of dilemmas, including if I am providing useful and nuanced information to offset the potential legitimization of a romanticized view of Inuit that my visitors may carry. I have yet to resolve this tension in myself. I suspect, if I am being responsibly reflexive, that I will never find resolution to that tension. I am also aware that the larger political climate will cause the ethical tension to evolve over time and force me to re-engage with it continuously. Similarly, with the Q'eqchi' Maya, I must balance my access to education and privileged spaces with the space that I am taking up and why, as well as specifically to my own relationship to the colonization of knowledge.

The other aspect of my identity that causes me ethical difficulty is the difference between my public and professional identities. I believe, in the current state of the world, that I am more effective presenting in my more privileged form, thus allowing me to convince and discuss both through speech and example that other privileged people have a responsibility to address their privilege. I cannot do so as effectively should I present as a visible member of any of the marginalized communities I am part of. Setting aside questions of whether it is my responsibility to convince people to treat marginalized people with more than nominal humanity, my question becomes whether speaking about or alongside "them" is more effective than speaking of "us" – the privileged, academic view or the displayed humanity. I am clearly conflicted, and I imagine my own position on this will change numerous times before publication of this book, but I highlight this issue not so much to speak exclusively of myself but to show through example that everyone who works for human rights in some capacity (paid or not) must continuously wrestle with the implications of their identity and resulting positionality. The complicated mess of relational power that identity illuminates is one of the foundations of human rights awareness, but it is also one of the most complicated aspects of human rights work.

In light of the Black Lives Matter movement and the other events ongoing at my workplace, my professional identity has become an even more pressing issue: Are my experiences of marginalization going to be addressed if I cannot tell my story freely? What will the impact be in terms of giving up clout by surrendering the title of "straight cis white male," specifically on those who have asked me to utilize my privilege to advocate for them?

Ultimately, I will need to wait for things to play out more before I can decide the appropriate course of action. It does highlight how severe the clash between contract and mandate can be. Erasing my own identity to breach my contract and provide quality education is not a dilemma anyone should have to face, yet the structure of my federally mandated human rights work requires it.

REPRESENTING THE FEDERAL GOVERNMENT AND THE ROLE OF A PUBLIC SERVANT

While my workplace status as an "arms length" organization means that the government, regardless of the party in power, should not be able to interfere in our operations, the influence of the federal government in the museum's early years was painfully obvious to many.

During my initial training, in 2014, I was instructed not to assert the rights of the 2SLGBTQIA++ community beyond what was protected by law, once again putting me in the difficult position of needing to silence my own identity and experiences to be able to teach people effectively, in this case being able to teach people at all. At the same training, I was told not to discuss abortion beyond the Morgentaler case, which is featured in our galleries. The most egregious issue at the time was the failure to acknowledge the Indian Residential Schools system and its ongoing legacy as genocide. While this omission has since been rectified, it was a challenging topic simply because honestly discussing it was not only in violation of my contract, but also in contradiction to the position of the federal government. This tension between the institution's eventual acknowledgment of the genocide in this country and the lack of support from the federal government further complicates commenting on something like the occupation of Indigenous Lands. In almost every interaction, I had to consider these issues: Who is the visitor, what is the quick assessment of their political views, how secure is my position, and what is my relationship and responsibility to the marginalized group in question? Much like with HudBay, this assessment often needed to happen on the fly.

While I could list many individual topics that I would like to publicly criticize, it is more succinct to say my contract contradicts my morals and education. Intellectual honesty, advocacy, and a search for justice are values that I have learned throughout my time at university. When those values inevitably bring me into conflict with a government that is rooted in the colonial endeavours of the British and French empires, I am faced with the ethical challenge of honouring the human rights abuses I have learned about and the people I try to support with my advocacy or bowing to the needs of that government. Fortunately, there is a way to navigate these dilemmas: by utilizing the "facts" of human rights. For most of the issues I come across, I can typically point to something in either the Canadian Charter of Rights and Freedoms, a supporting document, provincial human rights codes, or the Universal Declaration of Human Rights to justify my stance. All of these documents are featured in our galleries and thus give staff a sort of protection, wherein we can explain that we were simply interpreting content that our workplace endorses.

This same notion of being uncritical also applies directly to my museum workplace via the Code of Business Ethics. It states, among other things, that I cannot present my workplace in a negative light. This limiting of self-reflection creates a situation where any legitimate criticism that staff may make becomes a punishable offence, and it shelters the organization even further from necessary dialogue to help it grow. On a personal level, reflexivity is fundamental to my practice, and this directive prevents that process. It is difficult, at best, to engage in meaningful dialogue about human rights if I need to deliberately obfuscate when it comes to the museum that is enabling me to do that very work. Once again, the very best of my work can only come from a violation of my contractual obligations.

These two broad guiding statements get applied unevenly, typically along hierarchies of privilege across the organization, and require significant nuance and practice to navigate properly. Learning how to navigate this complicated invisible web is one of the critical steps in learning to facilitate quality human rights education. Fortunately, due to my professional identity, as long as I keep my wits about me and understand the context I am in, I can typically lean into my education, work around my contractual limitations, and produce the best work I am capable of – which would hopefully have a larger impact on my audience. Of course, this does not deal with the issue of my workplace itself not hearing criticism, but the process for that kind of feedback is being revised at time of writing due to the reckoning of 2020. It also leaves out the obvious question of how to navigate that dilemma for staff who do not hold the same level of privilege.

SOCIAL JUSTICE AND HUMAN RIGHTS

Social justice is defined by the Oxford Dictionary as: "the objective of creating a fair and equal society in which each individual matters, their rights are recognized and protected, and decisions are made in ways that are fair and honest" (Oxford Reference 2021), and human rights are defined as "the basic rights and freedoms that belong to every person in the world, from birth until death" (EHRC 2019). Government bureaucracy often necessitates the difficult task of separating these two concepts. While it is not clear from the definitions, the commonly accepted difference, at least in my corner of the world, is that social justice implies actively participating in and advocating for human rights, while the neutral noun "human rights" implies a more passive agreement, a first-generation understanding that not all rights need to always be supported by legislation and that people deserve to have access to certain rights or removal of threats guaranteed but not enshrined.

I draw attention to the difference because my federally mandated human rights work demands that I support human rights, without engaging in social justice activity. There is fear that advocacy would alienate potential partners, community members, stakeholders, donors, and visitors. Social justice often involves taking a critical lens to institutions, including governments and their corporate relationships, which, as discussed previously, has its own ethical challenges. When brought to this high-level understanding, however, we can see new challenges emerging, not just on an interpersonal interpretive interaction, but on a state level.

The ethical challenge of my position, though staggering, is clear: I cannot speak poorly of the federal government due to my position as a public servant, as doing so could be construed as partisan. Nevertheless, many of the actions taken by various government bodies, both historically and contemporarily, are negligent or in clear violation of human rights. Visitors look to me and my colleagues for answers on how to understand the actions taken by various government bodies, yet we are often unable to fully articulate the reality of those situations.

That, ultimately, is the source of nearly every ethical challenge I face in my work: balancing comments and education on the "facts" of human rights with advocacy, struggling to support the advancement of those rights and ideas. This obligation to separate the two also directly opposes my education. I was hired into the role of interpreter due to my education in the field of human rights and my passion about the subject. However, now in the role I am not allowed to utilize the portion of my education that requires us to act to support the struggle for human rights.

Anthropology takes a holistic approach to any given question, including that of human rights. While the discussion is still somewhat ongoing, I fall firmly in the majority group, wherein it is the professional and personal responsibility of anyone privileged enough to receive an education in anthropology (or anything else) to utilize that privilege to advocate for and amplify the voices of people who do not necessarily have that same access. In that sense "social justice" and "human rights" cannot be separated, which makes this directive of separation much more difficult to follow than it otherwise might be.

INTERPRETATION AND EDUCATION

In my role as an interpreter at a human rights museum, I interpret history, personal stories, legal implications, and any number of other aspects of human rights to different members of the public. Because of the breadth of a subject like human rights, there is very little that is "off the table," so to speak. Notably, I deliver to the public (usually adults), and to donors (and special interest groups and stakeholders), students (ranging from kindergarten to university), and, finally, Indigenous groups. Interacting with each of these groups highlights a different aspect of the ethical challenges outlined in the HudBay story above. As such I will be exploring the intricacies of each of the four groups to provide some more context in the overall issues present in federal human rights work.

Public Visitors

The "public" are easily the most varied group. Their visits tend to be the most politically contentious encounters, with groups ranging the breadth of the political spectrum in Canada. International visitors, too, bring their own views and political beliefs into the conversation, such as when a visitor from Turkey angrily spoke with me about the content regarding the Armenian Genocide, or when visitors from Russia debated the reality of the Holodomor, or when American visitors defended the travel ban targeting the Muslim population that was enacted by Donald Trump. There have also been numerous interactions wherein Japanese visitors question the portrayal of the "comfort women" system. Perhaps unexpectedly, the only topic of those listed above I find difficult to navigate from an ethical standpoint is the US travel ban on Muslim-majority countries, and broadly anything relating to the United States. While the Canadian government has made its stance explicit regarding the other topics, they seem bound to try to not ruffle our relationship with the US too much. Thus, some things about the actions of the United States government are not explicitly condemned, which makes broaching the subject while respecting some of the restrictions I mentioned difficult. There is also an expectation from some visitors to engage in dialogue about any ongoing political situations globally, which leads to a similarly challenging place.

The ethical challenge of considering both Canada's political relationship with these various nations and the need for justice and rights can be severe. Part of the challenge is due to my lack of knowledge about the visitor: I have had numerous interactions wherein someone asks me something seemingly innocuous, I answer in a vague or non-committal way, and they then reveal that they are affiliated with a foreign government. I found out that three men I was speaking with about the policies of the government of Bangladesh during the Rohingya crisis (as it was known at the time) were, in fact, ministers in that government. I have encountered numerous members of the US State Department and of the Canadian Parliament. I have spoken about companies who were involved in the production of items used in the Holocaust, in front of someone invested in one of those companies, who then reported me, trying to censor me.

This all emphasizes the dilemma between total honesty, abiding by my contractual obligations, and protecting my own employment. There is an inherent right to education that means the Rohingya should receive educational support from the Bangladesh government. But is it my place to voice that to these officials? When I was first confronted with this dilemma, Canada had not said much at the time about education, so there was little I could fall back on as a federal employee. As such, if the Bangladeshi ministers had decided to contact my employer, I could have been found to be in violation of our policies and risked my employment. On the other hand, I think it is important that they (and other politicians) hear from ordinary citizens, and I am aware that my personal privilege can afford me the opportunity to be a voice to amplify the Rohingya people's calls for justice. In the end I approached the discussion with the three of them through the lens of the humanity of the Rohingya, foregrounding the idea that the lives of the Rohingya exist beyond the scope of the genocide and that it is important they be enabled to engage in as fulfilling a life as possible. This was a political middle ground; I felt that stating explicitly that the Rohingya need educational resources may be judged as being too much of an agenda but that speaking to their well-being generally encompassed education. As with the other stories herein, I am stuck wondering if I did enough, or if the conversation had any meaningful impact.

Special Interest Groups, Donors, and Stakeholders

The next major group is special interest groups, donors, and stakeholders. The story about HudBay is an example of some of the challenges that exist in this context. The most infamous challenge, however, is discussing Israel and Palestine. The International Holocaust Remembrance Alliance, from whom the Canadian Government has adopted their definition of antisemitism, does make the distinction that policies of Israel may be critiqued but the right to Jewish self-determination cannot be (International Holocaust Remembrance Alliance, n.d.). Under this definition engaging in critique through an anti-Zionist lens is thus understood as antisemitism, which can be difficult for many to navigate.

My museum workplace has a number of donors who have, during various encounters, made known their support of Israel and the expansion of settlements at the expense of a dialogue about Palestinian rights. This makes discussing the violations of the rights of Palestinians in the occupation of the West Bank, Gaza, and other settlements extremely difficult. When engaging in dialogue with the donors who hold these views, it becomes extremely difficult to vocalize any concern for Palestinians without risking immediate shutdown and potential reports to management, due to a conflation of advocacy for the rights of Palestinians and the antisemitism that sometimes happens in this sort of discourse. Having said that, there are very serious human rights violations taking place in the Occupied Territories, such as the West Bank, Gaza, and East Jerusalem. If our mandate is to engage in education and dialogue then it is important that they be talked about, particularly by someone who is, again, positioned as an expert on human rights. As with the Q'eqchi' Mayan women who filed a lawsuit against HudBay, this is a situation where a group of people are only slowly gaining a voice within a human rights institution and, in the interim, rely on me and many others to provide accurate information, which is inhibited by the interests of stakeholders.

Once again, the valid need to maintain positive relationships with stakeholders and donors, the requirement for federal employees to be neutral, especially regarding a state that the government does not officially recognize, and the authentic need for dialogue are clashing in a way that can threaten my livelihood. There is no clear answer: leaning in any of these directions is a valid decision, and I have gone both ways during my employment, but none left me feeling as though I had taken a clearly ethical route. Most often I try to draw a parallel to other events and position the occupation as similar in practice to less controversial events without condemning the Israeli state as motivated by ethnicity in any way.

Student Visitors

The third major group I deliver to is students. There are, of course, different considerations depending on age, but with any minors there are many more concerns that come into play. My responsibilities as an educator are tested when the subject veers off the planned path, as it often does with young people. A moment that has stuck with me is when, while delivering a school program, a young girl of seven or eight who, when I casually mentioned transgender people, exclaimed in shock, "God says that's wrong!" Immediately I needed to assess how to best respond by balancing the need to respect the authority of parents and not overstep as a government employee with ensuring she understood that transgender people have the right to exist free of discrimination. I looked to the teacher for support, but I was met with a steely gaze that informed me I would also be fighting the teacher if I disagreed with the assertion. Particularly considering my institution's policy at the time of omitting 2SLGBTQIA++ stories for religiously affiliated school programs (which this was), the risk of censorship and punishment was quite high for me. If I said nothing, however, I would feel like I was shirking my responsibility as an educator and community member, not only toward the student but also the rest of her class, particularly if any of the students were members of the 2SLGBTQIA++ community. It would be important for them to see someone in a position of authority gently disagree with the moral judgments made about people's identities. I decided to say that some people believe different things about what God thinks about trans people and went on from there, ultimately linking it with the subject at hand. The student did not seem to think too much about my statement and continued with the lesson. While I stopped short of denouncing religiously motivated transphobia, not only because

I did not have enough time to have a nuanced conversation with her, but also because of the probability of retribution from the teacher and, consequently, my employer, I did try to complicate the issue so that the kids left with the idea that there are different ways of interpreting scripture. In retrospect and in consideration of my own identity, I do not believe I was pointed enough, but that was my compromise at the time. If I had the opportunity to redo this conversation I would be much more direct, however I also recognize that trans visibility and awareness has increased dramatically since this exchange happened in 2018.

There have been students who made assertions about vaccination causing autism, which ultimately is ableist and untrue, who made hateful comments about Black, Indigenous, and People of Colour populations, about women, Muslims, and a number of other identities that are discussed within media. If the child is stating something they believe or that they are hearing from the adults in their lives, there is always a momentary lurch wherein I must quickly judge how progressive the teacher is and how strong a correction I think I can "get away with." I have worked to learn how to navigate these moments in ways that enable me to counter harmful views, but it is never done without some concern about potential reprisal and a worry that I did not do enough.

Indigenous Visitors

The last group is the least challenging from an ethical sense: people specifically seeking information on colonization and Indigenous peoples. More often than not, groups of Indigenous peoples use the museum as a cultural and informational resource, rather than to gain "new" information. It is with other groups looking for this information that I have the clearest guidelines that match the ethical needs of the circumstances: with the Truth and Reconciliation Commission reports, the United Nations Declaration on the Rights of Indigenous Peoples, and the *Report of the National Inquiry into Missing and Murdered Indigenous Women and Girls* and *Supplementary Report: A Legal Analysis of Genocide,* there is a strong ability to make clear condemnations of the Residential School System and of ongoing colonization as a whole, including a recognition of Canada's genocidal policy. The only real ethical challenges I face with this content are linked to my own identity, my relationship with the Inuit, and my relationship with colonization and my own whiteness. Should I be the one teaching about these topics, given my privileged position?

CONCLUSION

All federally related human rights work and, really, any institutionally related human rights work, academic institutions included, face these kinds of politically charged ethical challenges in any number of given situations. My experiences are not unique, and while the details change, many of my colleagues have similar stories within the museum, and many of my classmates have similar challenges outside the classroom. It is overwhelmingly probable that these kinds of ethical issues will not be solved or, perhaps, are not even solvable. However, giving them real thought, even if no solution is reached, can only galvanize us to do better human rights work, although while there is an insistence on the artificial separation of human rights and social justice, this progress will be inhibited and, ultimately, will limit the impact that institutional advocacy work can have. Until there is more willingness to recognize that human rights are tied to justice, and that that requires some level of admission of culpability and responsibility from institutional actors, the challenges my colleagues and I face in situations like the HudBay stories (as well as others I talked about here) will not be resolved. Until these challenges are addressed, the Catch-22 of institutions both providing the platform and inhibiting the content will exist, and it will always be up to the smaller actors like myself to do their best to skirt the rules in order to be as effective as possible within the bounds of our roles. At this point it seems like a reckoning of some kind is inevitable, but whether this will make things less or more ethically challenging remains to be seen.

Since I wrote my first draft in early 2020 many things have happened. As it currently stands, donor tours are still not generally assigned to guides. This would sidestep some of the issues in a situation like HudBay, which I presented, though this mostly performative shift certainly does not address the deeper institutional and personal challenges I outlined here. Time will tell how these changes play out.

NOTE

1 *Choc v Hudbay Materials Inc,* 2011 ONSC 4490 (Amended Statement of Claim, 6 February 2012), online: *Choc v. HudBay Minerals Inc. & Caal v. Hudbay Minerals Inc.,* http://www.chocversushudbay.com/wp-content/uploads/2010/11/Amended-Statement-of-Claim-Caal-v.-HudBay-FILED.pdf. See also https://www.chocversushudbay.com/legal-documents/.

REFERENCES

EHRC (Equality and Human Rights Commission). 2019. "What are Human Rights?" Human Rights, June 19, 2019. https://www.equalityhumanrights.com/en/human-rights/what-are-human-rights.

International Holocaust Remembrance Alliance. n.d. "The Working Definition of Antisemitism." https://www.holocaustremembrance.com/resources/working-definitions-charters/working-definition-antisemitism.

Oxford Reference. n.d. "Social Justice." Accessed January, 2023. https://www.oxfordreference.com/view/10.1093/oi/authority.20110803100515279

12

The Oral Defence

SPEAKING BACK TO THE COMMUNITY

Yuriko Cowper-Smith

The Rohingya Canadian movement is a diaspora-led social movement working toward resolving the Rohingya genocide in Myanmar and the humanitarian crisis in Bangladesh. From December 2017 to December 2019, I used a community-engaged scholarship (CES)[1] approach to work within, and contribute to, the movement.[2] This chapter focuses on an ethical dilemma that arose during the final stages of my PhD. I first describe the ethical tension that arose. Then I explain my methodological approach to this chapter. Finally, I conclude with ideas on how the living principles adopted during this work can be incorporated more formally in future research.

THE VIGNETTE: WHY DID THE DEFENCE WEIGH SO HEAVILY ON THE RESEARCHER'S MIND?

My defence preparation crystallized two connected dilemmas around authorship and evaluation. To appreciate these dilemmas, I first describe the debate in the literature about co-production of knowledge, the methodology behind my dissertation, and the defence format.

There is a growing body of literature that explores the co-production of knowledge and community-engaged scholarship in forced migration studies, among other disciplines. Defined by Cerian Gibbes and Emily Skop (2020, 278–80), "co-production of knowledge is a methodological process that foregrounds the construction of knowledge and focuses on the contributions of and negotiations between key actors in producing science ... ideally the process complicates traditional research participation structures and the archetypal binary of the all-powerful researcher and the all-powerless subject."

Similarly, CES can be defined as a radical politics of solidarity, coalition, and co-resistance in active social justice struggles. Shirley Suet-ling Tang (2008, 248) writes on the goals of CES:

> For me to be accountable to community struggles over self-representation and self-advocacy means, in part, using my academic privilege to clear away potential obstacles that might discourage community practitioners from taking on the challenge of community knowledge production. Needless to say, as empowered, knowledgeable participants, community practitioners also advocated for themselves, so my role was to mobilize attention to their demands.

Related to CES, Clark-Kazak et al. (2017, 12) highlight that among the four ethical principles for working in situations of forced migration, partnership entails developing "appropriate protocols and mechanisms to ensure full participation of relevant partners," promoting "co-ownership of the research," and "respectfully acknowledg[ing] each partner's contributions." Co-production is essentially about admitting that the academy should not – does not – have a monopoly over the development of knowledge. It has always been a collaborative or multiple-sited endeavour despite boundary drawing and gatekeeping attempts (Gibbes and Skop 2020). Yet co-production is not without flaws. It must also grapple with the contextual power relations found within each research partnership, which may yield unforeseen challenges and complexity. In summary, the literature both praises the potentially radical and valuable aspects of co-production, in which power-sharing and mutuality are goals, but also holds that co-production can be messy and, troublingly, can be co-opted to serve the goals of the dominant power structures that the approach sets out to undermine (Gibbes and Skop 2020).

Explaining the CES aspects of the PhD research process underlines my immersion in the Rohingya social movement and the way community involvement played a substantial role during the information-gathering phase. During the research process, for me, reciprocity and accountability meant being receptive and answerable to the community's needs. In addition, reciprocity and accountability encapsulated responsibility toward partnership and self-determination, which is to "respect and support the right of people in contexts of forced migration to make their own decisions about their lives and the degree of participation in research processes" (Clark-Kazak et al. 2017, 12).

My process of building a long-term relationship based on reciprocity and accountability with members of the Rohingya community in Canada and abroad, and with other supporters, overlapped with the emergence of the Rohingya social movement after state- and military-led violence catapulted the Rohingyas' plight to public and political prominence. As I started my data collection only a few months after the violence of August 2017 (a pivotal point in the history of the movement), I witnessed central aspects of the movement's growth in real time. Bearing these CES principles in mind, I undertook a lengthier process of developing relationships with people in the movement, an experience that was drawn out over two years.

I conducted open-ended interviews to generate rich data by drawing on participants' perspectives, expertise, and experiences regarding their involvement in the social movement. I started by interviewing four different participants: a Bangladeshi professor who has worked with the Rohingya community in Bangladesh for his entire career; a lawyer who was a part of the Burmese democracy movement in Canada in the 1980s; a photojournalist who worked with the Rohingya community in Kitchener-Waterloo in 2015; and a group of representatives from Burma Task Force, an advocacy organization that has been working from Canada to address the Rohingya genocide since 2016. Then I asked one of *I Am Rohingya*'s producers and directors, with whom I became friends, to connect me with the Rohingya community members he knew. These early interviews and the support from the director helped me situate my work more appropriately in the dynamics of the movement and become more sensitively attuned to the types of discussions to have. This slow process eventually led to conversations with Rohingya activists; federal, provincial, and municipal politicians; senators; lawyers; academics; leaders; and movement allies from across Canada.

In parallel with interviews, I conducted participant observation. In the two-year period of the research process, the documentary *I Am Rohingya,* co-produced by a media company run by two young filmmakers and Rohingya youth, was showcased across Ontario. I attended the documentary's screenings, acting as a participant-observer for five screenings and as an organizer/panellist for three. Attending eight screenings of *I Am Rohingya* was, in part, what drove my increasing participation in movement events. Seeing how the Rohingya youth developed the initial

I Am Rohingya play and subsequent documentary[3] and observing their passionate advocacy led me to get to know the actors personally and learn about additional events. I also became involved in conferences, meetings, panels, and photography exhibits, respectively depicting the Rohingya communities in Winnipeg and Kitchener-Waterloo. In April 2019, two Rohingya peers and I organized a roundtable discussion at the University of Toronto. I additionally volunteered at three related organizations: the Canadian Rohingya Development Initiative, the Canadian Centre on Statelessness, and the Sentinel Project for Genocide Prevention. Researching during this period also meant that I could be present for significant government announcements such as the stripping of Aung San Suu Kyi's honorary citizenship in 2018; the unanimous vote in the House of Commons and Senate, in 2018, on supporting the findings of the International Fact-Finding Mission on Myanmar report, which called the crisis a genocide; the commitments of aid to Bangladesh and Myanmar in 2018; and the Senate motion on the Genocide Convention in 2019.

After I completed my interviews and participant observation, I conducted a qualitative thematic analysis. Throughout this phase, I stayed in touch with multiple research participants to continue personal friendships, support the movement and its goals, and refine my study's findings. More specifically, beyond mutual interest in maintaining relationships, the communication kept me abreast of movement dynamics and developments and allowed me to give back time and energy into the movement's activities after the completion of my research. It served the further purpose of revising my conceptual framework as I incorporated both direct and informal feedback from participants. Going back to the principles of reciprocity and accountability, by incorporating reactions, responses, and new ideas, the back-and-forth feedback process allowed for a rich explanation of the social movement's intellectual activities.

I now turn to the quandary.

The defence structure varies across disciplines and universities. There is also variation in the defence's significance or weight across universities in Canada and other countries. At the University of Guelph, in the Department of Political Science the defence is an oral examination of the student by their PhD thesis examining committee. It is presided by the chair of the department. The thesis examining committee comprises the student's supervisor, a thesis committee member, an internal-external examiner, and an external examiner. The internal-external examiner is a faculty member of the department. The external examiner is a faculty member of a different university, chosen broadly based on their discipline and knowledge of the research area. The student is expected not to have an existing professional relationship with the external examiner and does not contact the examiner during the examination period.

Usually, the defence is performed in a classroom for a total of two or three hours.[4] The student first presents their dissertation orally to their examining committee. The presentation is usually between twenty and thirty minutes, focusing on the work's main contributions. The student usually presents the fundamental components of the dissertation, which include the design, methodology, conceptual framework, results, contributions, and conclusions. Two rounds of questioning follow the presentation. The chair generally gives priority to questions from members of the examining committee. At the University of Guelph, in the Department of Political Science the external examiner is given the first opportunity to ask questions, followed by the internal-external examiner. Then the committee member asks their questions, finally followed by the supervisor. The second round follows in the same manner. Following these two rounds of questioning, the student leaves the classroom while the committee deliberates. The student is then summoned back into the room to hear the committee's decision on if they have passed the oral defence.

The defence is an opportunity to formally accord legitimacy to the PhD student. In the design of a conventional social science PhD in the Global North, completing the degree is the process by which a student becomes a scholar capable of undertaking an independent research project. Authorship is often a requirement of the PhD. In the world of peer-reviewed research, recognition of who deserves authorship is a significant ethical issue. Publishing is also a currency used to evaluate researchers, and it is also about value, recognition, and reputation. Sole authorship is often viewed as the most prized currency. The order of authorship takes into conscious consideration which one made the most substantial intellectual and labour-intensive contributions. For this reason, in this case – the final output of a PhD – the dissertation is usually deemed to be written by a single author.

Furthermore, the defence can be described as a culminating ceremonial performance where, if successful, the student becomes an authority on a given topic.[5] The defence allows the student to demonstrate their mastery of the study area while also presenting them with an opportunity to be subject to scholarly questioning and criticism by the academic community in their discipline. Through the process of defending the dissertation, the student demonstrates their ability to engage in a high-calibre scholarly debate. Through the defence structure, the student is accountable and evaluated by the other experts in the room, the established scholars from the same discipline, and the external examiner from the same field and a recognized authority on the topic.

The defence as a ceremony enshrines a particular scholastic and elite culture that is in tension with the principles of CES that I incorporated earlier in the research. In particular, these principles are challenged by both the requirement of sole authorship and the evaluative component of the PhD by non-members of the community.

First, when my dissertation was sent for examination and I was preparing for the oral defence, it felt like the project became more individualized and independent, almost wholly detached from the activist reality that I came to know so well. Throughout my work, participants' perspectives had been central during the analysis and writing phase; I constantly thought about how to acknowledge and recognize the community who granted me access and who shared their thoughts, knowledge, and ideas with me. However, sole authorship is a requirement of the PhD, which contrasts with the collaborative nature in earlier work stages. Since I had primarily been preparing alone, especially during the COVID-19 pandemic, this point was made even more palpable when isolated in my home office. The realization of the structure of the academic process of authorship truly dawned on me as I prepared for the defence.

Second, I had been steeped in the movement's activities for two years. It seemed logical, if I was to be scrutinized by academic experts, that I should also be scrutinized by those people I was claiming to represent. If the defence's central goal is for the student to speak to the academy, when does the student speak back to the research participants? Where do the ethics of accountability fit into this room of experts whom the research is *not* about? Who holds evaluative power? Still, when I was meant to defend my findings, the defence's conventional structure meant that I would be more accountable to the examining committee than to the community.

These related quandaries made me reflect deeply on how I could make the defence a more equitable and inclusive experience that continues to respect reciprocity and accountability. The inclusion of community voices in the last stage of my PhD, the oral defence, was of paramount importance.

HOW THIS CHAPTER CAME TOGETHER

This piece is based on the PhD research process, the defence, and discussions between three former research participants – Jaivet Ealom, Saifullah Muhammad, and Yusuf Zine – and the researcher. To develop this chapter, the author and contributors had a debriefing session after the defence and subsequent conversations about what the defence and the research meant to their activism more broadly. These discussions also revealed that the act of co-writing reinforces the challenges that someone who is not an academic may confront. The benefits of being involved in writing may not be apparent or even serve contributors' personal and professional goals. The contributors to this chapter come from various backgrounds, and writing is an addition to their already busy lives as activists and professionals in other sectors. As such, this chapter is also the product of a compromise.

Thus, the layout of the chapter reflects the available time that could be committed to the chapter, and the content illuminates what can be publicly said about allies involved in the same cause. As a PhD researcher, I am familiar with academic writing and professionally stand to benefit more directly from the writing process. And, as an ally, it is the researcher's responsibility to make room for the voices that they contend are at the centre of their research. The onus is on them to engage in a meaningful and non-tokenistic way with the community. This idea goes back to the point on sole authorship that I could not avoid in the dissertation, but which I intentionally sought to dispel in other publications such as this one. Yet, also due to the author's position as an academic and ally, the power relations make it so that, because the work is useful as a political tool, criticisms of the work may not be elaborated upon. And to achieve specific goals, it may be politically strategic to focus on the more positive qualities of the work and leave criticisms unsaid. Although this may not be the main reason why my actions are described positively by the contributors, it remains important to be transparent about these possible reasons and the power relations embedded within this chapter. This section thus underscores the chapter's methodology while also explaining the types of pressures that occur when navigating whose voices are included in writing.

ADDRESSING THE QUANDARY: AUTHORSHIP AND EVALUATION

Although procedural and standardized research ethics required by universities usually only cover the information-gathering and analysis phase, ethics are not neatly and linearly resolved after the conclusion of these phases. They are ongoing, perhaps particularly in research where the object of study is geared toward social justice ends, and the researcher is also social justice–oriented. So I knew that I would need to continue to engage with the principles of reciprocity and accountability, to chart the path forward. I took a few deliberate steps to ensure that ethics were included until the last stage of my PhD, the oral defence. I wanted to build a mechanism by which there was reciprocity toward and dual accountability for both measures of scholarly research and the people involved. The rest of the section describes the steps I took to make the defence more responsive to these principles that are in tension with the structure of the PhD.

Authorship

To establish continued reciprocity and accountability to participants, I attempted to settle the first tension on authorship. I invited many former participants who I was still in communication with to the defence. It was much easier for former participants who would otherwise have had to travel to join as it was a virtual defence. I also asked my supervisor if community members would be allowed to ask questions, similarly to how the examining committee would ask me questions. She agreed and asked the chair, who also built time into the defence for this purpose. I reached out again to the activists I was closest with and asked them if they were interested in attending the defence while clarifying that they could pose questions if they wanted to. Another step I took was to send my presentation to a Rohingya friend (a former research participant) and practice my defence in front of a group of Rohingya friends (also former research participants). This step served a triple purpose. First, I could practice my presentation in preparation for the defence. Second, I could fine-tune points and highlight aspects that were important to them based on their feedback. Third, doing a mock defence and then explaining the process about the defence to them also meant that the research participants would know what to expect and be prepared for the experience. I also asked research participants who would be present if I could attribute quotes from my dissertation to them in the presentation, to acknowledge their presence and contributions.[6]

Three former participants reflected on what the research project and inclusion in the defence signified to them. First, Saifullah Muhammad, one of the founders of the Canadian Rohingya Development Initiative, spoke to the relationship built throughout the years:

> Being a Rohingya, I feel delighted with her work, and on behalf of our entire community, I would like to thank her for choosing this topic. I

> have worked with Yuriko for three years. I can proudly say she is one of the few non-Rohingya researchers who personally knows Rohingya people, their leadership, the up-to-date situation, and the community's internal issues – more so than anyone else. She has dedicated her time to help Rohingya people in Canada, Bangladesh, and the refugee camps. She helped to establish the foundation of the Rohingya advocacy organization, the Canadian Rohingya Development Initiative. She still supports the initiative even after her PhD is complete. Most of the Rohingya leaders worldwide respect her and invite her to participate in different academic conferences. There is very little academic research on Rohingya. We look forward to working with Yuriko in the future, as her bold research will undoubtedly invite future collaboration and bring more awareness about our people. May she continue to inspire and enrich her future.

Second, Yusuf Zine, one of *I Am Rohingya*'s director-producers, noted the following:

> There are few other scholars I have come across who can successfully immerse themselves in the community that they are studying, like Yuriko – so much so that we, the Canadian Rohingya community, called her an honorary Rohingya. While Yuriko has successfully filled a knowledge gap with her research, which we hope many others will find helpful, I believe that it will not be the last. I can easily picture Yuriko connecting dots and making sense of academically untouched areas. I am eager to see more of her work in the near future.

This inclusionary process allowed the examining committee and the audience to witness the relationship that former participants had with me. Although there were only about twenty-five people among the total of seventy participants, and it was over the Microsoft Teams video, it was still an occasion for the examining committee to understand who was a part of the research and with whom I had built relationships, which provided insight into knowledge (co)production.

Evaluation

To continue with reciprocity and accountability, I then attempted to address the tension of evaluation. The defence was also a window of opportunity for community members to voice their approval or disapproval of my approach and the content of my presentation. The defence was a fairly standard procedure until the question period. I delivered a twenty-five-minute presentation to the audience. The three Rohingya participants who asked me questions had the chance to comment and to share information that they deemed critical to highlight that I either did not know, missed, or did not have time to broach. Another former participant, a key figure in Rohingya youth's early organizing efforts in Canada, also posed a question. The questions they asked were highly relevant and provided the group with more nuanced detail about the movement. They pointed out work that the movement had conducted that I had not mentioned in my presentation, and they raised points about the dynamics of the movement that I had not touched upon. And, the remaining twenty-one audience members were witnesses to the way I formulated my responses. Yusuf spoke to this point on the dynamic in the defence:

> It was an incredibly fulfilling experience to be in attendance at Yuriko's defence. Having witnessed her dogged research over the past few years and seeing it culminate into a powerful body of work was a joy. Her ability to reflect on every question asked during the defence demonstrated her carefulness, sensitivity, and in-depth analysis. We've spent a lot of time together discussing the nuances of this kind of work, and I can confidently say she has taught me a lot. I'm so glad her research exists to fill a gap in the academic literature relating to the Rohingya crisis.

Saifullah also shared his perspectives on the defence:

> I was extremely pleased to be invited to Yuriko Cowper-Smith's dissertation defence. The worst part about the virtual defence was that we weren't able to truly celebrate together. It was my first time attending such a dissertation defence. I felt like it was almost exactly the same as attending an academic talk. Pursuing a PhD is difficult, but I feel proud that her presentation was accurate with reliable information and brought up the Rohingya people's real situation.

Jaivet Ealom, another member of the Canadian Rohingya Development Initiative, noted his perspective:

> I had the privilege to witness Yuriko's work: collecting data from remote members of the Rohingya community and cleaning and making sense of them – in a spontaneous manner – while the crisis was ongoing. Yet

> it was a truly unique experience to watch her bring all the loose ends together and connect the dots and defend her work in front of some of the most respected scholars in the field.

The defence also supported some members of the community to appreciate a different view of their activism, as remarked on by Jaivet:

> While we are in the field – or the valley – of activism, we tend to miss the broader picture of our work. Yuriko's dissertation was a zoomed out, eagle-eye view of the whole movement. Her research helps us to see a more comprehensive picture. During the defence, the discussions provided some constructive criticism of some of the things we might have missed, could do better, or not looked at from her perspectives. We continue to reflect on what her findings mean for our work and what is useful to absorb for our goals.

Former participants asking me questions was an avenue of direct accountability to them and a way to address evaluation in at least two ways. First, having representatives of the movement in the room was deference to *their* mastery of the subject area, which is an argument that I make in the body of the dissertation. This is a central claim of my dissertation, but the writing is no replacement for their life's work, and their expertise and enthusiasm were evident through their presence in the meeting. Their being able to "test" me by asking questions and feeding the rest of the audience more information reinforced their position of authority on the topic of discussion – the Rohingya Canadian social movement. Second, the inclusion of community voices also allowed the examining committee and others to acknowledge the appraisal offered by the people represented in the dissertation.

Expect the Unexpected: Navigating Reciprocity and Accountability within PhD Parameters

There were several dynamics that I did not sufficiently anticipate. I did not fully brace myself, or the invited participants, for how the questions asked by the examining committee might make them feel. The questions were obviously valid scholarly questions. Still, it was also possible that *how* I answered the questions could have been upsetting and deeply personal for those participants in the room. As Clark-Kazak et al. (2017, 12) discuss under the principle of self-determination, research should "uphold the dignity of our respondents in our portrayal of them – individually and collectively." I wanted to ensure that I answered the questions to satisfy both academic requirements, including scholarly ethics,[7] *and* sensitivity to the power dynamics in the room. This consideration should always be the rule, but having former participants in the same room as the researcher heightened that requirement. If I were not careful, I could have tapped into very intimate intrapersonal dynamics based on gender, age, and political affiliations that former participants are a part of, and would implicate individual people in the room in my responses.[8] This self-imposed structure of the community-as-witness/participant defence made it so that I had to adhere to reciprocity and accountability to the people whom my research was about – yet fulfilling this requirement of authorship and evaluation compelled me to answer in some manner.

So when queries arose that implicated the dynamics of the people in the room, I had to make on-the-spot decisions about how to answer, to not raise any personal sensitivities. Indeed, for example, I was questioned about the "messiness" or "interpersonal" dynamics that occur during movement-building by my examining committee. I had not foreseen these questions, and any critical perspective of the movement would have directly impacted people in the room. So I answered the questions by pointing to generalized examples that, I hope, were broad enough not to cause embarrassment, annoyance, or harm, yet detailed enough to meet the examiner's expectation. If I sensed that the question would be impossible to answer without causing any of these feelings, I explained why I could not go further into the issue. For example, on a question related to age, because there were generations of activists in the room I did not want to be critical of either older or younger generations, or intimately discuss the dynamics between age groups. In this case, in my answer, I said that I could not go further.

This type of fumbling or awkwardness that I felt when answering the questions resulted from trying to bridge the tensions between reciprocity and accountability, and authorship and evaluation in perhaps a messy manner. And despite the above laudatory comments, in retrospect, when I sought to address authorship and evaluation by integrating former participants into the defence, there was little genuine inclusion. The former participants could ask questions and were witnesses but, ultimately, they had little weight in the formal evaluation. At best, I was able to achieve a tacit acknowledgment of their expertise and contributions and a simultaneous evaluation: the scholarly community conducting a conventional evaluation and some members of the community evaluating me through their questions, the presentation, and their witnessing of my handling of community questions.

CONSIDERATIONS FOR THE FUTURE?

In this chapter, we see that the principles of reciprocity and accountability are strained by the conventional academic structure of the PhD defence, namely in respect to authorship and evaluation. In an attempt to overcome these tensions, I tried to reconcile both the academy's requirements and the community's needs, which produced both positive and some unintended effects. Nevertheless, even in the culminating end performance, where students become "experts" and perform "their expertise" and are judged based on the merit of other scholars, it is possible for considerations of community-engaged scholarship to be included. In hindsight, I wish I had revisited the broader literature on CES research ethics in more depth to answer my dilemma and to offer me robust guidance in the moment of the defence. Although I revisited my methodology chapter, talked with my supervisor, and continued living the principles of reciprocity and accountability until the defence stage, I did not wholly map out what that process entailed with concerted intention. To attend to these principles and the built-in sensitivities in forced migration research, I propose that future CES studies include a CES component at the end of the research project. Upon this reflection, I now draw on Suet-ling Tang's (2008) work with Khmer (Cambodian) American communities in Massachusetts and the principles outlined by Clark-Kazak et al. (2017) to guide future practice.

What would such a scenario look like in the future? When reciprocity, accountability, authorship, and evaluation collide, there are several ways the research design can be built deliberately to serve both academic and community goals. Suet-ling Tang (2008) discusses sites of discussion and how they can be embedded in the research design. For Suet-ling Tang (2008, 243) "at the core of this theory/practice is the enabling of people from communities of struggle to have direct control and full power over how to explore and use their knowledge, skills, and capacities to imagine and build community." She continues:

> While some community practitioners already have the "tools" to engage in the critical analysis of social relations and the theoretical exploration of the work they do – perhaps in collaboration with scholar-activists who are seeking new forms of knowledge to advance their academic work – others do not have or prefer such tools. Those without such tools need to create, develop, and refine methodologies for promoting their Indigenous knowledge systems and for becoming better positioned and empowered to represent and advocate for their communities. (Suet-ling Tang 2008, 243)

Suet-ling Tang (2008) points out that creating opportunities – or sites – for dialogue and discussion with community members is a way not only to document, analyze, or present the needs/problems of the community but also to initiate conversation and further reflections to deepen their collective awareness of how to make progress. For instance, her story-sharing process "produced critical evidence about deeper, unresolved contradictions within the community, reflecting the larger cultural-historical context by which Khmer self-definitions as 'refugees' are intersecting with and challenging those of 'citizens,' 'minorities,' and 'Americans.' These multifaceted identities and self-representations complicate the evidence yielded about evolving communities" (Suet-ling Tang 2008, 255).

These sites are ever more critical for Suet-ling Tang due to community activists' personal and professional constraints; they are opportunities for participants to continue building capacity in their work. She shows that it is possible to create methodologies that can serve community purposes, and the process of research can be used creatively for the goals of a social movement. As Suet-ling Tang (2008, 261) concludes,

> I have always felt that the most intellectually stimulating and challenging place to carry out my publicly engaged work is not at the center of dominant academic and public discourses but rather in those in between spaces of *nepantla*[9] and constant transformation. In continually crossing disciplinary boundaries and connecting academia and wider publics, *nepantla* itself is a bridge, an always-in-transition space, a place where different sides and multiple perspectives can be simultaneously seen and heard.

Perhaps, as Suet-ling Tang (2008) proposes, the defence can become a site where activists could visualize and contemplate their years of work from different angles and other points brought up during the questioning. The defence can become, for a community, a moment "not only to uncover and articulate the knowledge that they [community members] possess but also to make their knowledge accessible to others" (Suet-ling Tang 2008, 245). It can become a planned site of conversation that serves as space to "develop, articulate, and assert their own critical, cultural, and analytical perspectives so that resources and strategies can be developed and allocated more fairly and creatively" (244). The defence, as a site, would offer opportunities for building "skills of collecting, validating, interpreting, and translating community data ... while making central and visible their own on-the-ground experiences and capacities as bilingual/bicultural leaders" (244). For Suet-ling Tang, there is a broader reach beyond said site's boundaries. By embedding this site into the research design, the study itself "emphasizes the goal of producing knowledge individually and institutionally across multiple arenas, including research, public policy, philanthropy, and, most importantly, communities at the grassroots level – all of which have important roles to play in the course of long-term community development" (245).

What are some other benefits of such an approach? In light of these views, broadly, including a CES component at the end of the research project will enhance reciprocity and accountability and get to these tensions of authorship and evaluation in several other ways. First, it becomes impossible to talk about a community, and their thoughts and perspectives, in an abstract, detached, and perhaps disingenuous manner when they are present in the same room as the researcher. This practice recentres the priorities to be more equitable toward research participants, as this requirement heightens the researcher's obligation to act with the safety of the participants in mind while also attending to the constraints and goals of the academy. Second, related to authorship, the approach places community representatives in a position of authority on the topic of discussion; having former participants in the room humbles the student and their peers by showing that the participants are also those with mastery of the subject area. Third, the inclusion of highly relevant and timely information and questions about the topic at hand offers another angle by which to evaluate the student. This may be the first opportunity for the student's supervisor and other faculty members to meet the people in the research. By virtue of former participants listening and asking questions, the evaluation committee would know if the researcher actually worked with the community they purported to represent and vice versa; community members would have insight into if the researcher was portraying the information given to them respectfully and in an accurate manner.

How would this play out in reality? The defence as a site of discussion would require that the researcher – and the university – consider the following, for example:

- Practising the presentation with community members and incorporating their feedback
- Formally acknowledging their contributions at the beginning of the defence
- Having a second external examiner who is of the community in the research

- Including a community member representative on the formal evaluation committee
- Inviting other community members as witnesses, and for them to ask questions
- Allowing for a formal discussion period after the student's examination
- Planning for sensitivities by recognizing the types of power relations within the room

This is by no means an exhaustive list and these are just examples of the way the process can be more formalized. It will be interesting to document how the defence evolves over time in the academy.

CONCLUSION: WHEN DO ETHICS END?

In this chapter, I use the case of the defence to demonstrate one researcher's attempts to reconcile the requirements of authorship and evaluation embedded within the conventional academic structure of the PhD defence with the CES-based principles of reciprocity and accountability. Perhaps even more importantly in research geared toward serving social justice ends, the researcher's prerogative is to reflect carefully on questions such as "When do ethics end in academic research?"; "Who holds evaluative power?"; and "Whom is the researcher accountable to?" I argue that the researcher's responsibility toward ethics of care exists until – at least – the end of the PhD project and does not stop after data have been collected and written about. Formally including community needs and priorities into the last stage serves to increase reciprocity and accountability to the people represented in the research and attends to other ethical principles inherent in research with people who have experienced forced migration. Though highly imperfect, it is possible, and future projects can continue to explore this tension.

NOTES

1 Clark-Kazak et al. (2017) point out that information-gathering with people who have experienced traumatic experiences, including forced migration, is laden with sensitivities that might not occur in other types of research. Clark-Kazak et al. (2017, 12) highlight the importance of four principles: equity, right to self-determination, competence, and partnership.

2 In my dissertation, I argue that the Rohingya Canadian social movement has developed four types of knowledge-practices (Casas-Cortés, Osterweil, and Powell 2008; della Porta and Pavan 2017) necessary to contend with the genocide in Myanmar and the refugee crisis in Bangladesh. The movement has established an

ethos and its political visions based on collective responsibility, awareness, and resolve. The movement has also figured out how to seize political opportunities and build coalitions with diverse sectors. Further, participants have presented policy options to the Canadian government. Finally, the movement has cultivated its transmission techniques based on affective solidarity to increase engagement (Johnson 2020). In other words, the movement is writing its "how-to" manual for resolving the genocide and refugee crises. The Rohingya Canadian social movement is building the intellectual foundations necessary to build and fuel their cause; they have the "tools to engage in the critical analysis of social relations and the theoretical exploration of the work they do" (Suet-ling Tang 2008, 243).

3 A play and documentary of the same name.

4 In 2020, during the COVID-19 pandemic, defences were performed over Microsoft Teams.

5 The defence is an exam, but the extent to which the defence is ceremonial or an assessment is contextual and depends on the student, their work, and the institution.

6 Although all of the research participants confirmed that this approach was fine, ultimately, I did not incorporate this information because I did not want to make anyone feel uncomfortable or risk the possibility of someone accidentally attributing quotes to them after the defence. The only quotes that I attributed were those that had already been made public.

7 A scholarly ethic is that one cannot falsify or suppress data.

8 I could have potentially broken their trust, which Clark-Kazak et al. (2017, 12) state is a key part of treating participants equitably.

9 As Suet-Ling (2008, 237) notes, "Nepantla, the space in between, is a dynamic place of transformation within which American studies and ethnic studies scholars have increasingly positioned themselves."

REFERENCES

Casas-Cortés, M., M. Osterweil, and D. Powell. 2008. "Blurring Boundaries: Recognizing Knowledge-Practices in the Study of Social Movements." *Anthropological Quarterly* 81, 1: 17–58. doi.org/10.1353/anq.2008.0006.

Clark-Kazak, C., Canadian Council for Refugees, Canadian Association for Refugee and Forced Migration Studies, and York University's Centre for Refugee Studies. 2017. "Ethical Considerations: Research with People in Situations of Forced Migration." *Refuge* 33, 2: 11–17. doi.org/10.7202/1043059ar.

della Porta, D., and E. Pavan. 2017. "Repertoires of Knowledge Practices: Social Movements in Times of Crisis." *Qualitative Research in Organizations and Management: An International Journal* 12, 4: 297–314. doi.org/10.1108/QROM-01-2017-1483.

Gibbes, C., and E. Skop. 2020. "The Messiness of Co-produced Research with Gatekeepers of Resettled Refugee Communities." *Journal of Cultural Geography* 37, 3: 278–95. doi.org/10.1080/08873631.2020.1759981.

Johnson, C. 2020. "Responsibility, Affective Solidarity and Transnational Maternal Feminism." *Feminist Theory* 21, 2: 175–98. doi.org/10.1177/1464700119859768.

Suet-ling Tang, S. 2008. "Community-Centered Research as Knowledge/Capacity Building in Immigrant and Refugee Communities." In *Engaging Contradictions Theory, Politics, and Methods of Activist Scholarship*, edited by C. Hale, 237–64. Berkeley: University of California Press.

13

"But Where Is the Violence?"

REFLECTIONS ON HONOURING RELATIONSHIPS AND TROUBLING ACADEMIA

Lara Rosenoff Gauvin

(A COLLECTION OF ACTUAL COMMUNICATIONS AND FEEDBACK FROM SCHOLARS AND INTERNATIONAL NON-GOVERNMENTAL ORGANIZATION WORKERS)

But where is the violence? Where is the violence?

How can you say that violence is unimportant?

Surely, this community is not as organized as you say?
As YOU say?

Or if they are … they are surely the exception … exceptional … exceptionally organized …

You mean, communal land rights

LAND

RIGHTS land rights land rights land rights

are important to post-war social reconstruction?

Oh, so maybe USAID shouldn't be having private-property workshops right now?

I believe that the community is as organized and as rational as YOU SAY … but that is incredible, as there are also witch burnings happening only three hours away …

BURNINGS, INFIGHTING, MURDER …

BUT … WHERE IS THE VIOLENCE in your article?

WHERE

IS

THE

VIOLENCE in the community?
BUT
BUT
BUT
WHERE
IS
THE
VIOLENCE
You can't tell me that people don't get into fights when drinking sometimes, can you?
?
?
?
How can you say that violence is unimportant?

INTRODUCTION

I have worked with an extended family (clan) in Northern Uganda for over fifteen years. I met members of *Kaka* Pabwoc (Pabwoc clan) while they were internally displaced in Padibe Internally Displaced Persons' (IDP) camp as a result of the war between the Ugandan government and the Lord's Resistance Army. Between 2004 and 2008, I was able to make annual visits to the IDP camp and then visited them back on their ancestral lands for the first time in 2010. In 2012, I conducted eight months of research on their ancestral lands of Pabwoc and continued, in 2015 and 2018, to work with this same community. As an anthropologist who prioritizes community-driven research, I strove at that time to highlight Acoli Indigenous concepts and practices of justice and social repair, in order to both support and understand how one rural-based extended family sought to rebuild their lives, homes, and community after two decades of forced displacement and intracommunity violence.

This chapter dwells in the spaces between research, relationships, and responsibilities. Specifically, I focus on why my research should amplify community *aspirations* of reconciliation and *ribbe kaka* (clan unity), rather than expose any clan disagreements. I take the opportunity, too, to delve into the dilemmas that arose from other academics' reactions to my choices and their feelings of being "troubled" by my personal and activist position as a working and living academic. I then take a moment to examine and reflect on some of the violence of the academy through a penchant for erasure – of my own research relationships and familial knowledge and relationships – and reflect on whether my idea and practice of "research" conforms to anthropological academic standards as a result of the choices I have made.

SOME BACKGROUND

In 2012 I conducted eight months of fieldwork in Pabwoc village, Northern Uganda, with people who self-identify as Acoli. I had known some of the residents of Pabwoc – members of Kaka Pabwoc (Pabwoc clan) – since 2004, when they were still living, displaced, in Padibe IDP camp, about eight kilometres from their ancestral lands. The extended family was first displaced from their lands in 1999, when the Lord's Resistance Army began attacks close by. Most of the families in Pabwoc went to the closest town of Kitgum and were hosted in tents in a primary school, but when cholera broke out and the fighting between the Lord's Resistance Army and the Ugandan government got more intense in their district, the government opened more IDP camps closer to rural villages, in their home subcounties. Newly displaced communities and those who had already fled to the town were guided to their local IDP camp (or so-called protected villages), in this case in Padibe subcounty. While some returned to their ancestral lands for some time in 2003, fighting and Ugandan government mandates forced them back into Padibe IDP camp after a few months.

The IDP camps in those years of intense fighting have been described by Chris Dolan (2009) as purposeful "social torture" by government due to a lack of funding and neglect that resulted in hunger and unsanitary conditions leading to massive amounts of disease. Life in the IDP camps also undermined Acoli Indigenous sustenance (economic), governance, and legal structures (Branch 2011), and "people from different clans were just all mixed up and squeezed together, away from their lands, relying on NGOS to survive" (Beatrice, personal communication 2008). The Ugandan Ministry of Health (2005) reported an excess mortality rate in the IDP camps of one thousand people per week.

Aside from these desperate, inhumane conditions, the Lord's Resistance Army would also abduct Acoli youth and force them to violence, often against their own families. The Ugandan military would also recruit other Acoli youth to fight the formerly abducted youth. This resulted in twenty years of what Acoli scholar Opiyo Oloya has called a time of "unprecedented Acoli on Acoli violence" (2013, 7).

When I finally arrived in Acoliland – the Ugandan districts primarily inhabited by people who self-identify as Acoli (Kitgum, Pader, Lamwo,

Gulu, Agago, Amuru, Nwoya, Omoro districts) – on my seventh visit, after all this, during peacetime, and with residents back home on their ancestral lands, most people were still trying to rebuild old huts and granaries, clear and plant new fields to feed their families, and pick up the pieces after about twenty years of the forced intracommunal war and, in many instances, forced intraclan violence. I was interested in what that looked like on the ground and was particularly interested – following the interests of the community – in the roles that intergenerational Indigenous knowledge played in these complex everyday processes (see Rosenoff Gauvin 2013 as to why). I was interested in this particularly, and in working with communities, because I was hearing a singular and very narrow discussion of "traditional justice" versus "transitional justice" in national and international academic and policy circles that I found excluded some of the very voices, and actions, of the people at the heart of the issues.

Although I engaged with community questions of youth being "out of culture" as a result of the war, I did not ask many specific questions about the war or the violence during my eight-month time in Pabwoc in 2012. My grandparents survived the Holocaust during the Second World War, and my own research is greatly informed by my location as (1) a granddaughter of survivors of mass violence and (2) a settler scholar in what is now known as Canada.

From the first location, growing up with my grandmother (my grandfather died when I was two), who experienced the murder of her family and who witnessed ever more horrifying violence, I learned that knowledge about these kinds of experiences is shared mostly in particular circumstances that cannot, and should not, be readily provoked by outside questions. Perhaps it is what some call a "trauma-informed" approach, but for me it was just navigating my somewhat intimidating and serious maternal grandmother. From her, I learned that stories are shared when and if people are ready to share and also that stories of survival and repair are sometimes more valued than those of violence and destruction.

The second location that influences my research is that of being a settler scholar in what is now known as Canada. Despite attending a Jewish day school that highlighted genocide and cultural survival, we never learned about the genocide of the Indigenous Peoples of Turtle Island and beyond. I only began later in life to consider my own complicity in the ongoing violence experienced by Indigenous peoples and examining my academic work and research in light of that complicity – as a white privileged woman enjoying the fruits of settler colonialism in Canada and of continuing imperialism globally – to actively strive to respectful and collaborative purposes, approaches, epistemologies, and methodologies in my work. Furthermore, an acknowledgment that my family was able to accrue wealth because of reparation payments from the German government (my grandmother worked in a garment factory and my grandfather died young), which allowed for my formal education, is also paramount to understanding my positionality. When thinking of my own understanding of my familial histories of violence, I also ponder how most people acknowledged the reality of the Second World War's holocaust while I was growing up, as opposed to rampant denial about the genocide of Indigenous people.

Upon reflection, these two stances are essential factors in my ongoing grappling with what it means, for me, to conduct ethical anthropological research, specifically, what research about violence should or could be and what it should not and cannot be.

WHERE IS THE VIOLENCE?

I had returned from my PhD fieldwork and in 2013 met with some professors at my university to talk about the time I spent in Pabwoc and my plans for writing it up. I remember presenting work that privileged the idea of ribbe kaka (clan unity) and explored different methods of Acoli Indigenous intergenerational knowledge transmission that were being used to rebuild life and community after the war. I took the professors through some chapter ideas that explored these practices of social repair – detailing Pabwoc's clan history and everyday life three years after their return to their ancestral lands.

Thinking with my host community's wants and needs in mind and heeding contemporary Ugandan scholars (for example, Nakayi 2011; J.J. Oloya 2015; O. Oloya 2013), it made sense to tell this story *of ongoing efforts* to rebuild home and community after twenty years of forced war and displacement and, thus, be part of those efforts, even if just in some small way through my methodologies and writings. I was particularly struck by the ideas and practices embedded in Acoli Indigenous law and governance and in the newly written clan constitutions I learned about while I was writing (see Bobi-Pabwoc Foundation 2014, as an example). Embedding these explorations of Acoli concepts of *roco wat* (restoring social relations or social repair) in dialogue with post-conflict ideas about transitional justice, I also found generative teachings in the work of Acoli scholar and poet Okot p'Bitek (1963, 1973, 1986, 2011), who wrote about Acoli oral tradition, cultural philosophy, and decolonizing perspectives.

Needless to say ... I received some pushback in that initial meeting.

But SURELY not EVERYONE feels this way, that clan unity is to be sought?
What about the youth?
Do they all AGREE?
What happens when people drink at night?
What do people argue about?
What are the histories of conflict and disagreement?
Don't some want to own their land privately, rather than communally?
And what about the women?
Do they agree?
WHAT ABOUT WOMEN'S RIGHTS?

Feeling flustered ... and a little angry – I remember thinking that I'm no tabloid reporter! – I answered honestly. Yes, there are disagreements, as all communities have. And yes, various people within the clan are fighting for what they believe in, which can be at odds with the majority, as everywhere. But the reason there is a functioning legal-political-economic system – at least from what I can see and learned in Pabwoc – is because enough residents believe in ribbe kaka (clan unity) and their accompanying Indigenous legal order (Napoleon 2007) that it has, in reality, helped restore stability after two decades of forced displacement and war. To be sure, the reasons for this belief are varied, but ribbe kaka, as I wrote, is not simply some utopian or spiritual ideal of togetherness and forgiveness. Rather, it is rooted in human-land relations and the necessity of clan unity in order for people to access land and be a part of a community that can help assure survival and that aspires to well-being on those lands. As John Jaramogi Oloya explains (2015), clans and subclans as "kin-based communal governance organizations" have always served these purposes in Acoli society, and so it is not at all unfathomable, unbelievable, or romantic, even, to acknowledge that they would aspire to the same after two decades of war and displacement.

Participating in the daily life of Pabwoc village (as much as I was able), I learned that an integral part of life at that time – or in rebuilding their lives, or social reconstruction, or social repair – was to somehow decentre the experienced forced wartime violence, to almost bracket it away, as much as humanly possible, from their everyday "post-war" lives. It was not to deny or ignore the violence per se, but to refuse (Simpson 2016) to be defined by the wartime's forced violences and the radical attack on self, home, community, and Indigenous governance and law that the war provoked.

I wrote about this refusal – what I learned from members of Pabwoc and from Mohawk scholar Audra Simpson – and modelled my PhD thesis and articles to also, in solidarity, refuse singular descriptions of "war-affected" communities. Consistently, however, I would get comments like those above questioning both the veracity and value of research that pointed to a resurgence in Indigenous governance and law upon a return to ancestral lands. I was even asked by a different university's committee on a grant application to be more skeptical or to point out the negative potentials of Indigenous governance, and I was asked to make detailed notes of what may go wrong within these forms of Indigenous sovereignties(!).

In the rest of this chapter, I would like to explore this odd, infuriating, dilemma in my research practice, examine what other work helped guide and assist me in naming the main issues and, finally, consider how the dilemma ultimately impacted the way I conceive of myself as a researcher today.

RESEARCH AS HONOURING RELATIONSHIPS

I held firm in not exposing and delving into wounds in my host community for several reasons, but the instinct was, at first, grounded not in ethics or ethos per se, but in the facts of "participant observation," the method upon which anthropology is based and in which I was trained. And those facts clearly show that the disagreements, ruptures, arguments, and fights, although present in Pabwoc over the eight months that I lived there (and which are, of course, present in any family or community), were not, in fact, very frequent or significant and did not detract from the overall efforts and everyday activities that served to bring the community together to rebuild, live, and perform social repair. In fact, the postwar and post-displacement, newly resurgent Indigenous governance structures have always been there to serve the community in this way and others: to respond to disagreement and conflict as all governance and legal orders aspire to do. Highlighting only disagreement and conflict never occurred to me, and my decision to explore and examine aspects of Indigenous knowledge, governance, and intergenerational relationships was not, at the outset, a result of any ethical considerations at all but of classic ethnographic methods.

However, the more I began to explore Indigenous and Afrocentric scholarship about methodologies (for example, Mkabela 2005; Parent 2011), coupled with the bewilderment I encountered in academia, the more I began to understand that my research practice, and any storytelling associated with it, was perhaps not the traditional academic norm that focused on violence and conflict on the African continent at that time.

When fellow academics ask incredulously, "Well, how can that be?" I am not quite sure what to answer. Why is it unbelievable for a community recovering from violence and upheaval to call for unity and to practise that unity through Indigenous governance? I do not think anyone would put the question that way. But if the description is of a rural patrilineal clan in post-war Northern Uganda emerging from twenty years of forced intracommunity war with the widespread use of child soldiers ... well, reactions have tended to be different. I can say that to speak of Indigenous governance and resurgence on the African continent and, generally, conversations of social repair (Shaw 2007) perhaps diverges from current anthropological concerns or general theoretical trends, or perhaps smacks of naive romanticism to some, but I also think that structural and theoretical racism play a role as well.

In response, I usually just point to my time living in Pabwoc as a participant-learner and speak about what people actually did in their day-to-day lives. Although interviews are important tools, and I did do many throughout the course of eight months and over the past fifteen years, it was, indeed, the relational day-to-day living and practices and casual conversations that formed the strongest, or most rooted, knowledge that was shared with me. This was the hallmark of anthropology, I had thought. This seems like an odd thing to defend in my chosen field. I further tallied the topics of casual conversations in my field notes, reviewed clan meeting notes, correlated answers from a village-wide survey, and corroborated time spent on everyday activities to prove or back up these teachings – as was requested of me by a university examiner. Indeed, I communicated the full "data" or knowledge I acquired through people's generosity and co-creation to back up these "bewildering" claims – as I was asked to do, and as I was made to doubt what I had been taught by my experiences with my host community.

But how could that be?
Surely "your" village is exceptional, then.

What about the women?
The youth?
Surely they cannot all agree?
Where is the discord? Where are the arguments?
Maybe they are hiding it from you?
???
Where is the violence?

I am going to recount here two conversations I had with people in Uganda as I was leaving Pabwoc after my main period of post-conflict fieldwork in 2012. The first was with a non-governmental organization worker in Kitgum town – a Dutch academic I met, who was coordinating efforts of a Ugandan-based advocacy and research group. This man, who had been working in Northern Uganda for a few years, asked me about my work and about village life. When I told him about Kaka Pabwoc and the degree of communal Indigenous governance and law practised – from land allotment to dispute resolution – and the way I, preliminarily at that point, understood social repair to be functioning within, he exclaimed that Pabwoc must be very "unique" in Acoliland. He had never heard of "that level" of governance and organization in rural communities despite the fact that he often worked with "traditional leaders" in addition to local government representatives.

The second conversation took place at Makerere University, in Kampala. I sat down for some tea in the university café with Professor Okello Ogwang, who self-identifies as Lango and was my supervisor when I was a research associate at the Makerere Institute for Social Research. He asked me, after all this time in Pabwoc, what my impressions were. I described that, primarily, I had learned how active and important Indigenous governance (the clans, sub-clans, and chiefdoms) was in moving on after the war, and in everyday life in general. Upon the residents' return to ancestral lands and the system of customary communal land tenure, these kin-networks – Indigenous governance – had quickly sprung back after their suppression in the IDP camps to organize daily life and provide relative social, economic, legal, and political order and stability. Unlike the Dutch academic, Ogwang showed little surprise. He replied that made a lot of sense. "After all, Lara, people project themselves onto and manage the land and themselves in ways that they know how to and in ways that they have done for centuries."

I wonder how outsiders, originally including myself, could not know (or have known) about the strength and range and persistence of Indigenous governance in Acoliland. I wonder how much these "invisibilities" may point to my (our) own cultural biases and, yes, theoretical racism regarding a supposed vacuum of capable governance, or Indigenous sovereignties, on what is now known as the African continent. And I wonder how much these biases are tied to enduring grand narratives, like *terra nullius* (as explored by Abbink et al. 2014; Makki 2014), the doctrine of discovery, and even "transitional justice," that perpetuate the continuing domination of the Majority World by the Minority World. I wonder to what degree the "fictions" of truth, named justice, serve to uphold the powers and narratives that actually work to dominate (Clarke 2009) and, important to my own research, to also dominate the role of knowledge production (and the researcher) therein.

The bewilderment and sometimes outright anger that I have encountered from many academics speaks, perhaps, to this racism and paternalism or, perhaps, even to the colonizing impacts and sometimes invisible or subconscious legacies of academic theoretical engagements. While the bias and racism of academia has been well documented (Smith 1999 is but one example) and the problem with damage-centred research insightfully detailed (Tuck 2009), pervasive, deep, arguably liberal forms of academic and institutional racism prevail.

Can you believe that these children are beaten?
BEATEN by their aunts when they return from the bush?
The stigma the women face
STIGMA from their OWN communities
force them into ever more precarious positions.
Women do not even have the right to own land!

While the preceding observations are indeed correct – some children did face enormous stigma and hardship when returning to their communities after escaping abduction, and unmarried mothers do face hardships, as examples – there are many, many, many more examples of both children and unmarried mothers who were helped by their families and extended kin-networks, and who themselves set up support networks and sometimes more formal civil society organizations to assist. For example, in the village-wide survey I conducted in Pabwoc in 2012, over one-third of the homesteads were occupied by adult daughters of Pabwoc, or maternal grandchildren of Pabwoc (Rosenoff Gauvin 2016). This means that though many of the actual residents of Pabwoc (these daughters and children of daughters) do not "strictly" have access to land (or "land rights") through so-called customary patrilineal land tenure practices, the lived reality of what one Western academic has even called "fundamentalist patrilineal ideology" (Whyte 2012) is a wholly inaccurate description of the living fluid systems of Acoli Indigenous governance and law. And so, while it is important to document those children and women who do fall through the cracks of "patrilineal" and "patrilocal" practices, should one not also document how kin-networks and Indigenous governance *actually* work to support the vast majority of their own people?

I make this point here because it is very common in so-called activist human rights research to document the difficulties faced by marginalized and precarious individuals and communities. And it is arguably important to do so. Yet Unangax̂ scholar Eve Tuck's warning about damage-centred research (2009) and key Afrocentric scholar Ama Mazama's work on Afrocentric theory (2001) both ask about the short- and long-term consequences of a singular focus on damage and oppression. Tuck further asserts that this type of documentation is actually founded on a false theory of change rooted in Western litigation.

I learn much from these incredible women and relate their work to a critical engagement with *terra nullius*, the doctrine of discovery, and other colonial and neo-colonial domination projects. If scholarship itself highlights only a lack of governance, a lack of social support, a lack of organization, a lack of knowledge, and a lack of compassion; if scholarship only highlights "a lack of" or "absence of" in *other* people's communities – the bread of some so-called activist human rights research – then the space described, the community, the often-Indigenous or marginalized or precarious community space is left open, "begging" to be controlled, or intervened in, and even researched by outsiders.

But I want to be clear here, too, and bring questions of ethical and community-led research back to the researcher themself and to an ethical reckoning with that role. What is the role of the researcher within all these nuances and textures of violence, domination, racism, resurgence, and repair? Which stories does the researcher tell, in what places, and for what purposes?

IN CONCLUSION, MY GRANDMOTHER

When I was writing up my PhD, I situated myself, my positionality, like I did here, so that the reader could better understand the story I was telling about Pabwoc and my ethical grappling with doing research with individuals and a community who have experienced extreme violence. I devoted a chapter in my thesis to "methods" in this way, detailing at the outset of the chapter my own familial history with violence, the wisdom passed down from my grandmother, Mania Singer, and how my own life history intertwined with my host family's and others in Pabwoc and Northern Uganda in the thirteen years I had been engaged there. My own upbringing influenced everything from how I ended up in Uganda in the first place, and the kinds of questions posed to me as a Jew for whom "religion and culture are still one" (Angelo, spoken personal communication, April 2012), to the knowledge I valued and the methods I ultimately used.

I was told by a representative of my PhD committee that I had to take the pages that detailed my experiences as the granddaughter of Holocaust survivors out of my final thesis. The reason given was that it was hard for the reader to consider the Holocaust alongside the violence and social repair I described in Northern Uganda.

What?

Well, I am very sorry for the poor dear reader ... but how could I fully and honestly grapple with forming relationships and learning about people's experiences of violence without explaining these formative experiences – how I encountered, understood, and approached relationships around mass violence and social repair in my own family and life? Indeed, these experiences were always shared with my host community and teachers in Uganda.

When I steadfastly refused in the editing period, the same committee member, after my defence, indicated that I would not be passed with it included (it was the revision they requested). My grandmother, and the effect of the Holocaust on her, her family, and me by extension, became a one-line footnote in one chapter of the story I had to tell about my relationships and experiences in Northern Uganda.

Aside from *feeling* awful, I wonder what the forceful erasure of my grandmother's experience has to do with sound academic research? And what else, consequently, is silenced into oblivion when academic practice and storytelling denies or de-values what your relationships– with both research participants *and* your own familial relations alike – teach you?

This is all. And this is not all.

These questions and other ethical questions continue. Who am I as a researcher, as a translator of experience, and as a storyteller engaged with violence and social repair? I know my responsibilities lie always with the people who share their experience and knowledge with me. But what really is my role in this translation and engagement, and in human rights work generally?

I am still working on it but am most grateful to and honoured by all my relations, and relationships, for the opportunity to learn from them and to ask these questions.

REFERENCES

Abbink, J., K. Askew, D.F. Dori, E. Fratkin, E.C. Gabbert, J. Galaty, S. Latosky, J. Lydall, H.A. Mahmoud, J. Markakis, G. Schlee, I. Strecker, and D. Turton. 2014. "Lands of the Future: Transforming Pastoral Lands and Livelihoods in Eastern Africa." Working Paper No. 154. Halle/Saale: Max Planck Institute for Social Anthropology.

Bobi-Pabwoc Foundation. 2014. "Constitution and Bylaws of the Bobi-Pabwoc Foundation." Draft on file with the author.

Branch, A. 2011. *Displacing Human Rights: War and Intervention in Northern Uganda*. New York: Oxford University Press.

Clarke, M.K. 2009. *Fictions of Justice: The International Criminal Court and the Challenge of Legal Pluralism in Sub-saharan Africa*. Cambridge: Cambridge University Press.

Dolan, C. 2009. *Social Torture: The Case of Northern Uganda, 1986–2006*. New York: Berghahn.

Makki, F. 2014. "Development by Dispossession: Terra Nullius and the Social-Ecology of New Enclosures in Ethiopia." *Rural Sociology* 79, 1:79–103.

Mazama, A. 2001. "The Afrocentric Paradigm: Contours and Definitions." *Journal of Black Studies* 31, 4: 387–405.

Mkabela, Q. 2005. "Using the Afrocentric Method in Researching Indigenous African Culture." *Qualitative Report* 10, 1: 178–89.

Nakayi, R. 2011. "Resolving Land Disputes in Post-Conflict Northern Uganda: The Role of Traditional Institutions and Local Courts." Working paper, December 2011. Copenhagen: Danish Institute for Human Rights. https://menneskeret.dk/files/media/dokumenter/udgivelser/rose_report_ok.pdf.

Napoleon, V. 2007. "Thinking about Indigenous Legal Orders." Research Paper for the National Centre for First Nations Governance, June 18, 2007.

Oloya, J.J. 2015. "How Did Governance in Acholi Dovetail with Violence? A Case Study of Multiperiod Communal Practices in a Fragile Situation in Uganda." PhD diss., University of Bradford.

Oloya, O. 2002. "Are the Acholi Mum for Fear of Rocking the Boat?" Editorial. *New Vision*, February 19, 2002.

–. 2013. *Child to Soldier: Stories from Joseph Kony's Lord's Resistance Army*. Toronto: University of Toronto Press.

Parent, A. 2009. "Keep Them Coming Back for More: Urban Aboriginal Youth's Perceptions and Experiences of Wholistic Education in Vancouver." Master's thesis, University of British Columbia.

p'Bitek, O. 1963. "Oral Literature and Its Social Background among the Acoli and Lango." Bachelor of Letters thesis, Oxford, St. Peter's College.
–. 1973. *Africa's Cultural Revolution*. Nairobi: MacMillan Books for Africa.
–. 1986. *Artist, The Ruler: Essays on Art, Culture and Values*. Nairobi: East African Literature Bureau.
–. 2011. *Decolonizing African Religions: A Short History of African Religions in Western Scholarship*. New York: Diasporic Africa Press.
Rosenoff Gauvin, L. 2013. "In and Out of Culture: Okot p'Bitek's Work and Social Repair in Post-Conflict Acoliland." *Oral Tradition* 28, 1: 35–54.
–. 2016. "'The Land Grows People': Indigenous Knowledge and Social Repairing in Rural Post-Conflict Northern Uganda." PhD diss., University of British Columbia.
Shaw, R. 2007. "Memory Frictions: Localizing the Truth and Reconciliation Commission in Sierra Leone." *International Journal of Transitional Justice* 1: 183–207.
Simpson, A. 2016. "Consent's Revenge." *Cultural Anthropology* 31, 3: 326–33.
Smith, L.T. 1999. *Decolonizing Methodologies: Research and Indigenous Peoples*. New York: St. Martin's Press.
Tuck, E. 2009. "Suspending Damage: A Letter to Communities." *Harvard Educational Review* 79, 3: 409–28.
Ugandan Ministry of Health. 2005. *Health and Mortality Survey among Internally Displaced Persons in Gulu, Kitgum and Pader Districts in Northern Uganda*. Geneva: World Health Organization.
Whyte, S.R., S.M. Babiiha, R. Mukyala, and L. Meinert. 2012. "Remaining Internally Displaced: Missing Links to Security in Northern Uganda." *Journal of Refugee Studies* 26, 2: 283–301.

Conclusion

MANY QUESTIONS, FEW ANSWERS

Christina Clark-Kazak, Shayna Plaut, Neil Bilotta,
Lara Rosenoff Gauvin, and Maritza Felices-Luna

Rather than offering a definitive conclusion to this book, we as editors wanted to return to some key questions that we asked ourselves throughout the writing and editing process. This book is about key dilemmas in human rights work. For many of the contributors, these dilemmas generated more questions than answers. In contrast to many books about methods, ethics, and human rights, we do not attempt to "resolve" these questions; rather, we find the process of questioning both productive and generative. Feeling unsettled, although uncomfortable, can be helpful when reflecting on ethics in our work and our relationships.

We wrote this conclusion collaboratively in response to the questions that emerged throughout the book. The dialogical style is intended to invite others – including you, as readers – into these conversations. It is fitting that Lara's last contribution to this section ends with a series of questions. We see this book as a starting point for many more discussions about ethics and human rights – a continuing process of reflection, learning, and questioning. So our concluding questions are not an endpoint but, rather, a beginning.

What drew us in to want to not only write this book, but to also seek out others' stories and experiences?

MARITZA: It has been over a couple of years that I am going through an "ethical crisis." I am uncomfortable with the traditional way of researching and teaching socio-political phenomena that produce suffering and harm to individuals and collectivities. I do not know how to engage in knowledge production and knowledge sharing that is non-exploitative, non-voyeuristic, and non-colonialist and that has a positive impact on those experiencing the harms I work on (and make my living out of). I am uncertain about everything, I question everything, and I doubt everything except for my commitment to engage ethically in human rights work. For me, this book is a way to create a space where we can open up about our uncertainties and unease, to share them with others, to listen to those of others, to sit in the unknown with others. It is also a space to challenge and question ourselves while simultaneously building an intangible fellowship with others striving through the tribulations of engaging in ethical human rights work. After reading the book, I am grateful to our contributors for being so candid in opening themselves up to us and sharing with us their own uncertainties.

SHAYNA: Over the years, in both my professional and personal life and in that messy space in-between, I have found that if you want to learn something, you have to make mistakes. As a journalist, academic (teacher and researcher), activist, colleague, partner, and mother, I have made A LOT of mistakes. Put bluntly, I have *really* fucked up. But this is generative because I found that the *learning* comes in the reflecting of those mistakes – particularly when you reflect with others. That said, although I have had many tear-filled and laughter-filled chats with friends and colleagues and students about my mistakes, I have rarely read about it in book form.

There are a few – *Taking Sides: Ethics, Politics and Fieldwork in Anthropology* (Armbruster and Laerke 2010) and some chapters in *Qualitative Research Methods in International Relations* (Klotz and Prakash 2008). Although these are excellent resources, it is rare to find a peer-reviewed text that offers candid reflections. And yet this is how I learn: to have an idea, to try it, to fuck up, to think about how I fucked up, to talk to others about how I fucked up, and to learn that they fucked up, too. In this space we then think through new possibilities: of doing things, imagining things, funding things, et cetera. This, to me, is where change comes from.

All this is to say, after working with the editors and contributors of this book on a variety of other projects (workshops, soliciting and editing articles, public presentations), I found that we had created a space of productive vulnerability and reflection where we could invite others – to share, to grow, and to create. It seemed like a needed and necessary space. And, not least importantly, the process itself would be fun – something that is, unfortunately, often very undervalued in academia.

LARA: Like Maritza, I also have been working in a space of critical uncertainty regarding how to work on, and advocate for, human rights in an equitable, respectful way that does not commit more violence in-process. Also, I have experienced parts of academia that are undeniably violent, and the privilege afforded to me as a white Jewish woman makes me very aware that many scholars experience much more regular and systematic forms of everyday violence. Add to this the relationships between participant-individuals and communities to ourselves as scholars, and to our institutions, professional organizations, funders, and others outlined in various chapters here, and, well, there are just a whole lot of difficult serious issues that are not usually engaged with publicly by academics and practitioners alike. Research and advocacy must grapple with these issues in a real way, and I believe that sharing these uncertainties, these lessons, these really problematic dilemmas that may be unresolvable is a very generative way to foster brave spaces and places for learning. Also, it is true that we learn from messing up, as Shayna unabashedly explained. But unless you have a very close relationship with a supervisor or mentor who is willing to share these complex and fraught moments, there is no real space to learn before your actions have real consequences for yourselves and your collaborators. I really think it important to learn as much as we can from each other's mistakes and dilemmas, and I am also grateful for the vulnerabilities shared here in hopes of better, more equitable, and more just human rights work.

CHRISTINA: Having taught research methods courses since 2007 and in my more recent experience developing ethical frameworks for researching forced migration, I have become increasingly unsettled by the ways in which ethics is framed in most standard textbooks and procedural ethics documents. Ethics are presented as, at best, a checklist, and, at worst, a barrier to doing research by requiring approvals and documentation. I was drawn to this book by its focus on practical dilemmas. By foregrounding "mistakes" and ethics-in-practice, the contributors help me to better understand messy relationships that resonate with my own research experiences. It is refreshing and cathartic to acknowledge that ethical praxis in human rights work is ongoing and reflexive.

NEIL: Throughout my social work education and career, I was fascinated by the number of culturally inappropriate conversations and "interventions" I engaged with, specifically with refugee young people. I yearned to learn more about the ways in which those who face substantial marginalization make sense of "us" (e.g., "professionals" and formal support systems). Why do I and those with similar identities and positionalities do the work we do? What happens if we make "mistakes"? Is all of our work a mistake? Who determines what is a mistake? How do others who work on issues related to injustice "act" when doing their work? Is there a "correct" way to work in contexts of "human rights"? Meeting this group of engaged and interesting scholars, activists, artists, educators forced me to think about how this work is extremely convoluted and ethically fraught. It is inspiring to know others are thinking about these difficult topics.

What is the role of emotion in working with human rights? What is the role of emotion when thinking/feeling/working through ethics of human rights?

SHAYNA: Emotions and I have a long and complicated history. I used to be scared of them. I used to pretend I did not have them because I thought it was a sign of weakness. I even (gasp – confession time) used to believe in the binary of emotional and intellectual and believed that intellectual equalled rational.

Life (and various critical theories – post/anti-colonial, feminist, queer) taught me otherwise: emotions can be very wise but they can also be very deceptive. So often emotions are what draw us to an issue, a cause, and are also what keep us in the work. But I still do not know where the (appropriate?) SPACE for emotion exists in academia. Is it context? Methods? Findings? Analysis? I have no answers for this, but I know that emotions are a strong motivator. As Alison Brysk (2013) and others have explained in the concept of "narrative politics," and as coined by students in my 2015 Framing of Social Justice course at Simon Fraser University, "the politics of empathy" are a powerful tool in engaging with others to make change.

LARA: Hmmm ... this is an interesting one. To me, human rights work is supremely interconnected with emotions, and what it means to be human. Indeed, what is more emotional than holding a young woman's hand to comfort her in the hospital after she had been shot by government soldiers ... or soothing a baby while his mother tells you of her experience of abductions and abuse at the hands of the rebels? But, phew ... emotions are also complex and changing as we experience, learn, and live in the world.

All this is to say, I think it is not at all useful, and rather impossible, to separate "emotions" from other intellectual or practical aspects of our beings. We are wholes, and if we do not engage with all aspects of ourselves with a critical, and compassionate, lens we can never hope for honest or, indeed, ethical engagement – whatever that may mean in situ and in relationship – in human rights work.

CHRISTINA: I agree with Lara that many people working with human rights are motivated by a deeply emotional – often visceral – response to injustice. We are angered by repression and human rights abuses. We fear for the safety, dignity, livelihoods, and security of ourselves or others. Care ethics validate these emotions, suggesting that they are indicators of normative values. However, researchers are sometimes penalized for transgressing norms of objective science, while those with direct experience of human rights abuses may be accused of bias. The contributors to this book help to disrupt these anti-emotion impulses by demonstrating that the ethical dilemmas usually emerged from a *feeling* that something was not right.

MARITZA: I totally agree with Christina. Professional codes of conduct and other ethical codes make us believe that through reason we can determine the correct or ethical course of action. Many of the chapters show that on the contrary, following those codes without questioning them can be the source of ethically questionable actions or of ethical dilemmas. Codes have been built through a colonial view of the world, and common practices within those codes can (re)produce relations of exploitation and domination despite their "ethical" grounding. Contributors' experiences reveal that the only way to escape that colonial worldview is by opening up to our emotions and to the emotions of others, not to rationalize them but to listen to them and explore them affectively rather than rationally.

NEIL: Do emotions not subsume all of our being? Yet, even in the field of social work, the notion of "emotions" is debated, particularly for researchers. When is it "okay" to share emotions with "Others"? When is it unacceptable? Who determines that? What if we, as scholars, allowed ourselves to tap into our emotions and feel them, without giving pejorative meaning to them, as we navigated our work?

Critical theories, especially feminist and post/anti-colonial theories, place a strong emphasis on the importance of context; given that, what are some ways we can think through ethical guidelines when we are teaching?

Mentoring? Organizing? Allocating, or denying funds or other aspects of leadership? And second, to that point do you think that "ethics" of human rights work can be codified as is the case in medical ethics or social work ethics? Do you think they should be? Why or why not?

NEIL: The notion of universal or codified ethics must be understood and interpreted with critical analysis. As I am learning, most "universal" or codified frameworks, guidelines, and protocols, are developed by those in positions of power who have very little connection or lived experiences with those we are "researching on" (let's be honest) or "working on" as medical professionals. Codifying ethics suggests that constructs such as "respect," "harm," and "justice" are universally culturally syntonic. Clearly, these terms vary across socio-political and historical contexts, culture, and values. This is not to suggest that I disagree with ethical frameworks, but what if "we" (as academics, doctors and social workers) discussed ethics with those we work with (participants and patients)? Would a collaborative process or more participatory approach to determining context-specific ethical codes not align more with anti-colonial and anti-hegemonic ideology?

CHRISTINA: I share Neil's skepticism of "universal" norms, but I do think there is some utility in highlighting principles of ethical research. There is an analogy here to the universal-cultural relativism debate within human rights more broadly. For example, I find helpful the "universal" belief in the inherent dignity of each human being that is at the heart of many human rights norms, but interpretations of what dignity means can vary by context. Similarly, I think it is helpful to frame ethics in principles – such as respect, relationships, and reciprocity – that can be the basis for a common point of departure when engaging in human rights work. But how these will be used and interpreted will vary.

MARITZA: I am uneasy with codification for two reasons. First, I find that either codes are too specific and dictate practices that take place in a variety of contexts and situations without being capable of taking into account those contexts or situations OR they are principles that can be interpreted in such varied (and sometimes even incompatible) ways that we can end up justifying opposing actions through the same principle. The second reason is that the existence of a code serves as a way to narrow our ethical gaze. If it is not dealt with by the code, then we tend to think of it as not an ethical question; or we assume that doing what the code says is enough and there is nothing else to worry about or to consider. Having said that, I would not oppose the existence of guidelines accompanied by resources (mentors, documents, members of communities) that have contextual and situational understandings and experiences that would be there to advise us through our work. Also, we would need to be trained to think about and to challenge codes, to not be limited in our thinking by the scope or the frame of the existing code. One of the highlights of the book for me is precisely the fact that contributors demonstrate what it means and how to go about critically engaging with ethics and ethical codes in human rights work.

SHAYNA: I have worked in the field of human rights since 1998, and in that time I have seen the increasing "professionalization" of human rights. What started off as a field of passion and experience increasingly became codified and reified, requiring specific certificates and degrees. This was partially based on the fact that there were often a lot of mistakes made: in bookkeeping/financing, in media relations, in policy making, and technology – all things that require particular skills and all things that *can* be taught. And so the early 2000s saw an increase in the codification of human rights as a field. MAs and then BAs began to emerge. Book publishers started to have a "human rights series."

I used to think this was a bad thing – a means of excluding people with lived experience for those with book learning. Now I am not so sure. I think there is a place for both to learn from one another. There is some basic human rights language, tools, and background that can provide a floor for people to start from – but that knowledge must, first, be accessible and, second, constantly evolve and shift based on the *changing realities* of real lives. And those with lived experiences (as activists, "victims," and even perpetrators) must be part of shaping this dynamic "canon" of human rights. This is one of my main goals of this book.

The same can be said for codifying *ethical guidelines* when engaging in human rights work. There is a place for checklists that can *help* people as they are thinking through a research or activist or artistic project that would aim to highlight, confront or demand accountability for human rights abuses. This can be very helpful in enabling the researcher/activist/journalist/artist to think through their own motivations, methods, and measures of success. That said, such guidelines and reflections should not be a static checklist but rather a dynamic and responsive starting point.

LARA: I agree with my thoughtful colleagues. I think something like "codification" can occur in different ways. I have seen Indigenous constitutions that have been written down for the first time, but with an emphasis on process, values, and ethos, rather than on specific rules and actions. Many chapters here speak to these values and processes, and as Christina and Neil point out, it is important to understand not only what a specific value means to you, but also what it means to the people you work with *in situ*. Negotiating these meanings, establishing understanding, AND a way to work together with these shared meanings, this is the goal, I think. With attention to process, without stipulating exact actions, this can be a good thing and a guide to work through with the people you are working with. A shared human rights ethics vision perhaps?

Given the diversity of submissions to this volume – in terms of content, location, profession – what are some commonalities that you see in terms of how people recognize they are in an ethical dilemma? What experiences did they draw on to make decisions? What are some of the differences?

LARA: I think discomfort is key here. And not simply disregarding the discomfort, but sitting with it, talking about it, analyzing it, dwelling in it ... this is it. Unsettling, in a way, as former research director for the Truth and Reconciliation Commission of Canada Paulette Regan (2010) puts it. In academia, as an example, we are not trained to deal with uncertainty or discomfort in this way. Everything must have an answer, a theory that explains, but the danger in always having an answer is to buy into ideas of progress, certainty, and the narrative of the forward accumulation of knowledge. Dwelling in discomfort interrupts this so-called experts' stance, offers humility, and admits that we are all still, and always, learners in this vital work.

NEIL: Reading through the material presented in this edited volume, I am drawn to the ubiquity of "ethical" struggles faced by researchers and practitioners. These deeply intriguing, powerful, and convoluted situations illustrate the depth and dearth of academic attention attending to ethical concerns. While many of our ethical dilemmas were not "solved" in the drafting of the chapters, perhaps finding answers or solutions was not our goal. Instead, offering a space where contributors were forced to critically reflect upon their experiences in ethical situations of precarity is a launching pad to engage in broader conversation with those on both sides of human rights discourse and experience. In other words, how will reflecting on these issues impact our next ethical dilemma?

CHRISTINA: One commonality that I see throughout the chapters is a commitment to deep reflection and humility. Each contributor has shown great courage to admit that they do not have the answers, especially in a professional context where doing so may discredit their authority and expertise. However, the ways in which people were able to respond to the dilemmas they faced varied greatly depending on their positionality within power relations. For me, this is a key difference across the contributions and reinforces my own sense of privilege as a white settler academic in a permanent job in the Global North.

SHAYNA: I find it interesting that many people in this volume are reflecting on the dance they feel when engaging with communities that are "not their own." Only one or two – namely Splicer et al.'s – reflect on the messy ethics of doing human rights work within one's *own* community. It reminds me of esteemed Māori scholar Linda Tuhiwai Smith's piece, "On Tricky Ground" (2005), and I would urge those of us who do work with communities for whom we do not identify (and I include myself here) to reflect on what we would do with(in) "our own." I do not know, but I do believe I *would* have much more visceral emotion, and that would make me more uncomfortable.

Whom do you see as an expert regarding the doing of human rights? What about the ethics of human rights? Whom do you consult? To whom, if anyone, do you defer?

CHRISTINA: I am uncomfortable with the idea of "expert" as all of us are continuously learning. I am especially uncomfortable with the notion of outside "experts" on other people's lives. This book shows that expertise is a constellation of experiences and positionalities, starting with people most affected by human rights violations. Ultimately, ethical human rights work will centre their experiences.

NEIL: The term "expert" is one that troubles me, too. I relate it to the construction of "cultural competence." To me, expert and "competent" imply a level of completion or one who fully and comprehensively understands a phenomenon, and, therefore, minimal effort for continued learning is required. Surely, as a white male academic from North America who studies forced migration and social work, I could and *should never* be referred to as an expert. Personally, I feel it is a disservice, an insult to those who experience forced migration, and a perpetuation of colonial and imperialist mainstream values of the world. Finally, similar to other areas of academia, I think this question is most applicable to those who have lived experiences of human injustices.

MARITZA: Aside from the points raised by Christina, my discomfort builds from Neil's point that the notion of expert is anchored on the notion of knowing something fully. To me, that is an impossibility and a lure that closes the door on different forms of knowing, different knowers, and different knowings. By expanding the notion of the expert or by flipping the script on who the expert is, we are still reinforcing the notion that someone can know (somehow) something fully. I prefer the notion of wisdom because it is about process (how to know, how to learn) instead of content (what you know); it carries with it the expectation of being consequential between our thoughts and our actions; it relies on emotions, reason, experience as well as on emotions, reasons, experiences of others. When we open ourselves up, we can benefit from the wisdom of so many different beings. Up to now, I have been too arrogant, too self-reliant, too closed-off to truly seek advice from others. I am working on that.

LARA: I also think that the term expert is extremely problematic. I like deep learners! All knowledge is co-created in some way, in some form. For too long, this co-creation, this learning and teaching, was not readily acknowledged. I hope this is changing. With regards to ethics in human rights work, I look to the people with whom I work. What is an ethical relationship to them? What is unethical to them? What does everyday responsibility to relationships look like, and how can I learn, honour, and respect this in the work?

"What are some of the benefits of working with/engaging with people with whom we may not share, and even have opposite, values? What are some of the strategies of working in these situations? Is there ever a time when we should walk away/cease working in this situation? If so, how do we know? How do we handle this?"

SHAYNA: One of the most fascinating and informative conversations I have ever had was with a neo-Nazi in southwest Ohio when I was nineteen years old. I am a queer Jew. Our first meeting was very random and we agreed to meet again to better understand each other's perspectives. By definition he should see me as the enemy and vice versa. The goal was not to change each other's mind or to argue but, rather, to understand where each of us was coming from ... What is the logic driving this fear and hate? Why do you hate me for who I am? As I drove up to the coffee house to meet him, I was shaking. I brought a friend with me as reinforcement. But in the end it was a fascinating, eye-opening, terrifying three-hour conversation that really shaped my way of engaging with the world.

If I want to contribute to changing the world, to make it a better, more just, more equitable, beautiful place, I need to better understand its dark underbellies. I need to understand the things that make me cringe, the things that disgust me, the things that I fear. For one, it will better clarify the things I find beautiful, vibrant, and essential. This knowledge will help encourage me to keep seeking and creating that elusive just world; for another it will help me better understand why not everyone agrees with me and thus help me devise strategies to either change or mitigate the impacts of their opinions. There is truth in the saying from *The Godfather,* "Keep your friends close and your enemies closer," but I do not want to become my enemy.

LARA: This is a tricky question but an important one. When I teach my Intro to Cultural Anthropology class, I stress the value of shifting the centre from which we view issues. This does not mean only shifting to understanding realities that you are already sympathetic to. That being said, it is extremely difficult to remain engaged with people long term, in dialogue, empathy, and research, if their viewpoints continue to aggressively target your own being, both existentially and physically. I think firm boundaries in these cases are really important, particularly a reflection on the length of time and intimacy of research methods used. Regular check-ins with your own mental health, and coming to terms with your priorities in doing research, would therefore be very important.

MARITZA: I believe the only way I can work with someone who holds opposing values is if we are able to agree on a short-term common goal or if I see it as an opportunity to push for things I deem important that I would not be able to achieve otherwise. I do not think, however, that working with people who do not share my core values is sustainable in the long term. This is not a normative stand. It is not a matter of "One should not"; it is a matter of "I cannot." I do not know how to, and I am not sure I actually want to work with those who see me as less than human because of who I am. My ability to choose to work or not with those whose values are contrary to mine is certainly a manifestation of structural privilege (most do not have the power, possibility, or opportunity to make that choice). My choice to avoid as much as possible working with people with opposing values does not mean that I do not engage with them. I agree with Shayna and Lara on talking with people we disagree with as a means to understand where they are coming from. In order to understand, we must be willing to listen, but how can we listen to thoughts, ideas, and emotions that dehumanize others, particularly when that other is me? Is dialogue even possible when one party is engaging in the conversation in order to be seen as human, to be recognized as human, to be allowed to exist, while the other is deciding on whether to grant that recognition or not? How can we navigate through apparently cordial and polite conversations where our counterpart takes for granted their own humanity but expects us to make a case for ours?

CHRISTINA: Conflict makes me uncomfortable. When confronted by people whose views are fundamentally opposed to mine, my first inclination is to disengage. As Lara points out, firm boundaries are important, and sometimes "muting" harmful and disrespectful views is an act of self-preservation and self-care. However, I agree with Shayna that I need to understand opposing views, and this requires listening to them, however difficult. I also acknowledge my privileged positionality and my responsibility, as Maritza notes, to speak out against dehumanizing discourses. For me, the challenge is to use my emotions productively. How do I channel my discomfort into taking a principled stand while still finding the humility to actually listen? These difficult conversations are still an area of learning for me. I find them particularly difficult in classroom settings, where, as the instructor, I need to honour the dignity of each person and allow for debate and disagreement, but also set clear guidelines on what is and is not acceptable. These are ongoing conversations.

NEIL: As one who holds all of the privileged identities (white, male, educated, able-bodied), I feel that I have a heightened responsibility to lean into the challenging and uncomfortable conversations with those whose identities and positions misalign with my own. As I can never experience the pain caused by an identity that is subjugated, I have to remain rooted in difficult discourse. While, sure, I need to be aware of physical harm, my privileged identities allow me to walk away from any and all situations without feeling dehumanized due to a part or all of my being. As Christina mentions, these are ongoing conversations. And I find myself consistently navigating ongoing conversations with myself around issues of identity, power, positionality, privilege, and oppression.

REFERENCES

Armbruster, H., and A. Laerke. 2010. *Taking Sides: Ethics, Politics and Fieldwork in Anthropology.* New York: Berghahn.

Brysk, A. 2013. *Speaking Rights to Power: Constructing Political Will.* New York: Oxford University Press.

Klotz, A., and D. Prakash. 2008. *Qualitative Methods in International Relations.* New York: Palgrave Macmillan.

Regan, P. 2010. *Unsettling the Settler Within: Indian Residential Schools, Truth Telling, and Reconciliation in Canada.* Vancouver: UBC Press.

Smith, L.T. 2005. "On Tricky Ground: Researching the Native in the Age of Uncertainty." In *The Sage Handbook of Qualitative Research*, edited by N.K. Denzin and Y.S. Lincoln, 85–108. Thousand Oaks, CA: Sage Publications.

Contributors

Neil Bilotta is a clinical assistant professor at the University of North Carolina at Chapel Hill School of Social Work. His work explores social inclusion and culturally responsive ethics of social work. He is interested in the ways racism, colonialism, and Eurocentric power inform research methodologies and social work interventions with communities who face substantiated subjugation, most specifically forcibly displaced young people (refugees, asylum-seekers, etc.).

Nick Catalano has worked in human rights education since 2014. Their anthropological focus is on the field of interpretation as fertile ground for human rights discourse, and the role public and non-traditional education can play in human rights projects broadly. They are also a staunch labour activist and believe that supporting workers in attaining security will enable those with less power to challenge the systems in place, ultimately allowing for greater equity for marginalized workers.

Claudyne Chevrier is an anti-racist, pro-choice, trans-inclusive feminist community organizer with a PhD in community health sciences. Her specific research interests lie in the interactions between social determinants of health, systems of oppressions, social inequalities, and accessibility to quality health care, particularly in relation to gender inequities. She is a proud founding member of the Sex Workers of Winnipeg Action Coalition. She now works in knowledge translation for public health and her love for evidence-based policies is rivalled only by her aggressive interest in felines and social justice.

Christina Clark-Kazak is a professor in Public and International Affairs at the University of Ottawa. She has previously worked for York University, Saint Paul University, and the Canadian government. Christina has served as president of the International Association for the Study of Forced Migration, president of the Canadian Association for Refugee and Forced Migration Studies, and editor-in-chief of *Refuge: Canada's Journal on Refugees*. Her research focuses on age discrimination in migration policy, young people's political participation, and interdisciplinary methodologies.

Yuriko Cowper-Smith holds a PhD in political science and international development from the University of Guelph. Her research focuses on the intersection of migration, statelessness, genocide, and social movements. She is currently the research and engagement officer at the Sentinel Project for Genocide Prevention.

Maritza Felices-Luna is a Peruvian criminologist working as an associate professor at the University of Ottawa. Her research focuses on political violence, armed conflict, and forced migration from a critical perspective using qualitative methodologies. Her goal is to contribute to postcolonial and feminist thought, to privilege "Southern" perspectives, to ensure open access to scholarly knowledges, and to develop a dialectical and dialogical ethics in contradistinction to a procedural ethics.

Sarah Fraser is a descendant of colonial settlers from Scotland, England, and France. She is a mother of amazing humans. She is also a psychologist, professor, and researcher affiliated to the School of Psychoeducation at the University of Montreal, the Centre de Recherche en Santé Publique, Myriagone chair of Youth Knowledge Mobilization, and Kahnawake Schools Diabetes Prevention Program.

Kristi Heather Kenyon is an associate professor in the Human Rights Program at the University of Winnipeg's Global College. Her work focuses on health and human rights advocacy, mobilization, and innovation, with a regional focus on sub-Saharan Africa. She also has a strong interest in research methods and ethics and experiential pedagogy. Her book, *Resilience and Contagion: Invoking Human Rights in African HIV Advocacy,* was published in 2017.

Jennifer M. Kilty is a professor in the Department of Criminology at the University of Ottawa. A critical prison studies scholar, her research examines criminalization, punishment, and incarceration – often at the nexus of health and/or mental health. She has published works on conditions of confinement, carceral segregation practices, the criminalization of HIV nondisclosure, prison education and pedagogy, and the mental health experiences of criminalized people.

Cougar Shakaien'kwarahton (He Clears the Smoke) Kirby is Coast Salish and Nuu Chah Nulth from Tsawout, BC, on his mother's side. His father is Kanien'kehá:ka from Kahnawà:ke. He completed a BA in sociology and Indigenous studies at McGill University. He was a member of the men's varsity lacrosse team in Montreal and a research assistant for Indigenous Youth Empowerment.

Sandra Lehalle (Sandy to most) is an associate professor in the Department of Criminology at the University of Ottawa. Her research interests lie in the policies and practices of detention by the state. Through her research, she unveils the complex relations between state authority and society by focusing on the role played by politics and the law in the legitimizing process of state power and of its privileged repressive device: the prison. She also works at breaking the social invisibility and stigma that characterize the loved ones of incarcerated persons, an important, albeit overlooked segment of the Canadian population (www.prisonricochet.ca).

Juliane Okot Bitek is a poet and assistant professor of Black Studies at Queen's University where she is joint-appointed in English and Gender Studies. Her *100 Days* was nominated for several writing prizes and won the 2017 IndieFab Book of the Year Award for poetry as well as the 2017 Glenna Lushei Prize for African Poetry. Her book *A is for Acholi* was on Brittle Paper's 100 Notable African Books list for 2022, and her most recent book, *Song and Dread,* was released in spring 2023. Juliane lives in Kingston, Ontario, on the lands of the Anishinaabe and the Haudenosaunee people.

Myrto Papadopoulos is a photographer, educator, and filmmaker. Her work tends to focus on issues surrounding gender, identity, and trauma. Her clients include *Smithsonian Magazine,* nationalgeographic.com, *TIME, GEO, New York Times, WSJ, Le Monde, Guardian, Washington Post, Die Zeit,* BBC, and ARTE TV, among others. Myrto was born and raised in Athens, Greece, and studied at the International Centre for Photography in New York City.

Jason Phillips is an independent consultant and adjunct research professor at the Norman Paterson School of International Affairs at Carleton University. He has worked in the humanitarian sector for twenty-five years and is currently part of the International Rescue Committee's Global Surge Team. Jason is a member of the Humanitarian Quality Assurance Initiative's General Assembly and was a member of InsideNGO's (now Humentum) Board of Directors.

Shayna Plaut is the director of research at the Canadian Museum for Human Rights and a research manager for the Global Reporting Centre. Her work is at the nexus of academia, journalism and activism, and motherhood. Specifically, she is interested in how people represent themselves in their own media, with a particular focus on peoples who do not fit neatly within the traditional notions of the nation-state. Shayna has researched and engaged with Romani media, migrant media, and Indigenous media in Canada, the US, and Europe since 2002.

Lara Rosenoff Gauvin is a mother, activist, curator, and assistant professor of anthropology at the University of Manitoba. She is currently co-chair of the University of Manitoba's Respectful Repatriation Ceremony – seeking peace and home for Indigenous Ancestors, belongings, biological materials, and tangible and intangible cultural expressions that have been stewarded by the university without proper and ongoing consent from Indigenous families, Nations, and communities. She also continues long-standing relationships with one extended family in Acoliland, Northern Uganda, working together on public dialogues about Acoli Indigenous governance and law.

Katsi'tsí:io (Brooke) Splicer is Onkwehón:we from Kahnawà:ke. She is a research coordinator for youth-led, action-based research that explores how to engage youth in community. She is passionate about the journey of decolonization and re-indigenizing aspects of life, in particular her mind and way of living. She has a six-year-old daughter and a dog-daughter. Although she pursued Western education, she is learning that there is much more to life than Western understandings of "work" and is learning how to live sustainably, including keeping chickens and bees, gardening, and foraging. She is a yoga instructor, studying to be a clinical herbalist, and currently in Kanien'kéha Ratiwennahní:rats, a two-year adult language immersion program.

Index